Westminster Aids to the Study of the Scriptures

THE WESTMINSTER HISTORICAL ATLAS
TO THE BIBLE

WESTMINSTER AIDS
TO THE STUDY OF THE SCRIPTURES

THE WESTMINSTER DICTIONARY OF THE BIBLE

Edited by John D. Davis

Fifth edition revised and rewritten by Henry S. Gehman

THE WESTMINSTER HISTORICAL ATLAS
TO THE BIBLE

Edited by G. Ernest Wright and Floyd V. Filson

(OTHER TITLES IN PREPARATION)

THE WESTMINSTER
HISTORICAL ATLAS
TO THE BIBLE

Edited by

GEORGE ERNEST WRIGHT

Associate Professor of Old Testament, McCormick Theological Seminary

AND

FLOYD VIVIAN FILSON

Professor of New Testament Literature and History
McCormick Theological Seminary

WITH AN INTRODUCTORY ARTICLE BY

WILLIAM FOXWELL ALBRIGHT

Professor of Semitic Languages, Johns Hopkins University

PHILADELPHIA

The Westminster Press

1945

PRINTED IN THE UNITED STATES OF AMERICA
THE LAKESIDE PRESS, R. R. DONNELLEY & SONS COMPANY
CHICAGO, ILLINOIS, AND CRAWFORDSVILLE, INDIANA

PREFACE

THE study of geography cannot give the ultimate explanation of human life. Nevertheless, life has a geographical basis which the study of history cannot neglect. For example, the peculiar conditions within Palestine and its setting in the Near East provided a background for a people who lived in the world, yet were never quite united with the world. They enjoyed enough detachment to preserve and develop their gifts, but in their constant contact with the stream of significant events they faced the deepest and most vital problems of life.

Careful study of the historical geography of Biblical lands is imperative for two reasons. First, these regions have exercised an immense influence upon our Western World. Indeed, the foundations of modern civilization are to be found in the heritage which the ancient civilizations of the Mediterranean area have left to us. This is true not only in such details as the alphabet, pen and ink, metallurgy, astronomy, medicine, and mathematics, but more basically in the heritage of the Judaeo-Christian religion, Greek philosophy, and Roman law. Hence he who would understand the major factors which have shaped our faith, thought, and life cannot neglect the historical geography of Biblical lands.

Second, the study of geography is necessary for understanding the Bible. The Scripture is not a treatise on philosophy or theology, nor does it present a manual of abstract ethics. It is primarily a historical literature, which tells how God confronted men at particular times and places. Geography, history, and religion are so inextricably bound together in it that the religious message cannot be truly understood without attention to the setting and conditions of the revelation. In this respect the Bible is unique among the world's scriptures; it is the only one for whose comprehension the study of historical geography is basic.

I. GEOGRAPHICAL INFLUENCE ON BIBLICAL HISTORY

The focal center of Biblical history is the small land of Palestine, and the geographical influence upon the Judaeo-Christian movement may be suggested by a brief discussion of four facts about this country's situation:

A. The basic cultural ties of Palestine were with Syria and the rest of the Fertile Crescent. From this region, which lay along the great Arabian Desert, came the dominant factors in the cultural life of Palestine. No permanent or thorough shaping of Palestinian life ever came from the west. Moreover, it was separated from Egypt by the barren coastal desert and the wilderness of Sinai. This does not mean that there were no contacts between Egypt and Palestine. The influence of Egypt on her northern neighbor was constant; in nearly every excavation of ancient Palestinian ruins, objects imported from Egypt have been found. Yet that influence was always superficial; it did not affect the basic elements of the native culture.

The conceptual life and material civilization of Palestine were oriented mainly toward the Fertile Crescent on the north and northeast. When we examine the Israelite beliefs about life after death, about the essentially anthropomorphic rather than theriomorphic nature of God, about man as created for the service of the Divine, and about the divine requirements concerning both the ritualistic and the moral law, it becomes clear that the closest kinship of these beliefs is with the conceptual life of the Fertile Crescent. In Egypt, on the other hand, as indeed also in Greece, the fundamental doctrines about human and divine life were very different. Similarly, the arts and crafts, architecture, agriculture, metallurgy, and ceramics of Palestine were dependent upon Syria. It was in the latter country that new inventions, new styles, and new fashions originated. From Syria they gradually filtered down into Palestine, where, however, they never possessed the same brilliance. In material culture Palestine was the borrower and imitator, rarely the originator.

This culturally dependent region of Palestine was never a center of wealth. It was comparatively poor in natural resources, and as a result was not fought for with quite the same intensity as were the richer portions of the ancient Near East. None of the world's large cities were located within its borders. A sophisticated urban culture, of a type common in such centers as Tyre, Byblos, Ugarit, and Babylon, did not exist in Palestine except as a weak reflection or imitation of the cultured and wealthy north. Here, therefore, was the providentially provided setting, in which the prophetic minds of Israel could understand that the real purpose and blessing of God for his people were not to be found in riches, political power, and cultural distinction. The prophets reacted against contemporary culture because of its pagan character and the easygoing, compromising tolerance which it promoted.

B. Proximity to the Arabian Desert was a second noteworthy feature of the geographical situation of Palestine. Between that land and the Desert to the east there was no barrier. Hence here, as in the other countries of the Fertile Crescent, there was the eternal struggle between the nomadic and the settled peoples.

The struggle between the Desert and the Sown seems to be a perpetual one. The moment that the central political authority weakens or is destroyed, that moment the Bedouins sweep in . . . . Like the waters of the ocean, the Bedouins may be held in check, but the moment the barriers are weakened, in they sweep with a destructive force that cannot be stemmed. . . . They can always retreat into the desert whither few can follow, and they are always prepared to break into the fertile lands at the first appearance of weakness there.*

Before Israel invaded Palestine, the comparative poverty and culturally dependent nature of the country meant that there was no real political strength and no deeply seated urban culture which could successfully resist nomadic invasion and influence. The incoming Israelite hosts constituted a nomadic group with the typical patriarchal organization of Arabia, and in later times they continued to look back upon this organization as the ideal one. In addition, later Israel preserved the relatively high moral purity and austerity of the patriarchal, nomadic religion, so that when the people settled down to agriculture and became increasingly urbanized, the family God of the Fathers did not become another nature or weather deity. The close relation of God and people, as symbolized in the covenant, was Israel's nomadic heritage, and the most important factor in saving her from idolatry. These basic elements of patriarchal religious life were idealized in later Israel and always remained as a purifying agent, not only among such extremists as the Nazirites and Rechabites, but among the great prophets as well.

This does not mean, however, that we can explain away Israel's unique conception of God simply by reference to the Arabian Desert or nomadic life. Before the days of Mohammed, Arabs were polytheists. Geography may explain the conditions of divine revelation, but cannot provide a substitute for it. What can safely be said, however, is that the patriarchal influence upon Israel remained dominant throughout her struggle with Canaanite polytheism. The ideal background of her religion lay in the desert, not in the scenes of urban civilization, and to that background the prophets constantly appealed.

C. A third important geographical fact about Palestine was its situation on two of the most vital trade routes of the ancient world: one between Egypt and Asia, and the other running west from Arabia to reach the coastal plain and there branch off to Egypt or Syria. By reason of this involvement in the economic life of the world, Palestine inevitably was drawn into world affairs. The period of Biblical history was the first great epoch of empire-building. It witnessed the impressive rise and rule of such mighty empires as Egypt, Assyria, Babylonia, Persia, Macedonia, and Rome. Each in succession reached out to seize and dominate the trade routes which passed through Palestine. This little country was thus inescapably forced within the bounds of each succeeding kingdom. It is not surprising, therefore, that the prophets deal with the international situa-

*Glueck, Nelson, The Other Side of the Jordan (New Haven, 1940), pp. 6 f.

5

tion and see the far reach of the power of God. Nor is it strange that along the many lines of trade and travel Jews moved out from their homeland until in the early days of the Christian movement, settlements of Jews were found in every important city of the known world.

D. The geographical features of Palestine and the character of its borders offered its inhabitants the possibility of a definitely limited but nevertheless real detachment. It would be easy to exaggerate that detachment; indeed, this has often been done. Palestine was too much involved in the currents of the ancient world to live in "splendid isolation" at any period of its history, and the study of its life always requires attention to the surrounding world. In spite of this immensely significant fact, however, Palestine was set apart from every neighboring region. On the south and east were uninviting wilderness and desert. The almost unbroken shore line of the Mediterranean Sea severely limited maritime contacts with lands to the west. On the north the massive heights of the Lebanons and Hermon rendered complete identification with the life of Syria impossible.

Thus on every side the borders of Palestine marked it as destined to have its own peculiar history. This provision for detachment was further effected by the lack of geographical unity within the country itself. Galilee was separated from Samaria; the hills were distinct from the plains; Transjordan was divided from western Palestine by the deep cleft of the Jordan Valley. Thus when the Canaanites were in control, no unified state ever came into being. Instead, there were numerous city-states. Even the deities became localized and pluralized, so that we hear of Baals and Ashtoreths, although in the official religion Baal and Ashtoreth were a single god and goddess. The basic geography of the country, therefore, created divisive forces which naturally tended to separate people into groups.

When Israel entered the country, she possessed a common religious and historical tradition, but throughout her existence she had to struggle against the geographical factors which divided north from south and east from west. Yet the partial isolation of the country as a whole provided sufficient detachment to enable Israel to develop a unique spiritual heritage. In Judaism this detachment was magnified into a national and religious exclusiveness. So basic did this element become that it continued to shape the lives of Jews even when they moved out into Gentile lands, and the Jews as a strong religious and cultural group continued to exist even when deprived of homeland and political independence. Under the stimulus of Hellenistic influence and Roman rule, however, the setting was created in the first century for a fuller revelation of the world scope of God's purpose. The days when detachment could be creative and fruitful were past; it was the time for Israel to give her gifts to the world.

II. THE PLAN OF THE ATLAS

In this volume the Editors and Publisher have sought to supply a series of maps which will set forth clearly and vividly the geographical setting of the Biblical story. The explanatory chapters which accompany the maps attempt to provide the essential facts needed to comprehend the historical and geographical framework of Scripture. Carefully selected photographs supplement the maps and text.

A new Biblical atlas is urgently needed. In recent decades extensive exploration has added greatly to our geographical knowledge of the Biblical lands. The last generation has seen an epoch-making advance in the methods and achievements of archaeological work. A new degree of mastery of the languages of the ancient Near East, a hitherto unattained correlation of the discoveries in the Mediterranean and Near East, and the development of adequate methods of excavation have all combined to make this advance possible.

The volume begins with an introductory article on the methods that have been employed in the rediscovery of the Biblical world. Professor W. F. Albright, the acknowledged authority in this field, has been kind enough to supply it. Following this article is a table of dates for convenient reference; it places the persons and events of the Biblical story in the full setting of the ancient world.

In the main body of the book each map plate is accompanied by an explanatory discussion. Chapter I deals with the general geography of Palestine. Chapters II-VII are primarily historical, and cover the period beginning with the world of the Patriarchs and ending with Judah in Nehemiah's time. At this point the historical maps are interrupted to give enlarged section maps of Palestine and their accompanying geographical discussion in Chapters VIII-X. Chapter XI, with its four section maps, continues the historical discussion, dealing with the great empires between the ninth and second centuries B.C. Chapters XII-XVI carry the story to the fourth century A.D., discussions of Palestine alternating with discussions of the Mediterranean world into which Christianity spread. Chapter XVII traces the history of Jerusalem, and Chapter XVIII surveys the archaeological excavations in Palestine during the past century.

It is hoped that the Index of Sites at the close of the volume will prove to be one of the most useful features of the work. It is not limited to the sites that appear on the maps, but is enlarged to provide a geographical index to the Bible (the spelling used is generally that of the A.V.). It gives directions for finding any site shown on the maps, and in the case of other places gives the approximate location, if it can be determined. With the expert aid of Professor Albright, an attempt has also been made to present the accurate spelling of the modern Arabic names of the places with which the ancient Palestinian sites are identified.

The Editors have divided responsibilities as much as possible. In general, Professor Wright's work extended through the Old Testament period. Professor Filson was responsible for the later period, beginning with the time of Alexander the Great. Plates I-VII, XI: A-C, XVII:A, and XVIII, together with Chapters II-VII, X, XVIII, and portions of Chapters XI and XVII have been done by Professor Wright. Professor Filson edited Plates XI:D, XII-XVI, and XVII: B-D, and prepared Chapters VIII, XII-XVI, and parts of Chapters XI and XVII. They collaborated on Plates VIII-X and Chapters I and IX.

The Editors are greatly indebted to their advisory committee, consisting of Professors W. F. Albright, of Johns Hopkins University; Millar Burrows, of Yale University; and O. R. Sellers, of McCormick Theological Seminary. These scholars gave generously of their time and interest in examining the material in the volume and making many suggestions. To Professor Albright in particular we owe a great debt for his sympathetic counsel and advice at every stage of the work. Professors George Cameron and I. J. Gelb, of the Oriental Institute of the University of Chicago; and Professor A. A. Hays, of McCormick Theological Seminary, also gave scholarly aid in connection with the preparation of Plates II, III, XI, and XVI.

Constant aid has come from the Rev. L. J. Trinterud and Mr. John Ribble, of The Westminster Press, and from Mr. W. R. Bowes and the technical staff of the R. R. Donnelley and Sons Company in Chicago. The interest of these men went far beyond the usual function of publisher and printer, and the results of their expert and patient counsel appear on every page. To them is due also the revolutionary method of map making, developed especially for use in this atlas. It provides skillful reproduction of complicated geographical factors and beauty of appearance, and makes possible the publication of the atlas at a price within the reach of the student.

Dr. Georges Barrois, of Princeton Theological Seminary, drew the relief map of Palestine which was used on Plates I, IV, VI, VIII-X, XII, XIV, and XVIII. He began work on the relief map of the Mediterranean world, but pressure of other duties prevented him from completing it. Mr. Hal Arbo, of Chicago, completed this map, which is used on Plates II, III, XI, XIII, XV, XVI; he also prepared the special maps used on Plates V, VII, and XVII. Mrs. Jean Arbo prepared the maps for the engravers by lettering sites, drawing in roads and boundaries, et cetera, on the basis of original copy supplied by the Editors. To these artists we express our sincere appreciation for their painstaking and highly competent work.

G. ERNEST WRIGHT.
FLOYD V. FILSON.

McCormick Theological Seminary
August 31, 1944.

TABLE OF CONTENTS

TABLE OF ILLUSTRATIONS

ACKNOWLEDGMENTS *We gratefully give credit to the following sources for the illustrations used in this volume:*

Oriental Institute, University of Chicago, Figures 1 (Aerial Survey of the Oriental Institute), 3, 5, 10, 11 (Painting by M. Bardin after Unger), 12 (Cast in Oriental Institute), 16, 17, 18, 20 (Cast in Oriental Institute), 28, 29, 32 (Cast in Oriental Institute), 49 (Cast in Oriental Institute), 51 (Painting by M. Bardin after Unger).
Ewing Galloway, ©, Figures 2, 4, 6, 8, 13, 15, 34, 35, 38, 39, 40, 42, 54, 57, 58, 59, 60, 61, 65, 67, 68 71, 72, 73.
Philip Gendreau, ©, Figures 7, 36, 37, 50, 56, 62, 63.
Lepsius, *Denkmaeler*, Part 2, Pl. 133, and Part 3, Pl. 40, Figures 9, 22.
Petrie, Sir W. M. F., *Hyksos and Israelite Cities* (Bernard Quaritch Press), Pl. IVa, Figure 14.
Boreux, *La Sculpture égyptienne au Musée du Louvre*, Pl. XXVIII, Figure 19.
Syria, Vol. 17, Pl. XXI, Photograph by C. F. A. Schaeffer, for the French expedition to Ugarit, Figure 21.
Wilson and Palmer, *Ordnance Survey of the Peninsula of Sinai*, Photographs, Vol. I, Numbers 48–50, Figure 23.

American Schools of Oriental Research, Figures 24, 25, 43, 44, 45, 47, 76; Figures 25 and 47 being by courtesy of the Air Officer Commanding, Royal Air Force, Middle East.
H. G. May, Figures 26, 27, 30, 55.
Watzinger, *Denkmaeler Palaestinas*, Vol. I, Pl. 16, Figure 31.
Wellcome-Marston Archaeological Research Expedition to the Near East, Figure 33.
G. Ernest Wright, Figures 41, 46, 52, 69.
O. R. Sellers, Figure 53 (from the Beth-zur Excavation; courtesy, Royal Air Force Official, Crown Copyright Reserved).
Oxford University Press, Figures 64 (from Sukenik, *Ancient Synagogues in Palestine and Greece*, Pl. XVI:A) and 70 (from Rostovtzeff, *Dura-Europos and Its Art*, Pl. II).
W. A. McDonald, Figure 66.
Illustrated London News, ©, Figure 74.
University Museum, Philadelphia, Figure 75.
Palestine Institute, Pacific School of Religion, Figure 77.

THE REDISCOVERY OF THE BIBLICAL WORLD

WILLIAM FOXWELL ALBRIGHT

I. INTRODUCTORY CONSIDERATIONS

THERE are few fields where the progress of discovery makes constant revision of handbooks and other aids to study more necessary than in Biblical research. This is not easy, even for scholars, to realize, since one instinctively feels that old books are more useful as guides to the study of old subjects than new books. On the other hand, there is danger in seeking new discoveries and novel points of view at the expense of more solid earlier work. This is particularly true in fields like Biblical archaeology and geography, where mastery of tools and of methods of investigation is so arduous that there is always a temptation to neglect sound method, substituting clever combinations and brilliant guesses for slower and more systematic work.

Since it is only in our generation that the progress of research has made real synthesis possible, all standard books appearing earlier are in imperative need of revision, often of complete rewriting. Moreover, many of the latest books and articles have been written by men who are not really competent. The reader who is not a specialist is naturally helpless in selecting a reliable authority to follow. The mere fact that an author occupies a distinguished academic position or has made some remarkable discoveries in the field or museum does not prove his scholarly competence. Hence the value of such an organization as the American Schools of Oriental Research, which is not tied to any one university or organization but gathers the best skills and selects only the most reliable scholars to present the results of excavation, exploration, and interpretation to the educated public.

In evaluating the information contained in standard Biblical handbooks, it is well to compare the dates of their publication with the dates of the most significant archaeological discoveries. To begin with standard English works of conservative character, Clarke's great *Commentary*, which is still used by many, appeared in 1810–1826; Kitto's famous *Cyclopaedia* came out in 1843–1845. If we consider fundamental German works, Eichhorn's *Introduction* (with which the history of the so-called higher criticism really begins) was published in 1783, while the first scientific Hebrew dictionary and grammar were brought out by Gesenius in 1810–1813. The most important developments in literary criticism of the Old Testament came in 1805 with De Wette's contention that Deuteronomy was composed in the reign of Josiah, in 1853 with Hupfeld's successful revival of Ilgen's view that there were three documents instead of two in Genesis, and in 1876 with Wellhausen's consolidation of the Graf-Kuenen view that the Priestly Code was the latest of the four documents of the Pentateuch.

Turning to compare the most important dates in the history of modern Biblical archaeology, we note that the Egyptian hieroglyphics were not deciphered until the years 1822–1841 and that Assyrian cuneiform was not decoded until 1845–1851. Systematic excavations were not begun in Assyria until 1843 and in Egypt until 1850; the first scientific excavations from our present point of view were undertaken by Flinders Petrie in Egypt (since 1883) and Palestine (1890). But it was not until 1887 that the Amarna Tablets (see p. 35) were found, while the Elephantine Papyri did not become available to scholars until 1911. The great Hittite archives of Boghazköy were unearthed in 1907, but it was not until the middle twenties that enough material became available to make synthesis possible. The long-lost Canaanite religious literature has been excavated only since 1929, while successful interpretation of its remains cannot be said to have begun until 1932. Scarcely any original Sumerian literature from the third millennium was available for scholarly research until S. N. Kramer began to publish in 1938. It was not until 1939 that the present writer felt that the time had come to begin the preparation of real syntheses of ancient Near-Eastern history and civilization. During the preceding decade our knowledge of archaeological chronology had increased so rapidly that it was then possible for the first time to date events and cultural phenomena in different lands correctly in relation to one another.

This tremendous improvement in knowledge and method applies not only to the broad field of ancient civilization but at the same time to such special aspects as geography and topography, with which this book is primarily concerned. Even in the field of map making there has been great advance since Robinson began his epochal researches in 1837. At that time few points in the entire Near East had been precisely located in latitude and longitude, while details were left to be roughly sketched in by cartographers who utilized naval observations and explorers' records of distance and direction.

FIG. 1. The Behistun "Rock" in Iran (Plate III, E-3). On the jagged face of this mountain the Persian monarch Darius I (522–486 B.C.) carved an inscription, twenty-five feet high and fifty feet wide, to commemorate his first victories. It was written in the three most important languages of the eastern portion of his realm, Old Persian, Babylonian, and Elamite. An English army officer, Sir Henry Rawlinson, copied the three versions of the inscription between 1835 and 1847. The monument is three hundred feet above the plain, and Rawlinson's deed was a most difficult one. Yet it was by this means that Babylonian was deciphered. The inscription cannot be seen on the photograph, but it is located on the left side of the vertical fissure in the center of the photograph, just above the road.

The Holy Land was the first country of southwestern Asia to be systematically surveyed, yet the Survey of Western Palestine was not undertaken until 1865 and was not finished until 1877. Schumacher's much sketchier survey of northern Transjordan, begun in 1885, was not finished until 1914. The region of Moab and Edom has never been properly mapped. In recent years considerable progress has been made with the detailed cadastral survey of Palestine, and a number of sheets are now available. Moreover, a century ago nothing was known about geological formation, and little about soils and water supply, rainfall and temperature, etc. Above all, however, from our present standpoint, we have learned how to use archaeological data to locate, date, and often identify ancient sites. How this is done will be concisely explained below.

II. HOW WE EXCAVATE IN THE NEAR EAST

It is often supposed that the archaeologist digs merely for the purpose of unearthing monuments and finding museum objects in the buildings or tombs which he excavates. It is true that much excavation of the nineteenth century was undertaken for these ends; the outstanding example of it is Mariette's work in Egypt from 1850 to 1880. Fortunately, however, not nearly so much harm could be done in Egypt as in Mesopotamia by such rough-and-ready methods, since there was almost no stratification in the temples and tombs of the Nile Valley which Mariette cleared of their silt and sand. From the very beginning of the work of Botta and Layard in Assyria, about a century ago, much more care was devoted to the recording of the finds as they were made, to the planning of excavated buildings, and to the prompt publication of the principal objects discovered. Yet scientific archaeology cannot be said to have commenced until 1890, when Flinders Petrie dug for six weeks at *Tell el-Ḥesī* in southern Judah (Plate XVIII, B-5). At that time he was able to demonstrate once for all that most important ancient sites of southwestern Asia consist of more or less regular, superimposed layers of debris, and that it is possible to date them by the artifacts (objects made by man) which each layer contains. The most valuable artifacts for dating are pieces of pottery, whole or broken. These broken pieces are found in enormous numbers on these ancient sites. Pottery was fragile and seldom was usable for any great while. Moreover, pottery styles changed rapidly. In his brief season in Palestine, preceded and followed by many years of excavation in Egypt, Petrie showed that archaeological chronology could be based on a careful study of the relation of objects to one another in the light of the deposits in which they occur, as well as on equally systematic study of the evolution of pottery forms or styles (sequence dating). The study of the physical relationship of artifacts in the light of the strata in which they are found is called "stratigraphy," and the study of the relation between the forms of objects is called "typology." All scientific modern archaeology is based on the application of these two basic principles, to which we shall return presently.

The best recent archaeological method is associated with the name of George Andrew Reisner, a native of Indianapolis, who became the foremost excavator of modern times. Reisner combined the methods employed by the leading German excavators, who stressed the architectural and engineering side of archaeology, with the stratigraphy and typology of the Petrie school, employing both with the aid of American filing cabinets and recording systems. Fortunately, Reisner was always supplied with adequate funds to provide for assistants and apparatus, so he was able to set an example of comprehensive and accurate recording of his work in the field.

Today archaeological treasure hunts are no longer permitted in the Near East. In all the countries of this region, whether independent nations or mandatories, there are organized departments of antiquities, headed by Government appointees who are generally scholars of distinction. The directors of antiquities are assisted by staffs of trained archaeologists, who care for the archaeological museum or museums, inspect ancient monuments and see that they are protected against injury, watch over the trade in antiquities and prevent illicit digging and smuggling as far as practicable, and control the excava-

tions carried on by native and foreign institutions. In Palestine the officials of the Department of Antiquities are British in the higher grades and Jewish or Arab in the lower grades; there is also an international archaeological advisory board consisting of representatives of domestic and foreign archaeological interests. There are detailed ordinances which control archaeological matters affecting governmental organization and the rights of individuals. For the best recent approach to a uniform archaeological system in the Near East, we may refer to the text of the resolutions of the archaeological conference in Jerusalem, July, 1943, as published in the *Bulletin of the American Schools of Oriental Research*, October, 1943.

The excavator of today is expected to undertake his work with an adequate staff of assistants, who are provided with all necessary equipment, such as surveying instruments, photographic apparatus, drawing tools, picks, hoes, baskets, and sieves. In large sites light railways and cranes may be required. The work of the native diggers, who are generally untrained, must be supervised directly by the members of the excavating staff or by trained native foremen, whose own supervisory activity is carefully controlled by the director of the expedition. The site and its environs are surveyed first, if possible, and a survey grid, composed as a rule of squares twenty meters on a side, is prepared. All excavated remains are recorded on this grid as exactly as possible, in order to avoid errors. All artifacts found during the excavation are labeled with the number of the room or other locus where they were found. If desirable, the exact spot, as well as the precise level above the floor, is noted. Many photographs are taken to show the exact appearance of the ruins as they are cleared, and especially to record the relation of objects to one another as well as to the adjacent walls. The levels of the excavated ruins are also duly recorded, attention being concentrated mainly on tops of walls in each locus, floor levels, and foundation levels. When this task is finished and the excavator has taken careful notes on details, such as peculiarities of construction and indications of repair or reoccupation, the entire stratum may be removed down to its foundations and the next stratum below may be cleared in the same way. Sometimes, of course, there was so much reuse of older walls and so much partial reconstruction that it is not practicable to remove any walls until the excavator has cleared a sufficient number of superimposed foundations to make a systematic analysis of their relation to one another possible.

All significant objects of human manufacture found should be recorded summarily, with brief descriptions and identifying drawings or photographs, on cards or in a record book, the objects themselves being correspondingly labeled. When possible, objects are restored and cleaned, though final cleaning and restoration are generally left to be done in the museums where they are later deposited. It is particularly important, moreover, that pottery be cleaned and put together on the spot, since it is all of chronological interest and since most broken pottery is discarded after the close of an excavation. Accurate outline drawings and clear photographs are prepared on the spot as far as possible, so that errors and losses may be averted. Chemical treatment of objects and detailed technical study of them must nearly always be left until later, since few expeditions possess the necessary facilities or technologically trained staff.

In interpreting his finds as sources of historical information the archaeologist must be particularly careful not to allow his judgment to be biased by preconceived ideas. In other words, he must remember that archaeology is primarily an inductive science, and that the careful use of factual data precedes all deductive reasoning. Hence the importance of distinguishing throughout between stratigraphy and typology, which we have defined above. First of all, he must be sure of the limits and relations of his strata and must determine whether any unique piece from a given stratum really belongs there or is an intrusion from above or below. Strata are not always level, and later pieces were sometimes washed down from a higher level on a site, or earlier pieces were dropped on the surface after being brought up from an ancient pit, excavated for a cistern or silo. The trained excavator has little trouble with such intrusions, but care

FIG. 2. The Sphinx and Pyramids at *Gizeh*, Egypt (Plate V, C-3). The great age of pyramid-building in Egypt was during the Old Kingdom between the twenty-seventh and the twenty-second centuries B.C. The pyramids are the most spectacular and tremendous tombs ever built by man. The Sphinx, while possessing the body of a lion, is actually the portrait head of Pharaoh Khafre, the builder of the pyramid behind it. The great Pyramid of Khufu stands just to the right of the photograph.

is obviously required in making deductions from the appearance of a singular object in a given stratum. Unwritten objects, such as pottery, must first be dated relatively to other comparable objects which recur in higher or lower deposits. Then one can give them a date in absolute chronology (B.C. or A.D.) by noting what kind of datable objects (inscriptions, scarabs, coins, etc.) are found with them or in known relation to them. For such evidence we may have to turn to another site, where identical objects may occur together with intrinsically datable remains. Typology is of the greatest importance in fixing chronology, since it enables the scholar to group archaeological objects into classes and species, to identify given types wherever they may recur—sometimes hundreds of miles apart—and to trace the evolution of a given form. When the successive steps of evolution of form are once known, it is possible, for instance, to assign approximate dates to objects which are a little later in type than objects found in a given datable stratum and a little earlier in type than corresponding objects found in the next stratum above. By the combination of inductive reasoning from stratigraphy and deduction from typological indications the archaeologist gradually builds up a coherent chronological system. After such a system has been built up it may be rectified and adjusted by reference to formal historic chronology (see below, section IV).

Once the excavator has accurately described and interpreted his data, they can be used for a great many historical purposes. Particularly significant, of course, are written objects and documents, since they enable the scholar to reconstruct the life of religion, politics, and commerce. But other remains have great and steadily increasing significance. Through them we learn about the arts and crafts of antiquity, how men built and where they lived, how they made pottery, practiced metallurgy, what crops and animals they possessed. Through them we also learn to follow the history of human settlement. Once the archaeologist has determined the pottery chronology of a given region by excavating a number of sites, he can proceed to date all other occupied sites of antiquity by the potsherds with which they are strewn. The outstanding illustration of the successful application of this principle is Nelson Glueck's archaeological survey of Transjordan, in which he has examined and described more than 1,500 ancient sites, dating them by their sherds.

III. HOW WRITTEN DOCUMENTS ARE INTERPRETED

As stated above, written documents form by far the most important single body of material discovered by archaeologists. Hence it is extremely important to gain a clear idea of their character and of our ability to interpret them. Just as in all archaeological work, the question of method takes first place. It must be remembered that every single script employed in the ancient Near East has had to be deciphered in modern times. Curiously enough, for every ancient script to be deciphered two new ones seem to be discovered. We have deciphered Assyro-Babylonian cuneiform and various other independent cuneiform scripts, three principal varieties of Egyptian hieroglyphics, and many other alphabetic and syllabic scripts, but an even greater number remain to be interpreted, and new ones turn up every few years.

As a characteristic example of the nature of our task, we may point to the cuneiform alphabet of Ugarit. First discovered in 1929, many hundreds of tablets in this script have been excavated by C. F. A. Schaeffer at *Râs Shamrah* (Ugarit) on the Syrian coast opposite Cyprus (Plate II, E-2). The first fragmentary tablets were published by Virolleaud in 1930 and almost immediately deciphered by Bauer and Dhorme, both of whom were distinguished as Semitic philologians and as cipher experts. First Bauer correctly identified over half the letters, then Dhorme added five more, after which Bauer made various corrections in his own system, raising the total number of letters identified by himself to nineteen. Subsequently, on the basis of a vastly increased body of texts, Virolleaud and others added six more characters, making thirty in all. However, decipherment was here again only the beginning, and it is characteristic of the difference in the type of skills required that neither Bauer nor Dhorme, in spite of their outstanding ability as Semitists, contributed much to the task of interpretation as such. The next step required schooled imagination, held constantly under control by a rigid sense of grammatical form. Many scholars now entered the field; outstanding among them was H. L. Ginsberg, whose keen grammatical instinct had been cultivated by a thorough training in Semitic philology. Thanks to Gordon's *Ugaritic Grammar*, which appeared in 1940, we now have a solid grammatical basis for further work. Students of Ugaritic are

FIG. 3. The ruins of Persepolis, the magnificent capital of the Persian Empire begun by Darius I (522–486 B.C.) and completed by his successors. The low building in the center is the royal treasury, which has been reconstructed as the expedition headquarters of modern excavators. Columns of the royal palaces can be seen as they were left standing by Alexander the Great, who wantonly set fire to the beautiful capital.

now concentrating on the explanation of passages in the texts hither-to published, with special attention to the meaning of words.

We must distinguish sharply between the earlier and the more recent periods of philological research in our field, since the transla-tions of documents written in different languages depend for accuracy on the progress of grammatical and lexical knowledge. Thus it is unsafe to rely on any translations of Egyptian historical texts which appeared before Breasted's *Ancient Records* (1906), since Breasted was the first historian to take full advantage of the tremendous progress in the knowledge of Egyptian achieved by Erman and Sethe after 1880. It is equally unsafe to depend on any translations of Egyptian religious texts made before about 1925, since that year marked the publication of the first volume of the great Berlin dictionary of Egyptian, while the year 1927 saw the appearance of Gardiner's monumental *Egyptian Grammar*. The first reliable English translations of Egyptian religious texts appeared in Blackman's *Literature of the Ancient Egyptians* (1927) and Breasted's *Dawn of Conscience* (1933). Turning to Mesopotamia we find ourselves in a worse situation, since no English translations of cuneiform texts adequately represent the great progress in scientific philology marked by the brilliant work of Landsberger and his pupils since about 1923. Luckenbill's *Ancient Records of Assyria and Babylonia* (1926–1927) was far below the standard set twenty years earlier by Breasted in the corresponding Egyptian field. Scarcely any Accadian (Semitic-Babylonian) religious text of importance is now available in an up-to-date English trans-lation. The student who does not wish to be misled by antiquated renderings must, accordingly, study recent German work, though even in German no comprehensive translations from the past fifteen years are available. Assyriologists are handicapped by the lack of a comprehensive and up-to-date Assyrian dictionary, the latest lexicon being the sketchy and antiquated glossary of Bezold, edited by Goetze in 1926. The field of Sumerian took a forward step in 1923, when Poebel's grammar was published. Fortunately the publication of the valuable Sumerian religious literature from the temple library at Nippur (Plate II, F-3) in Babylonia is in the hands of Poebel's gifted student, S. N. Kramer, who in 1938 began to edit and translate reconstructed Sumerian epics from the third millennium. Since this is the oldest body of narrative literature in the world, and since it influenced much of the religious literature of the Semites of later times, its importance can scarcely be overestimated.

Our understanding of cuneiform Hittite is now abreast of our knowledge of Sumerian, in spite of the fact that cuneiform Hittite was not deciphered until 1915 and that workers are few. On the other hand, decipherment of hieroglyphic Hittite was brought to an abrupt stop by the outbreak of the current world war after a decade of steady progress. We are still unable to translate a single inscription in hieroglyphic Hittite satisfactorily, though most of the phonetic characters and many ideograms can be read and a good deal is under-stood about the grammar. At present Ignace Gelb, of the University of Chicago, is the leader in this elusive field. The study of Horite (Hurrian), though begun more than fifty years ago after the publica-tion of the first cuneiform tablets in that language, is still hampered by the small number of texts, which come from half a dozen different excavations, in Egypt, Syria, Mesopotamia, and Asia Minor. E. A. Speiser's excellent *Introduction to Hurrian* (1941) represents the high-water mark in this field.

IV. HOW ANCIENT DATES ARE FIXED

Since chronology is the backbone of history and since it is impos-sible to get a clear idea of the relationship of events and movements unless we know their dates, it is extremely important for the thought-ful student of the past to get a clear idea how dates are fixed. Since 1938, Mesopotamian chronology has gradually become stabilized until it is probably correct to within half a century as far back as the twenty-fifth century B.C. Egyptian dates for the Old Kingdom have had to be rather drastically reduced to agree with the lower Meso-potamian chronology, and the archaeological chronology of Syria and Palestine has been adjusted to harmonize with the concurrent evidence from both sides. For the first time since the beginning of excavations we are, accordingly, in a position to validate our chronol-ogy of the ancient Near East. On what basis can we make this affirmation?

Assyrian chronology is now fixed back toward the middle of the second millennium B.C., thanks to the publication by Arno Poebel, in 1942–1943, of the so-called Khorsabad List of Assyrian kings, which begins in the late third millennium and ends in the eighth century B.C. Moreover, the latter part of this list overlaps other lists of annual magistrates, or eponyms, which are preserved intact from the early ninth century to the middle of the seventh. Part of the period is also covered by a terse chronicle, giving each eponym with the outstanding events of his year. Under one year a solar eclipse is recorded, thus enabling the astronomer to compute the precise date —763 B.C. In this way it is possible to fix the precise date of all the dated events recorded in the Babylonian Chronicle, covering the years from 745 to 667 B.C.—and the accessions of the kings of Babylon agree throughout to the year with the data of the Ptolemaic canon, compiled from Babylonian sources by the famous Greek astronomer of the second century A.D.! Further, thanks to many thousands of dated business documents, we are able to control practically all intercalary months employed in the Neo-Babylonian and Persian periods to adjust the calendar. With the aid of exact astronomical data, it thus becomes possible to give the Julian equivalents of nearly all dates in Mesopotamian records of the first millennium B.C. This means that we have invaluable pegs on which to hang our Biblical chronology from the ninth to the fifth century B.C.

Thanks to the agreement of the Khorsabad List (checked and controlled by numerous other Assyrian sources) with the astronomically fixed chronology of the New Kingdom in Egypt, we can be sure of our approximate dates back to the reign of Asshur-uballiṭ (c. 1362–1327), who came to the throne not long before the death of Amenophis IV (c. 1377–1360). Dead reckoning on the basis of the Khorsabad List brings us to about the middle of the eighteenth century for Shamshi-Adad I, the older Assyrian contemporary of the great Hammurabi of Babylon. The contemporaneity of these outstanding figures in ancient history was not discovered until 1937, with the sensational find of the Mari tablets, which flooded the age in question with historical illumination (see p. 24). Since lists of the annual events by which years were then dated in Babylonia have been recovered—confirmed by many thousand dated business documents of the age—we possess a record of the chronology of Babylonia from the beginning of the Third Dynasty of Ur to the end of the First Dynasty of Babylon, a period of over five centuries, so we can now fix the chronological position of every year in this series with reference to the Khorsabad List within thirty years or so. Moreover, in 1912 the German scholar F. X. Kugler discovered that a cuneiform table of movements of the planet Venus had originally been drawn up under King Ammiṣaduqa of Babylon, as proved by a date formula from that king's reign. This table makes it possible for the astronomer to calculate possible alternative dates for the reign of Ammiṣaduqa, and it becomes easy to show that only one of them fits the data provided by the Khorsabad List and the Mari documents. Employing this astronomically calculated date, the reign of Hammurabi falls between 1728 and 1686 B.C. and the beginning of the Third Dynasty of Ur between 2070 and 2050 B.C.

Turning from Mesopotamia to Egypt, we find one great advantage in the existence of the Sothic cycle, a period equivalent to 1,460 Julian years. When the Egyptian calendar was formally regularized, perhaps about 2780 B.C., it opened each year with the first day on which the star Sirius was visible on the eastern horizon before sunrise, which then coincided roughly with the appearance of the annual Nile inundation in Lower Egypt. But since there were only 365 days in the Egyptian civil (vague) year, each year the calendar fell behind about a quarter of a day. In the course of 1,461 vague years the date of any astronomically fixed event in the calendar returned to its original place in this calendar, so 1,461 vague years = 1,460 Julian years of 365¼ days each. Since the Egyptians celebrated the festival of the heliacal rising of Sirius every year, to the accompaniment of elaborate ritual and mythology, they could not help becoming aware of this discrepancy and its cyclic character. Fortunately for us, we have a definite, though not entirely clear, statement about the end of a Sothic cycle in the second century A.D. in Censorinus, and a probable allusion to the commencement of the same cycle in the monuments of Sethos I, toward the end of the fourteenth century B.C. These fixed dates, combined with new moons and other data, enable us to give fairly exact dates for the kings of the Twelfth Dynasty, between c. 1989 and 1776 B.C., for Amenophis I of the Eighteenth Dynasty, c. 1546 B.C., and for Tuthmosis III, c. 1490 B.C. (These dates follow the correlation of Borchardt, corrected in part

by Edgerton, and may have to be moved up or down a few years.) For years many scholars fought the "low chronology" of Borchardt, Meyer, and Breasted, until overwhelmed by the weight of new evidence. I know of no competent ancient historian today who places the beginning of the Middle Kingdom before 2000 B.C. Thanks to the corroboratory evidence of Mesopotamian chronology, there can be no doubt about the substantial correctness of Borchardt's date.

All our chronology of the lands of the Aegean, including Crete, as well as of Palestine and Phoenicia during the Bronze Age, depends upon direct or cultural synchronisms between these regions and Egypt. The archaeological chronology of the entire Bronze Age in Palestine is based on Egyptian. The results are so reasonable throughout and are now so beautifully confirmed by Mesopotamian evidence (through Syria) that they cannot be changed more than a century or two in the future. Since our Palestinian dates depend largely on pottery, they are generally somewhat fluid, but even so they remain fixed within narrow limits. Before 3000 we are again reduced to conjecture on the basis of cultural periods and geochronology.

V. HOW ANCIENT SITES ARE IDENTIFIED

Few scholarly matters have been as cavalierly handled as the identification of ancient sites. Owing to the intense interest of pilgrims and travelers in the Holy Land, well-meaning clergy and helpful guides have made many hasty identifications, generally on the flimsiest pretexts. Moreover, few of the modern scholars who have identified Biblical sites have possessed the necessary scholarly training. Most of what has been written on the subject of Palestinian topography since the seventeenth century is now virtually worthless. However, here and there are some outstanding names of men who made valuable contributions to our knowledge of the topography of the Holy Land. In 1714, Adrian Reland published a careful and comprehensive account of Palestine and its ancient towns, compiled from all available ancient literary sources—the Bible, Graeco-Roman literature, and the Talmud. In 1837, Edward Robinson undertook his epoch-making trip to Palestine, in the course of which he vastly

FIG. 4. A cedar of Lebanon. The cedar forests of the Lebanon range are now greatly diminished in size, but they were once extensive and the most important source of excellent furniture and building wood in the ancient East. Egyptian, Mesopotamian, Canaanite, and Israelite monarchs drew heavily from these forests for their luxurious palaces.

improved existing maps and located hundreds of modern sites, besides identifying for the first time scores of Biblical towns whose location was completely unknown. Dozens of Western scholars followed his footsteps during the following half century, but few of their identifications have stood the test of sound method. In 1865–1877 Conder, Kitchener, and others carried out the great Survey of Western Palestine, followed by an abortive American expedition and later by a successful one-man German undertaking (see above). In 1894, George Adam Smith published his *Historical Geography of the Holy Land*, which became astonishingly popular and passed through many editions. From the scholarly point of view it was abreast of the times when it first appeared, but it has become more and more antiquated with the progress of investigation. The next important step forward came in 1902, when the German Evangelical Institute for the Archaeology of the Holy Land was founded under the direction of Gustav Dalman. He and his pupils introduced much greater precision in their treatment of the material, observing the physical facts as accurately as possible, reproducing modern Arabic names correctly, and dealing with the literary and documentary sources as exhaustively and critically as possible. The German school added some good identifications and discarded many bad ones, as may be seen most conveniently from the *Atlas* of Hermann Guthe (latest edition: 1926). Dalman was succeeded in 1922 by Albrecht Alt, who has improved Dalman's method by utilizing inscriptions and results of archaeological excavations and surface explorations. Since 1922 the American Schools of Oriental Research has taken the lead in surface exploration, dating sites by the potsherds with which they are strewn. The high-water mark of its investigations is marked by the explorations of Nelson Glueck, who began a systematic examination of all ancient sites in Transjordan in 1932, and has continued it ever since with occasional interruptions. No such thorough archaeological survey has ever been made in any other comparable area in the Near East. For the first time we can analyze the fluctuations of population in Transjordan, from period to period, and delimit the boundaries of Edom, Moab, and Ammon on purely archaeological grounds.

The topographical student of today can begin with an admirable French work, Father Abel's *Géographie de la Palestine* (two volumes, 1933–1938). But he will soon find that this is only a convenient starting point for further research, especially on the basis of the rapidly accumulating archaeological and inscriptional material. The serious investigator must consider the following aspects of his problem: (1) criticism of the written sources in which ancient place names occur; (2) approximate location of sites from documentary indications; (3) toponymy, or the analysis of place names and their linguistic transmission; (4) archaeological indications; (5) the evidence of tradition.

The first requirement boils down to a very simple yet often neglected principle: all ancient literary works must be edited with the greatest possible exactness, after a methodical comparison of all preserved manuscripts (whose variant readings must be recorded); all inscriptions must be accessible in photographs or in good copies by scholars of recognized competence and precision. In the case of important places, such scientific editing of passages where they are mentioned frequently gives a clearer idea of their relation to other places in the neighborhood. In the case of less important places, it is well to know the most reliable form of their names before proceeding to locate them. Textual criticism becomes a matter of primary value in dealing with long lists of names such as we have in Joshua, where the Greek translation of the third or second century B.C. often corrects the Hebrew Bible, though it is sometimes not possible to restore the original Greek reading with any degree of confidence. The topographer is thus heavily dependent on the laborious work of textual critics of the Greek Bible. As one out of many possible illustrations we select Josh. 19:45, in a list of towns of Dan. The Hebrew text reads, "And Jehud, and Bene-berak," whereas the oldest Greek manuscript, from the fourth century A.D., offers, "And

(I)azor and Banaibakat." The Taylor Prism of Sennacherib, in its account of the campaign of 701 B.C. against Hezekiah, offers, "Azuru and Banai-barqa." Today we find the two Arab villages of *Yazûr* and *Ibn-ibrâq*, with ancient names, only a mile and a half apart, thus proving the correctness of the Iazor of the oldest Greek text against the Jehud of the much younger Hebrew text of the Masoretic Bible (see Plate IX, C-4, where the traditional name Jehud is placed at modern *Yazûr*).

Our second approach depends more upon knowledge of the country, ancient and modern, as well as upon common sense, than upon any other considerations. The topographer must analyze accounts of journeys and campaigns, comparing routes and lists of different periods with one another; he must be able to select the most suitable location for an ancient town on the basis of terrain, communications, water supply, etc. If he can find different references to a place, he can often locate it approximately by the simple method of drawing lines or circles and noting where they intersect. The greatest danger here is that the scholar will content himself with the application of this method and perhaps the third one, without taking other approaches into consideration.

The third approach to topographic problems begins by comparing ancient place names with modern. Since this method is the most obvious of all, it has been sorely abused by amateur topographers, as well as by many scholars who should know better. Thus Palmer proposed the identification of Zephath (Hormah in the south) with modern *Isbeitâ* (*Subaita*), though all Semitic vowels and consonants are different (Plate XVIII, B-7). It is quite true that both vowels and consonants shift in the course of history (thus Hebrew *g* becomes Arabic *j*), but these shifts are subject to regular phonetic laws, which can never be stated arbitrarily but must always be worked out inductively by first collecting all certain examples of correspondences between ancient and modern names. It is also true that popular etymology often modifies an ancient name slightly: e.g., ancient Shefar'am in Galilee is now called *Shefa'amr*, which means, "Healing of 'Amr." Note, however, that even here all the consonants and vowels are kept; the only change is in transposing two consonants. There is little excuse save ignorance for the frequent disregard of sound linguistic method by topographers, especially by archaeologists without any philological training, since Kampffmeyer published an admirable—now slightly antiquated—monograph on the subject as far back as 1892.

The fourth approach consists in utilizing the results of surface exploration and excavation for identifying sites. Thus, for instance, Palmer's identification of Zephath was disproved by the results of the Colt expedition ten years ago. No pottery or other remains from the Israelite period were discovered either at *Isbeitâ* (*Subaita*) itself or in the vicinity, thus confirming the objections to the identification previously made by philologians and territorial geographers, who considered the site as much too far south of the mountains of Judah and the arable lands of the tribe of Simeon. An increasing number of identifications have been made on an archaeological basis and subsequently confirmed from other sources: e.g., *Tell ed-Duweir* as the site of Lachish (Plate XVIII, B-5). The archaeological method may be used together with territorial geography: if a town can be limited to a certain district, an exhaustive examination of all possible sites in the area in question often yields the correct identification without any further ado. In this way Garstang discovered the site of Hazor in Galilee (Plate XVIII, D-2).

Our final approach is that of tradition, which can be very valuable but must be employed with great caution. Modern "traditions" are often worthless: e.g., Masterman identified ancient Tarichaea on the Sea of Galilee with modern *Khirbet Kerak* (Plate XVIII, D-3) because the Jewish colonists of Chinnereth—established in the nineteenth century—told him that their ancestors had pickled fish there. Naturally the facts are that the colonists had learned about this once popular but quite erroneous identification from travelers or teachers!

CHRONOLOGICAL OUTLINE OF ANCIENT HISTORY

(c. = circa = about)

I. THE ANCIENT WORLD BEFORE THE PATRIARCHS

A. The Stone Age, beginning 200,000 to 500,000 years ago.
1. The Paleolithic or Old Stone Age, coming to an end c. 25,000–12,000 B.C. Neanderthal man, the first distinguishable race, spread over Europe and Western Asia in the middle of the period; represented in Palestine by Mt. Carmel man. In Europe the first appearance of modern man (*homo sapiens*) was Cro-Magnon man at the end of the period; best known for his remarkable cave paintings.
2. The Mesolithic or Middle Stone Age, c. 12,000–8000 B.C. In Palestine Natufian man was the first to engage in agriculture and domesticate animals. He represents the first historical race.
3. The Neolithic or Late Stone Age, in the Near East c. 8000–4500 B. C. Pottery invented and the first villages founded.

B. The Chalcolithic Age, c. 4500–3000 B.C. Copper introduced; the first great buildings erected; and writing begun (in Babylonia c. 3500 B.C.).

C. The Early Bronze Age, or first historical period, c. 3000–2000 B.C. —the age when the first great states emerged.
EGYPT:
1. The Early Dynastic Period (Dynasties I–II), c. 3000–2700.
2. The Old Kingdom or Pyramid Age (Dynasties III–VI), c. 2700–2200. Close commercial relations by sea and land with Syria and Palestine, involving also, perhaps, political control of these countries by Egypt.
3. The First Intermediate Period, c. 2200–2000—a dark age caused by Asiatic, perhaps Amorite, invaders.
BABYLONIA:
1. The Early Dynastic or Sumerian Age, c. 2800–2400.
2. The First Semitic or Accad Dynasty, c. 2400–2200, of which the chief ruler was Sargon I. The world's first great empire was founded, and expeditions were sent as far away as Syria and the Taurus (Silver) Mountains.
3. The Guti (highlander) rule, and Sumerian resurgence in the Third Dynasty of Ur, c. 2200–2000 B.C.

II. THE ANCIENT WORLD BETWEEN THE AGES OF ABRAHAM AND DAVID, c. 2000–1000 B.C.

A. The Middle Bronze Age, c. 2000–1500 B.C.
EGYPT:
1. The Middle Kingdom (DYNASTY XII), c. 2000–1780. Palestine and Syria under Egyptian control.
2. The Second Intermediate Age, c. 1780–1550. Dynasties XIII–XIV, c. 1780–1720. The Hyksos Period, composed of Dynasties XV–XVII, c. 1720–1550, during which Asiatic rulers (probably mostly Canaanite) seized control of Egypt and established a great empire including Palestine-Syria. War of liberation led by Kamose and Ahmose, c. 1600–1550.
3. Beginning of the New Kingdom under Amenophis (Amenhotep) I, c. 1546.
MESOPOTAMIA:
The Amorite invasion and establishment of Amorite dynasties from the Mediterranean to Babylonia, c. 2000–1700. The Mari Age, known from the archives found at the city of Mari, 18th century. The First Dynasty of Babylon (Amorite), c. 1850–1550 (according to the new "low" chronology), with Hammurabi reigning during the latter part of the 18th and perhaps early 17th century. Irruption of non-Semitic Indo-Iranian and Hurrian (Horite) peoples from the highlands into northern Mesopotamia, 18th and 17th centuries. Destruction of Babylon by the Hittites of Asia Minor, c. 1550.
PALESTINE:
Controlled politically from Egypt during most of the period. The wandering of the Patriarchs in the hill country and Negeb, c. 2000–1700. Descent into Egypt of the family of Jacob, c. 1700. Country exceedingly prosperous under Hyksos, c. 1720–1550. Conquered by native Egyptians under Ameno-phis (Amenhotep) I, c, 1546–1525. Some portion of the House of Joseph (Ephraim and Manasseh) may have returned to Palestine from Egypt when the Hyksos were expelled.

B. The Late Bronze Age, c. 1500–1200 B.C.
EGYPT: This was the period of the New Kingdom, when Egyptian rulers expanded their empire to its greatest extent in all directions.
1. Dynasty XVIII, c. 1546–1319. According to the Borchardt-Edgerton chronology, the chief Pharaohs ruled as follows: Thutmose (Thothmes) III, c. 1490–1436, under whom some of the most brilliant campaigns in Egyptian military history were launched. After the capture of Megiddo, c. 1468, he had little Canaanite opposition, and controlled all territory between Egypt and the Euphrates, where his border touched that of Mitanni. Amenophis (Amenhotep) III, c. 1413–1377, and Amenophis IV (Akhnaton), c. 1377–1360, were the Pharaohs to whom the letters from Canaanite, Hittite, Mitannian, Assyrian, and Babylonian kings found at *Tell el-Amarna* (Akhetaton) were written. After the capture of Megiddo, Akhnaton instituted a monotheistic religious revolution in Egypt; as a result of his concentration on that project, the Egyptian hold on Asia was greatly weakened.
2. Dynasty XIX, c. 1319–1200, during which energetic efforts were made to re-establish the empire in Asia, into which the Hittites had extended their control. The chief Pharaohs were: Sethos (Seti) I, c. 1319–1301; Rameses II, c. 1301–1234, who fought the drawn battle with the Hittites at Kadesh in Syria, c. 1297, and concluded the formal treaty with them which established the Syrian boundary, c. 1280; Merenptah, c. 1235–1227, who claims to have defeated Israel in Palestine, c. 1230. Moses and the Exodus of Israel, probably shortly after 1300 B.C.
MESOPOTAMIA:
Babylonia weak under Kassite (non-Semitic) rulership, c. 1500–1150. The Hurrian (Horite) or Mitannian state in northern Mesopotamia, c. 1500–1370. During the major part of that period almost continuous, but indecisive, warfare between Egypt and Mitanni. The state was conquered by the Hittites, c. 1370, but was kept as a buffer between Asia Minor and Assyria; finally taken over by Assyria, c. 1250.
ASIA MINOR:
The Hittite Empire, c. 1600–1200. A Hittite army raided Babylon, c. 1550; conquered northern Syria in the first half of the 14th century. Battle of Kadesh, c. 1297, and treaty with the Egyptians, c. 1280.
PALESTINE:
A province of Egypt, nominally at least, throughout the period. The Amarna Age, illuminated by the letters from Canaanite kings to the Egyptian court, c. 1400–1360. Final destruction and abandonment of Jericho, 14th century. The main phase of the Israelite Conquest, c. 1250–1225.
THE GREEK WORLD:
The golden age of Crete and the Minoan civilization achieved its peak in the 15th century. The downfall of Crete, c. 1400. The Mycenaean civilization in Greece and establishment of active trade with Asia, 14th–13th centuries.

C. The Beginning of the Iron Age, c. 1200–1000 B.C.
EGYPT:
Dynasty XX, c. 1200–1085. Invasion of the Sea Peoples (among whom were the Philistines) thrown back by Rameses III, c. 1190. After c. 1150 the power of the Pharaohs declined and the priests became the real rulers, and the Asiatic empire was lost.
MESOPOTAMIA:
No strong rulers, except the Assyrian Tiglath-pileser I, who c. 1100 held northern Syria for a time.
PALESTINE:
The Period of the Judges, c. 1225–1020. The Aramean invasion of Bashan (and eastern Syria), 12th–11th centuries. The Philistines, thrown back from Egypt, settled along the southern coastal plain, early 12th century. The great battle with the Canaanites in the Valley of Jezreel and the Song of Deborah, c. 1100. The struggle with the Philistines, 11th century, with the fall of Shiloh and the death of Eli, c. 1050. Saul and the beginning of the Israelite monarchy, c. 1020–1004.

III. THE PERIOD OF THE HEBREW KINGS, c. 1000–587 B.C.

A. Palestine: The dates of the Israelite and Judean kings are not fixed with absolute certainty, though the margin of error has been reduced to a very few years. The following chronology is from one of the latest systematic treatises, by J. Begrich:
(1) The United Monarchy: David, c. 1004–998 (as king of Judah), c. 998–965 (over all Israel); Solomon, c. 965–926. The division of the kingdom, c. 926.
(2) The Divided Monarchy, c. 926–587 (the cross lines mark changes of dynasties).

ISRAEL				JUDAH		
RULER	REIGN	PROPHET	EVENTS	PROPHET	RULER	REIGN
JEROBOAM I	926–907		*Shishak's invasion, c. 922*		REHOBOAM	926–910
Nadab	907–906				Abijam	910–908
Baasha	906–883				ASA	908–872
Elah	883–882				JEHOSHAPHAT	872–852
Zimri	882				Jehoram	
OMRI	882–871				(or Joram)	852–845
AHAB	871–852	} ELIJAH			Ahaziah	845–844
Ahaziah	852–851		*Battle of Karkar; coalition vs. Assyria, 853*		Athaliah	845–839
Jehoram	851–845				Joash	
JEHU	845–818	} ELISHA			(or Jehoash)	839–800
Jehoahaz	818–802				Amaziah	800–785
Joash	802–787				UZZIAH	
JEROBOAM II	787–747	AMOS			(or Azariah)	785–747
Zechariah	747–746				Jotham	
Shallum	747–746	} HOSEA	*Syro-Ephraimitic war, c. 734*		(regent and king)	758–743
Menahem	746–737		*Tiglath-pileser III's invasion, 733–732*	ISAIAH }	AHAZ	742–725
Pekahiah	736–735		*Siege of Samaria by Assyrians, 724-Feb., 721*	MICAH }	HEZEKIAH	725–697
Pekah	734–733		*Sennacherib invasion, 701*		MANASSEH	696–642
Hoshea	732–724		*Deuteronomic Reform, 621*		Amon	641–640
Fall of Samaria	721		*Josiah killed by Pharaoh Necho, 609*		JOSIAH	639–609
			Nebuchadnezzar's first invasion, 598	JEREMIAH }	Jehoahaz	609
			Nebuchadnezzar's second invasion, 589–587	EZEKIEL }	Jehoiakim	608–598
					Jehoiachin	598
					Zedekiah	598–587
					Fall of Jerusalem	587

15

B. Mesopotamia:

The Assyrian Empire, c. 1000–612. Conquest of northern Syria, early ninth century. Beginning of the push southward under Shalmaneser III (859–824) checked by the drawn battle with the Syrian coalition (in which Ahab of Israel participated) at Karkar, 853. A new attempt to seize southern Syria and Palestine succeeded under Tiglath-pileser III (745–727), who in 733–732 conquered the Plain of Sharon, Galilee, Gilead, and Damascus, turning them into subject provinces and leaving the small kingdoms of Palestine as client states. As the result of rebellion, Israel was reduced by Shalmaneser V (727–722) and Sargon II (722–705), and 27,290 leading citizens were carried into exile, 721. Sennacherib (705–681) invaded Judah in 701. Esarhaddon (681–669) succeeded in the conquest of Egypt, but he and Asshurbanapal (669–626) were engaged chiefly in defensive warfare against threatening powers on all sides. Fall of Asshur to the Medes, 614, and of Nineveh to the Medes and Babylonians, 612.
The Babylonian Empire, c. 612–539. Defeat of the Assyrians and Egyptians under Pharaoh Necho at Haran, 609. Nebuchadnezzar (605–562), after his defeat of Pharaoh Necho at Carchemish in 605, took over Syria-Palestine, leaving small principalities like Judah as client states.

C. Egypt:

The Libyan Dynasties (XXII–XXIV), of which the first Pharaoh was Shishak, c. 935–712. Shishak's raid on Palestine, c. 922. The Ethiopian Dynasty (XXV), c. 712–663. Assyrian conquest of Egypt, c. 670.
The Saite Dynasty (XXVI), c. 663–525. Pharaoh Necho (609–597) and Hophra (588–569). The former attempted to recover the Egyptian Asiatic empire, defeating Josiah in 609, but being defeated by the Babylonians at Haran in 609 and decisively at Carchemish in 605.

IV. THE EXILIC AND POST-EXILIC PERIODS, 587–333 B.C.

A. Palestine:

Leading Judean citizens exiled from the country in 598 and 587, among them Ezekiel. The Edict of Cyrus, permitting the return from Exile, c. 538. Temple rebuilt by Zerubbabel, 520–516. Ezra's return, 458 (some scholars date it later). Nehemiah's return, 445. Malachi, c. 500–450.

B. The Persian Empire:

Cyrus united Persia and Media, 549; conquered Lydia, 546; conquered Babylon (which was ruled by Nabonidus and the crown prince Belshazzar), 539. Cambyses (530–522) conquered Egypt, 525. Darius I (522–486); campaign against Greece and defeat at Marathon, 490. Xerxes I or Ahasuerus (486–465); campaign against Greece and defeat at Thermopylae and Salamis, 480. Subsequent rulers: Artaxerxes I (465–424); Xerxes II (424–423); Darius II (423–404); Artaxerxes II (404–358); Artaxerxes III (358–338); Arses (338–336); and Darius III (336–331).

C. Greece:

The defeat of the Persians at Marathon, 490; at Thermopylae and Salamis, 480. The golden age of Pericles, 460–429. Herodotus (c. 484–425). Socrates (c. 470–399). Plato (c. 428–348). Aristotle (384–322).

V. THE HELLENISTIC PERIOD, 333–63 B.C.*

A. Macedonian Empire: Period of rapid expansion.

Philip (359–336) extended power over Greece; battle of Chaeronea (338) marked end of power of Greek city-states.
Alexander the Great (336–323) conquered Persia and extended rule to western India; decisive battles: River Granicus (334), Issus (333), Gaugamela (331). He reached India (327); died in Babylon (323).

B. Hellenistic Empires Which Emerged From Alexander's Empire:

Alexander's Generals Compete for Power. At first Perdiccas was in control in Asia, Antipater and Craterus in Europe. By 301 Cassander held Macedon, Lysimachus Thrace and Asia Minor, Seleucus Mesopotamia and Syria, and Ptolemy Africa. Conditions remained unsettled. By 277 three leading empires had emerged; they remained until absorbed by Rome.

THE THREE GREAT HELLENISTIC EMPIRES:
1. Macedonia: Antigonus Gonatas (277–239). The line of kings ends with Perseus (179–168); in 168 Macedonia became dependent upon Rome, and in 146 was made a Roman province.
2. Egypt: Ptolemy had been satrap since 323; he founded the dynasty which bears his name. Ptolemy I (323–283); Ptolemy II (285–246); Ptolemy III (246–221); Ptolemy IV (221–203); Ptolemy V (203–181/0). Thereafter the line of Ptolemies continued, under Roman dominance, until 30 B.C., when Egypt became a Roman province.
3. Syria: Seleucus gained control of southern Asia Minor, Syria, and the eastern portions of Alexander's empire, and founded the Seleucid dynasty: Seleucus I (312–280); Antiochus I (280–262/1); Antiochus II (261–247); Seleucus II (247–226); Seleucus III (226–223); Antiochus III, the Great (223–187); Seleucus IV (187–175); Antiochus IV, Epiphanes (175–163), Antiochus V (163–162); Demetrius I (162–150); Alexander Balas (150–145); Demetrius II (145–139/8); Antiochus VI (145–142/1); Antiochus VII (139/8–129). The weak, unsettled Syrian kingdom continued until 64 B.C., when Pompey took over Syria and made it a Roman province.

SMALLER KINGDOMS WHICH EMERGED FROM ALEXANDER'S EMPIRE:
1. Pergamum: Continued under the Attalids until Attalus III (139/8–133), who willed his kingdom to Rome.
2. Bithynia: Established by Ziboetes (327–c. 279) and Nicomedes I (c. 279–c. 250); continued until Nicomedes III (94–75/4), who willed his kingdom to Rome.

C. Other Kingdoms of Asia Minor:

1. Pontus: Under the Mithridatids beginning with Mithridates I (337/6–302/1); mastered by Rome in middle of first century B.C.
2. Galatia: On the Halys River in Asia Minor; settled by the Gauls, c. 278; passed to Rome on the death of Amyntas (37–25).

*The dates from this point follow the *Cambridge Ancient History.*

D. Parthian Empire:

Threw off the rule of the Seleucids (tradition says this happened under Arsaces); the Parthian era began c. 247 B.C. The Empire grew until it reached from the Euphrates to the borders of India. In 53 the Parthians defeated Crassus and threatened Syria and Asia Minor; in 40 they succeeded in entering Jerusalem; but in 39/38 the Romans repulsed the threat. Their kingdom continued, but with declining power, until A.D. 224.

E. The Greek Cities:

Resisted Macedonian rule; made alliances with Rome. But Rome gradually took Greece over; the destruction of Corinth (146 B.C.) ended resistance. Greece organized as the Roman province of Achaia, 27 B.C.

F. Palestine:

Continued under Egypt until 198 B.C., when Syria gained control. In 167 the Maccabean revolt against Syria occurred. The Maccabean leaders were: Judas Maccabaeus (166/5–160); Jonathan (160–142); Simon (142–134); John Hyrcanus (134–104); Aristobulus I (104–103); Alexander Jannaeus (103–76); Alexandra (76–67); Aristobulus II (66–63). In 63 Pompey established Roman control over Palestine.

VI. THE ROMAN PERIOD, 63 B.C. to A.D. 325

A. Earlier History of Rome:

Etruscan control from about 750 B.C. Establishment of Roman Republic about 500. Rome dissolved the Latin League in 338, and controlled central Italy. Subjugation of Italy to Po Valley complete about 266. Period of Punic Wars, 264–146; destruction of Carthage, 146. Achaian League crushed, Corinth destroyed, 146. Wars against peoples in Spain, Numidia, Helvetia, etc., spread Roman rule in western Mediterranean world. Wars against Mithridates VI of Pontus (121/0–63) and against pirates in eastern Mediterranean extended Roman rule in east. In 64–63 Pompey organized as provinces Pontus, Cilicia, and Syria; he took over Palestine (63).

B. Period of Conspiracies and Civil Wars:

Catiline's conspiracy; opposed by Cicero; Catiline slain (62). First Triumvirate: Pompey, Caesar, Crassus (60). Caesar's Gallic Wars (58–51). Civil war between Caesar and Pompey (49–46). Assassination of Julius Caesar (44). Second Triumvirate: Antony, Octavian, Lepidus (43); defeats republican forces under Brutus and Cassius at Philippi (42). Battle of Actium (31); Octavian, later called Augustus, sole ruler.

C. The Roman Emperors:

The Five Julian Emperors: Augustus (31 B.C. to A.D. 14); division of provinces into senatorial and imperial; golden age of Latin literature, e.g., Virgil; birth of Jesus. Tiberius (14–37); ministry of John the Baptist and Jesus. Caligula (37–41). Claudius (41–54); Paul leads missionary expansion of Church. Nero (54–68); Rome burned; Christians persecuted there (64). Rival Contenders for Power: Galba, Otho; Vitellius, Vespasian (68–69). The Three Flavian Emperors: Vespasian (69–79); Jewish revolt (66–70); destruction of Jerusalem (70). Titus (79–81). Domitian (81–96); persecution of Christians in latter part of reign.
Emperors in Period of Maximum Expansion: Nerva (96–98). Trajan (98–117); provinces Dacia, Armenia, Mesopotamia, Assyria, and Arabia added to empire; letters of Ignatius, Bishop of Antioch, c. A.D. 115. Hadrian (117–138); revolt of Jews (132–135); Jerusalem rebuilt as Aelia Capitolina. Antoninus Pius (138–161); Marcion in Rome, c. 138–140; Polycarp and Justin Martyr important Christian leaders. Marcus Aurelius, Stoic philosopher-king (161–180).
Emperors in Century of Disorder: Commodus (180–192); leadership of Irenaeus in Church. Septimus Severus (193–211). Caracalla (211–217); grant of universal citizenship. Severus Alexander (222–235); new Persian empire, 226. Decius (249–251); general persecution of Christians. Death of Christian scholar Origen, c. 254. Aurelian (270–275).
Emperors with Absolute Power: Diocletian (284–305); reorganization of imperial administration; removal of imperial residence to the east; general persecution of Christians. Contest for power after Diocletian's death. Constantine the Great, sole ruler (323–337). First ecumenical council, Nicaea (325).

D. Palestine Under the Romans:

Rule of the Herods: Hyrcanus appointed ethnarch and high priest under Roman control (63 B.C.). Antipater, the Idumaean, virtual ruler of Palestine under Roman grant (c. 55–43). His sons, Herod and Phasael, tetrarchs (41). Antigonus, son of Aristobulus, high priest and king by aid of Parthians (40–37). Herod the Great, king of Judaea by grant of Roman Senate (40–4 B.C.). Upon his death, kingdom divided: Archelaus, tetrarch of Judaea, Samaria, and Idumaea (4 B.C. to A.D. 6); Herod Antipas, tetrarch of Galilee and Peraea (4 B.C. to A.D. 39), until banished for suspected plotting against Rome; Philip, tetrarch of Gaulonitis, Trachonitis, Batanaea, Auranitis, and Panias (4 B.C. to A.D. 34).
Roman procurators ruled (A.D. 6–41) after Augustus deposed Archelaus. Of these procurators, Pontius Pilate was in office 26–36.
Herod Agrippa I was made king by Caligula in 37 over the former tetrarchies of Philip and Lysanias (Abilene); in 39 or 40 he was given the tetrarchy of Herod Antipas, in 41, the rest of Palestine. He died in 44.
Roman procurators again ruled Palestine, 44–66: Cuspius Fadus (44–?); Tiberius Alexander (?–48); Cumanus (48–52); Felix (52–60; or, 52–c. 55?); Festus (60–62); Albinus (62–64); Gessius Florus (64–66).
Herod Agrippa II, made king of Chalcis (A.D. 50), exchanged this realm for the former tetrarchy of Philip about 53. Nero later added to this kingdom some cities of Galilee and Peraea. His long reign lasted until c. 93.
Jewish revolt against Rome (66–70). Destruction of Jerusalem and the Temple by Titus (70). Judaea again under Roman procurators.
Renewed revolt, led by Bar-Cochba (132–135). Jerusalem rebuilt, after revolt was crushed; renamed Aelia Capitolina; only Gentiles allowed in it.

E. Nabataean Kingdom:

By the beginning of the Hellenistic era the Nabataeans were in possession of the territory of the ancient Edomites. From their capital at Petra they extended their control in all directions. Their independence was limited by the Romans from 63 B.C. on, but their land did not become a Roman province until A.D. 106. Aretas IV was their king from 9 B.C. to A.D. 40.

FIG. 5. Esdraelon or the Valley of Jezreel. This plain separates Galilee from Samaria. In the background are the Galilean hills, in which, just left of center, some houses of Nazareth can be seen. At the top right is Mount Tabor (see Fig. 35). In the left foreground the pass of Megiddo (Fig. 26) opens out into the plain. At the left, above the pass, the flat-topped mound of Megiddo, comprising some thirteen acres, juts out into the plain. Megiddo was the fortress city which guarded the pass.

THE GEOGRAPHY OF PALESTINE

PLATE I

PALESTINE has wielded an influence in world history quite out of proportion to its size and natural resources. Its prominent role in determining the cultural and particularly the religious life of the modern world is the more surprising in view of its remarkably small dimensions. West of the River Jordan (Plate I, D 2-5), its total area is only 6,000 square miles. If the portion east of the Jordan is included, there are but 10,000 square miles in the entire region. Thus in its full extent Palestine is barely larger than the State of Vermont, and exceeds the size of Wales by only twenty-five per cent.

With patriotic pride the Israelites spoke of their country as extending "from Dan even to Beer-sheba" (I Kings 4:25). Yet from Dan (I, D-2), at the southwest foot of snow-capped Mount Hermon, to Beer-sheba (I, B-6), where the Hill Country ends and the southern desert region begins, it is slightly less than 150 miles. The distances from east to west are even smaller. From Accho (I, C-3) to the Sea of Galilee (I, D-3) it is only 28 miles. Even in the south, where the shore line curves gradually toward the southwest, it is but 54 miles from Gaza (I, A-6) to the Dead Sea (I, C-D 5-6).

Within such meager limits occur surprising contrasts of terrain and climate. Along the coastal plain a mild climate prevails; the average annual temperature is about 67° F. at Joppa. Only thirty-four miles from the Mediterranean Sea, at an altitude of nearly 2,600 feet, Jerusalem (I, C-5) enjoys a delightful temperate climate with an average annual temperature of 63°. To the east of the "holy city," however, there is such a sharp drop in altitude that fifteen miles away, at Jericho (I, C-5), one stands 3,300 feet below the level of Jerusalem, and nearly 700 feet below the level of the Mediterranean Sea. In this region a warm, virtually tropical climate prevails. Indeed,

the heat of the summer months is so intense as to enervate the natives who live there. Farther east, however, where the plateau of Transjordan (I, D-E 3-7) stretches away at an altitude some 3,500 feet above Jericho, snow falls in winter and the rather temperate climate approximates that of Jerusalem.

The same striking contrasts of altitude and climate may be traced from north to south. From the heights of Mount Hermon (I, D-2), 9,100 feet above sea level, where the temperature has an alpine range and snow lies on the mountaintop the year round, the land slopes down in a rapid descent until the Jordan Valley, just after leaving Lake Huleh (I, D-2), reaches sea level. Continuing to the south, the valley offers a mild climate about the Sea of Galilee (I, D-3), 685 feet below sea level, and when it finally reaches the Dead Sea, 1,275 feet below sea level and the lowest body of water on the surface of the earth, the summer climate is intensely hot. From this deep gorge the Arabah ascends rather steadily until at a point just west of Petra (I, C-8) it is 300 feet above sea level.

Climatic conditions, however, depend not only upon altitude but also upon other factors. Of great importance are the winds, which usually blow from the west. In the winter, coming from the west or southwest, they bring the clouds which drop their moisture as they reach the cool Hill Country, and thus cause the rainy season, which extends from October to April. During the summer season, the northwest breezes bring a welcome coolness but almost no rainfall.

In addition to the prevailing breezes from the west, winds from other directions blow occasionally. Particularly in the early fall, cool winds come down from the north. More important, however, is the occasional sirocco or hot "east wind," which blows in from the eastern desert. Because of its excessive dryness, heat, and violence, it

FIG. 6. The Plain of Shechem in the heart of Samaria. In the center, surrounded by a modern wall, is the ancient Well of Jacob. In the left background is the modern village 'Askar, which may be the site of ancient Sychar (John 4:5). This view looks northeast from the eastern slopes of Mount Gerizim. Behind 'Askar, the slope of Mount Ebal begins its rise to the left. Between these two mountain slopes is the mouth of the important pass for roads leading west and north. The mound of ancient Shechem, which once guarded the pass, is just left of the area here shown. The road running up past 'Askar leads to Beth-shan (Scythopolis) in the upper Jordan Valley. The road to Jerusalem runs to the right at the very foot of Mount Gerizim.

is the country's chief climatic curse (cf. Job 1:19; Jer. 18:17; Ezek. 17:10; 27:26).

For a more detailed study of its physical features, resources, and climate, Palestine may be divided into four main sections: (1) the *Coastal Plain;* (2) the central *Hill Country,* including its spur, Mount Carmel (I, B-C 3), which juts out northwest into the sea; (3) the deep cleft of the *Jordan Valley;* and (4) the *Plateau of Transjordan.*

I. THE COASTAL PLAIN

The almost unbroken coast line of Palestine distinctly discouraged commerce on the Mediterranean Sea. In this respect Palestine was in a quite different situation from her northern neighbor Phoènicia. The latter possessed harbor facilities in such places as Tyre (I, C-2) and Sidon (I, C-1). Moreover, the rough terrain of Phoenicia comes down practically to the sea, and deprives its people of adequate opportunities for agriculture. Inevitably, therefore, the Phoenicians became a seafaring people.

With their interest in the sea, the Phoenicians often reached southward and took possession of Accho (I, C-3). This port, called Ptolemais in New Testament times (Acts 21:7), though poorly sheltered from sea winds, was the most attractive harbor location afforded by the coast of Palestine proper. By including Mount Carmel in her borders Phoenicia could completely control the Bay of Accho and the port.

However, even when the Israelites controlled Accho and its bay, they had there no adequate harbor. It was not until recent years, when British engineers built a breakwater running out from the northeast side of the Carmel spur, that this bay provided a really safe anchorage. South of Mount Carmel the coast line was even more discouraging to sea trade. Dor (IV, B-3) was used as a port in Biblical times, but it had no stormproof harbor. Joppa (I, B-4) likewise could boast no real harbor; a line of irregular rocks a short distance from shore appeared to offer a little protection, and with this meager encouragement Joppa has rendered mediocre service through the centuries as a fair-weather port.

Perhaps the most striking proof of the fact that Palestine did not face the sea is the location of Gaza (I, A-6). It was the greatest trading center of ancient Palestine, yet it lay some three miles inland, and no attempt to provide it with a port proved permanently successful. It was land trade from south, east, and north that made Gaza rich.

Yet, although Palestine could never develop a maritime people, it did possess, except where Mount Carmel made its northwest thrust into the sea, a fertile coastal plain. This plain may be divided into three sections. To the north of Mount Carmel was the *Plain of Accho* or Acre (I, C-3), located on the small bay north of Carmel. In Biblical times this small but fertile area was dotted with many important towns, only a few of which are shown on Plate VIII.

Between Mount Carmel and Joppa lay the *Plain of Sharon* (I, B-4). This was a well-watered region which in spots, partly because of the drainage barrier of low hills along the coast, was even marshy. In ancient times it probably possessed extensive forests, and the combination of marshy tendencies and forests kept it from being thickly settled. Its maximum width was a little over twelve miles.

By far the most important section of the coastal plain in Biblical times was *Philistia* or the *Philistine Plain* (I, A-B 5-6). Here once lived those ancient enemies of Israel, the Philistines, who subsequently gave their name to the whole country, for the word "Palestine" is derived from "Philistia." In this well-watered and generally level plain there were few trees, and almost everywhere the rich brown soil invited agricultural development (see Fig. 39). Recently the success achieved in extensive citrus groves has demonstrated anew the fruitfulness of this plain. The one threat to the productivity of the area was the drifting sand, which tended to encroach upon the region near the coast.

Attractive as the Coastal Plain has proved to modern agricultural groups in Palestine, it is noteworthy that this section was never a center of Israelite strength in Old Testament times; nor in the New Testament period was it dominated by the Jewish people and culture. The chief center of Israelite population and interest was not the Coastal Plain but the Hill Country.

II. THE HILL COUNTRY

The rough and rocky Hill Country forms part of an almost continuous range of hills which runs south through southern Syria and extends almost unbroken down the length of Palestine until it drops to a lower level in the desert country south of Judah. In this range the continual outcropping of rock vividly reminds the observer that limestone prevails throughout the extent of Palestine.

Within the limits of Palestine, the three divisions of the Hill Country are Galilee, Samaria, and Judah. *Galilee* (I, C 2-3), in its northern portion, is quite rugged, and at one point, near Merom (VIII, E-5), attains an altitude of nearly 4,000 feet above sea level. The southern half, however, is less hilly, and enjoys a somewhat milder climate. Much of its rolling land can be tilled; level plains a few miles north of Nazareth (I, C-3) and just northwest of the Sea of Galilee invite intensive cultivation. The entire series of hills in Galilee, sloping down from north to south, constitute in reality extensive foothills of Mount Lebanon (I, D-1).

At the southern end of Galilee the range of the Hill Country is cut by the great *Valley of Jezreel* or Esdraelon (I, C-3). From very ancient times important cities were built in this valley; of these Megiddo (VIII, D-7) was of particular significance, because it guarded and controlled the pass which permitted the easiest movement of caravans and troops from the Plain of Sharon to the Valley of Jezreel (Figs. 5 and 26). Mount Carmel, to the northwest, pushed its foot to within two hundred yards of the shore of the sea (Fig. 30) and if its slopes were manned by a hostile army, the use of the shore road around the point was impossible. To save time and distance and to secure safety of passage, it proved desirable to keep control of the pass which led directly from the southern Coastal Plain to the Valley of Jezreel. Megiddo was thus a location of strategic military importance. Control of the Valley of Jezreel was likewise crucial in military maneuvers in Northern Palestine. Hence it came about that again and again this region became a decisive battleground, until, according to the probable interpretation of Rev. 16:16, it gave its name to the scene of the expected final battle of God's hosts with the powers of evil. "Har-Magedon" seems to be the Mount or Hill of Megiddo.

This fertile and inviting valley, in which today several prosperous agricultural colonies of Zionists are to be found, is drained to the west by the River Kishon. The latter is in reality a small brook which may overflow and prove impassable in the rainy season. It flows out to the Mediterranean Sea through the Plain of Accho. To the east two valleys lead down to the Jordan. Their ancient names are unknown. One of them passes between Mount Tabor (I, C-3 and Fig. 35) and the Hill of Moreh (VIII, E-7); the other runs between the Hill of Moreh and Mount Gilboa (I, C 3-4). Thus, except in the heavy rainy season, Esdraelon offered easy, unimpeded passage from the coast to the Jordan Valley.

The hills of *Samaria* form the geographical center of the country. They rise abruptly at the north in Mount Gilboa and the southern extension of Mount Carmel, and reach their highest point at Baalhazor (I, C-5). The two most conspicuous peaks, however, are Mount Ebal and Mount Gerizim (I, C-4), which stand in the heart of the district of Samaria. They were always heights of great military importance, because between them ran the main pass on the north and south road, and at the eastern mouth of this pass was a crossroads from which highways ran in all directions (Fig. 6). Religious significance was soon attached to these twin peaks, and in later days the Samaritan religious group had its center on Mount Gerizim.

The third main division of the Hill Country is *Judah*. In this district the hills are not quite so lofty as in Samaria. Approaching Jerusalem (I, C-5) the hills descend to 2,500–2,600 feet above sea level, and then rise as they go south until the highest point (3,370 feet) is reached just north of Hebron (I, C-6). On the western, more gentle slope of this central watershed, clouds coming in from the Mediterranean bring considerable rainfall and thus sustain plant life on a reasonably adequate level. To the east of the watershed, however, is found the bleak "Wilderness of Judah" or wasteland, deprived of adequate moisture, deeply cut by the valleys leading to the Dead Sea, and dropping down so sharply as to offer little opportunity for agricultural development (see Fig. 42).

The natural result of this contrast was that population and history centered much more upon the fertile western slope of the Judaean Hill Country. Here geographical considerations compelled the people of the upper Hill Country to take deep interest in the *Shephelah* (I, B-5) or Lowlands. The latter region was a distinct district, formed by the broken foothills of the Judaean plateau, but partially severed from it by longitudinal valleys. The Shephelah was important to Judah, not only because of the grain of its valleys and the vineyards and olive groves of its hills, but even more for defensive reasons. In Israelite times such strongly fortified towns as Lachish, Debir, Libnah, Azekah, and Beth-shemesh were situated in it.

To the south the hills gradually descend to the *Negeb* or Southland, which centers in the area between Beer-sheba (I, B-6) and Kadeshbarnea (I, A-7). In this broken, semiarid country people can exist only with the most careful conservation of the water supply. At one time in early Christian history careful water conservation and irrigation systems made possible the support of a considerable population. Life proved precarious in this region, however, and the general dryness of the Negeb is shown by the fact that in recent years a number of ancient papyri, which survive only in very dry climates, have been found there (see pp. 63 f.).

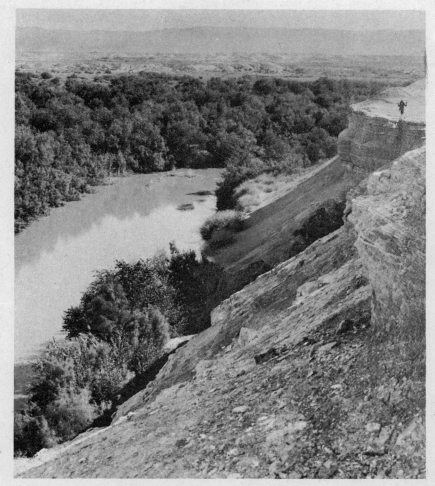

FIG. 7. The Jordan River shortly before it enters the Dead Sea. In the background may be seen the wilderness of the Jordan Valley and the steep slopes of the Hill Country on the west.

FIG. 8. The northern tip of the Dead Sea where the Jordan flows into it.

III. THE JORDAN VALLEY

The Jordan Valley is part of a great rift or geological fault. This rift extends down through Syria, where it divides Mount Lebanon from the Anti-Lebanon range known in the Bible as Hermon and Amana; it continues through Palestine as the Jordan Valley; farther south it forms the Arabah (I, C 7-8) and the Red Sea, and thence extends into Africa.

The sources of the River Jordan are located on the western side of Mount Hermon (I, D-2 and Fig. 34). In its upper course the river runs above the level of the sea, but by the time the stream arrives at Lake Huleh (I, D-2), or Lake Semechonitis, as the first-century Jewish historian Josephus calls it, it is but seven feet above sea level. Thence it drops swiftly to the Sea of Galilee, a beautiful fresh-water lake some 685 feet below sea level, which in the days of Jesus supported a considerable fishing industry.

The one area on the lake shore which invited extensive cultivation was the fertile Plain of Gennesaret, located at the northwest shore and aided by mild climate in yielding a year-round supply of fruits, grains, and vegetables. Elsewhere around the lake the surrounding hills come down to the shore on almost all sides (Fig. 36). Down from these hills rush the winds which cause the sudden storms mentioned in the Gospels (e.g., Mark 4:37). On the east side of the lake the slope rises sharply to the high plateau beyond. Since communication with the plateau region is therefore not easy, the Sea of Galilee has been linked almost entirely with life on its western side.

Other names for the Sea of Galilee are the Sea of Chinnereth, a name used in Old Testament times; the Lake of Gennesaret, a New Testament designation derived from the fertile plain on its northwest; and the Sea of Tiberias, a name derived from the city which Herod Antipas built on the western shore c. A.D. 20.

Leaving the Sea of Galilee as a clear and quiet stream, the Jordan winds down its serpentine course toward the Dead Sea (Fig. 7). By the time it has reached the traditional site of the baptism of Jesus by John the Baptist, it has become a muddy carrier of the soil picked up on its journey. When it empties into the Dead Sea it has reached a level some 1,275 feet below the Mediterranean.

The Jordan was naturally somewhat of a barrier to free communication between east and west Palestine. Yet the ancient Israelites and the later Arabs found many places where the river could be forded except in time of high water, and government and trade have often proved able to bind the two sides of the valley together. In the early Christian period the Romans first bridged the Jordan, at a point not far below Lake Huleh; a bridge centuries old still stands at that spot. There are also modern bridges just south of the Sea of Galilee and at a point east of Jericho.

The Valley of the Jordan, both to the north and south of the Sea of Galilee, was intensively cultivated throughout ancient times. Tributary streams were utilized in the construction of networks of irrigation channels. Such settlement and cultivation, like the occupation of the Valley of Jezreel and the Coastal Plain, occurred before the coming of the Israelites. Precisely in these fertile plain areas the early centers of civilized life developed, and the invading Israelites found the inhabitants already in control of the level land. Hence the newcomers first seized the comparatively undeveloped Hill Country, and only gradually obtained control of the plains. The grazing of flocks and herds, the cultivation of olive, fig, and vine, and the less-crowded life of the hills seemed better to suit the nomadic Israelites; and they found it easier to defend the Hill Country with their more individualistic ways of war than to cope with the professional military forces and equipment which they met in the plains.

The Dead Sea (Figs. 8 and 38), like the Great Salt Lake in Utah, has no outlet. Hence about 25 per cent of the water consists of salt deposits, from which it has recently proved profitable to extract potash and other chemicals. In ancient times the sea did not extend so far south as it does today. The peninsula which extends out into the sea west of Kir-hareseth in Moab (I, D-6) is called the "Tongue." South of this "Tongue" is the area which the Israelites called the Vale of Siddim (Gen. 14:3). Here were situated Sodom, Gomorrah, Admah, Zeboiim, and Zoar (x, H-3). About 2000 B.C. or shortly thereafter (in the time of Abraham) a great catastrophe occurred, presumably an earthquake. Following this event the Vale of Siddim was filled with water, the extent of which has been increasing ever since (see pp. 65 f.).

In Old Testament times the Dead Sea was called "Salt Sea" or "Sea of the Arabah." Josephus speaks of it as "Lake Asphaltitis." However, the Dead Sea had little importance in the history of Bible times. Its oppressive heat in summer, its unnatural saltiness, and the forbidding heights on east and west combined to make it a rather desolate place.

IV. THE PLATEAU OF TRANSJORDAN

The Plateau of Transjordan is divided into five sections by four main streams; the Yarmuk (which is not mentioned in the Bible), the Jabbok, the Arnon, and the Zered. To the north of the Yarmuk was the Biblical *Bashan* (I, D-E 2-3), roughly identical with later Haurân. Signs of prehistoric volcanic activity are frequent in this region; extinct craters, large patches of lava, and a layer of black basalt over the common limestone of Palestine still witness to early eruptions. Trees are rare but the soil is rich. While a somewhat limited rainfall prevents the fullest agricultural development, the region is noted for extensive grain production.

Stretching both north and south of the Jabbok (I, D-4) was *Gilead*. Since it was well watered, possessing a larger number of streams and springs than Bashan, it was capable of sustaining a larger population. This fact, coupled with its greater nearness to the western Hill Country, caused it to play a more prominent role than Bashan in the history of Israel. The most important stream in Gilead was the Jabbok, which took its rise near Rabbath-ammon (I, D-5) and flowed east and north in a semicircle before descending to the Jordan Valley. In the upper reaches of the Jabbok watershed centered the kingdom of *Ammon* (I, D-E 4-5). To the north of the Jabbok are well-wooded regions, but farther south trees become fewer and are not found on the plateau south of Mount Nebo (I, D-5). The area east of Gilead and Ammon is a rather dry region of gently sloping low hills, beyond which is the great desert.

South of the deep valley of the Arnon (I, D-6) lay the original area of the kingdom of *Moab*. To its high and level plateau Israel rarely laid claim. Farther south was *Edom* (I, C-D 7-8), which centered in strategically located and picturesque Petra (I, C-8). Apparently doomed to unimportance by the semidesert climate in this region, Edom was strong for two reasons. It controlled the trade from the desert to Gaza and other western points. Furthermore, it possessed what Palestine proper lacked—quantities of copper and iron ore (cf. Deut. 8:9 and Fig. 44). This ore is found along the border of the Arabah, where the valleys have cut into old sandstone underlying the heavy deposits of limestone, which are never far below the surface in Palestine.

PLATE I

RELIEF MAP OF
PALESTINE
Copyright, The Westminster Press
International Copyright Secured. All Rights Reserved
SCALE OF MILES

CITIES AND TOWNS   o
MOUNTAIN PEAKS   +
ELEVATIONS IN FIGURES   1264

Sidon

MT. LEBANON
c.6000

River Abana

Damascus
2264

River Litani

MT. HERMON
c.9100

Tyre

Dan
505

S E A

Lake Huleh
7

Accho

G A L I L E E

Sea
of
Galilee
c.-685

B A S H A N

Karnaim
1526

MT. CARMEL
1810

River Kishon

MT. TABOR
1843
+
Nazareth
1144

VALLEY OF JEZREEL
200-250

Yarmuk

River

G I L E A D

MT. GILBOA
1698

Ramoth-gilead O
2205

PLAIN OF SHARON

MT. EBAL
3077
+
MT. GERIZIM +
2849

S A M A R I A

Jordan

River Jabbok

T R A N S J O R D A N

M E D I T E R R A N E A N

Joppa o

Baal-hazor
3317

River

A M M O N

Rabbath-ammon
2820

Jericho
-700

PHILISTINE PLAIN

Jerusalem
2593

+ MT. NEBO
2644

SHEPHELAH

Gath
363

Dead
Sea
c.-1275

P L A T E A U   O F

M E

Gaza o

+3370
Hebron
3040

J U D A H

River Arnon

Gerar
180

M O A B

Beer-sheba
1013

Kir-hareseth
3115

N E G E B

River Zered

E
D
O
M

Kadesh-barnea?
c.3300 +

A R A B A H

▲ 288   Sela (Petra)
3805

PLATE II

THE WORLD OF THE PATRIARCHS
(c. 2000–1700 B.C.)

Copyright, The Westminster Press
International Copyright Secured. All Rights Reserved

SCALE OF MILES

0   100   200   300   400   500

CITIES AND TOWNS	○	●
MAIN PATRIARCHAL ROUTE OF TRAVEL		
MAIN PATRIARCHAL CENTERS		

Ancient sites mentioned in the Bible appear under Biblical names. Other sites have names taken either from contemporary literature or, if these are too difficult to transcribe, from later literature.

Sites known to have been occupied at this period but the names of which are unknown, appear under later names and are underlined in block.

Names inserted for Geographical Orientation—   in Parentheses

THE HEBREW TABLE OF NATIONS
(From Genesis 10 and Related Sources)

JAPHETH or INDO-EUROPEAN PEOPLES	RED
HAM, or AFRICAN PEOPLES	BLUE
SHEM, or SEMITIC PEOPLES	ORANGE
ALLOTTED to both HAM and SHEM	BLACK

THE WORLD OF THE PATRIARCHS

(C. 2000–1700 B.C.)

PLATE II

IF ONE were to draw a line from Egypt up through Palestine and Syria, then down the Euphrates to the Persian Gulf, he would have marked out an area in the shape of a semicircle which has been called "the Fertile Crescent." This was the center of civilization from the Stone Age to the golden age of Greece in the fifth century B.C. In the time of Abraham (c. 2000–1700 B.C.) world history centered in this region. The farther we move from it in any direction, the more primitive were the people. The two great foci of political and cultural energy were Egypt and Mesopotamia. There the first great states were established during the early third millennium because the Nile, Euphrates, and Tigris rivers made irrigation and a stable economy possible. Acting as a bridge between them was the narrow coastal strip of Syria-Palestine, across which moved caravans and armies, involving its peoples in the economic, political, and intellectual life of the two states. East and south of this bridge lay the arid Arabian Peninsula, joined to Asia on the north by the Fertile Crescent and to Africa on the west by the Sinai Peninsula. This peninsula was the home of the Semites, or the children of Shem (Plate II, Inset), a proud, nomadic people who throughout history have treasured their patriarchal society and their pastoral traditions. Arabia is not a desert of shifting sand like the Sahara west of Egypt; it is a tableland, with sufficient rainfall in the interior and in the south for the needs of a considerable population. The Israelites, Canaanites

(native inhabitants of Palestine-Syria), Babylonians, and Assyrians were all Semitic peoples, who in successive waves had moved from the Arabian Desert into the fertile lands.

North and east of the Fertile Crescent lay the highland regions of the children of Japheth (II, Inset, and Gen., ch. 10). These were the Aryan or Indo-European peoples. The history of the lands of the Bible, both before and during the period of Israel in Palestine, is largely the story of the successive invasions from Arabia on the one hand, and from the highland zone on the other, together with the conflicts of these invaders with each other and the kingdoms and civilizations which they developed.

A study of Plate II will reveal quite clearly the state of our knowledge about the world of Abraham's day. The cities and towns which are known to have existed are concentrated in the Fertile Crescent and in Egypt. Comparatively little is known about the peoples of the highlands surrounding the Fertile Crescent, of Europe to the northwest, or of Africa to the southwest. Between 1900 and 1600 B.C. an early Hittite state was formed in central Asia Minor, but we know very little about it. The records of an Assyrian trading colony at Kanish (II, E-2) have been recovered, revealing that before 1800 B.C. a highly developed trade was in existence between Assyria and Asia Minor, its chief object being the exploitation of the silver mines of the Taurus Mountains (III, B-2).

FIG. 9. This picture, painted on the wall of the tomb of an Egyptian noble at *Beni-hasan* (II, E-3), is the best representation from antiquity of Asiatics, probably Amorites, of the time of Abraham. It shows the family of a chieftain named Absha entering Egypt about 1900 B.C. Note the elaborately woven, many-colored woolen clothes (compare Joseph's "coat of many colors"), the shoes and sandals, the skin water bottles, the bows, javelins, heavy throw sticks (upper left), ax and eight-stringed lyre (lower left). Asses were used for transportation, since so far as is known the camel was not yet domesticated. In the upper right corner are two Egyptian scribes who are introducing the family to an official who is not here shown. They wear the white linen skirts so common in Egypt. At the top is a good example of Egyptian hieroglyphs cut in stone. At the right the scribe shows a letter written in ink on papyrus, which was the Egyptian method of communication. On the bottom line of the letter the number in the family is given as thirty-seven.

The European areas on Plate II are marked with a number of archaeological terms which are not derived from contemporary records. In the time of Abraham, Europe had not yet emerged from the comparatively dark prehistoric age into the historical period when the people began to write about themselves and to achieve a high degree of social organization and intellectual advancement. Consequently, all that we know about the country has been discovered by archaeologists, who have given to various cultural units names which serve as convenient designations to aid in the discussion.

Greece and the island of Crete were far in advance of the rest of Europe at this time and in the following centuries were to emerge into the historical period. The Balkans were still in the "Early Bronze Age": that is, in a period when metal tools and weapons were coming into use, though the people had been living in villages and engaging in agriculture for some time. Farther west the manner of life was more primitive. In western Spain and southern France the cultures were still in the Chalcolithic Age: that is, in the transitional period when metal was first being introduced, though agriculture, pottery, and domesticated animals were known. Western France and Sardinia were still characterized by megalithic tombs; these were tombs constructed of stones so large that later peoples believed that their predecessors in the land had been giants. In Palestine also such structures had been built, but by a pastoral people in the late Stone Age, some three to four thousand years earlier. In England during this age some part at least of the famous Stonehenge was in existence, but on the whole the great age of megalithic dolmens (tombs), menhirs (upright stone shafts), and cromlechs (stone circles) was coming to an end.*

THE AGE OF THE PATRIARCHS

During the period following 2000 B.C. the whole Fertile Crescent was flooded with Semitic invaders from the Arabian Desert (Figs. 9,

*For more detailed information about prehistoric Europe, the reader is referred to V. G. Childe, *The Dawn of European Civilization* (1939) and C. F. C. Hawkes, *The Prehistoric Foundations of Europe to the Mycenaean Age* (1940).

FIG. 10. Canaanite captives in Egypt being led before the Pharaoh. This relief, which portrays the general appearance of Israelites as well as Canaanites, is a good representation of the typical Semite of the day. Note the noble, aristocratic features, particularly the finely cut noses, and the long hair and beards. It is commonly thought that Israelites had "hooked noses," but this was originally a Hittite or Armenoid feature. (From the Temple of Rameses III at *Medinet Habu* in Egypt.)

10), who in Mesopotamia were called "Westerners," a name which appears as "Amorites" in the Old Testament. By 1750 B.C. the main cities from Syria to Babylon were ruled by Amorite dynasties. The chief source of our knowledge is the city of Mari (II, F-2), the capital of the most important state of the area. This kingdom extended some three hundred miles from the frontier of Babylon to the border of Syria. Its king was a man named Zimri-Lim, whose remarkable archives have been recovered, consisting of over 20,000 clay documents. Some 5,000 of them were letters written to him by kings, officials, and commoners from various parts of Syria and Mesopotamia. These documents and others like them have caused a revolution in our knowledge of the age, including a reduction in the date of the great Babylonian king, Hammurabi, by some three hundred years.

Zimri-Lim's palace was one of the show places of the day. It contained nearly three hundred rooms, and comprised more than fifteen acres. The detailed records and reports which were kept indicate that it was both the commercial and political center of a most efficient state. Other discoveries show the widespread interest in divination and "fortune telling." While in Egypt there was a firm and sure faith in a beautiful hereafter, the Mesopotamian people paid less attention to the matter. In fact, they appear to have varied between faith and doubt. One of their great epics was concerned with the adventures of a hero named Gilgamesh, who was overtaken by a morbid fear of death and began a long search for immortality, but never quite found it. Consequently, the Mesopotamian (and the Canaanite and Israelite as well) was primarily interested in living this life as successfully as possible. To do so he developed elaborate techniques for piercing the veil of the future, and Babylonian diviners became so famous that they were soon scattered throughout the Fertile Crescent. Balaam, hired by the king of Moab to curse Israel, is a good example (Num., chs. 22 to 24). (Cf. the stern prohibition of these practices in Deut. 18:9–14.)

Mari was conquered about 1700 B.C. by the greatest king of the age, the illustrious Hammurabi of Babylonia. Under his rule the small village of Babylon became an even more impressive city than Mari, and the commercial center of a rich empire which extended from Nineveh (II, F-2) and the Upper Euphrates to Ur (II, F-3). The most famous building of Babylon was the temple-tower named *Etemenanki*, one of the wonders of the ancient world (Fig. 11). Babylon, being the polyglot city that it was, and possessing the great temple-tower second in size only to the great Pyramid of Egypt, was the perfect setting for the Israelite story of the confusion of tongues. It was indeed a city with a tower whose top reached the heavens (Gen. 11:4).

One of Hammurabi's notable achievements was his code of laws, a collection and adaptation of old Sumerian laws and customs (Fig. 12). This code has long interested students of the Bible, for many of its provisions are similar to those found in secular Israelite law. The latter, however, is no copy of the former. The Code of Hammurabi is merely typical of the common law of the day, and from this law Israel later adapted much that she needed.

Palestine and the coast of Syria during the age of the Patriarchs appear to have been largely under Egypt's control. Monuments belonging to important Egyptians have been found at Gezer and Megiddo in Palestine (IV, B-5 and C-3) and at Byblos and Ugarit in Syria (II, E-3 and E-2). Recently discovered Egyptian texts on which are listed numerous Asiatic enemies mention a number of towns, among them Jerusalem, Shechem, and Hazor (II, E-3)—the earliest reference to these important places outside the Bible. Each town is ruled by one or more chieftains, and the implication of the documents is that the social organization was patriarchal and quite different from the city-state system in vogue after the seventeenth century (see pp. 33 ff.).

A most interesting Egyptian story, the Tale of Sinuhe (c. 1900 B.C.), describes contemporary life among the Amorites in eastern Syria. Sinuhe was a high Egyptian official who had to flee from his country for political reasons. He found refuge with an Amorite chieftain in the country of the "East" (*Kedem*), presumably the same gen-

eral territory as "the land of the children of the east" to which Jacob
went, according to Gen. 29:1. The comparative wealth of the seminomadic life which Sinuhe lived in this region is vividly described.
It is the same type of life as that of the Patriarchs described in Genesis, who lived from flocks and herds while occasionally engaging in
simple agriculture. Further illustration of patriarchal life is to be
found in a beautiful Egyptian painting which pictures a family of
Asiatics, presumably Amorites, entering Egypt about 1900 B.C. (Fig.
9). The families of Abraham and Jacob undoubtedly looked and
dressed very much like these people when they journeyed to Egypt
during periods of famine (Gen., chs. 12; 42 ff.).

Egypt at the time of Abraham was ruled by the Pharaohs of the
illustrious Twelfth Dynasty (c. 2000–1780 B.C.). Besides exercising
political control over Palestine and Syria they organized an extensive
sea trade with Syria, Cyprus, Crete, and Punt (II, F-4). The southern
boundary of the country was pushed southward to the second cata-
ract of the Nile, where a border fortress was erected at *Semneh* (II, E-4).
Expeditions were sent to Sinai to exploit the copper and turquoise
deposits existing there (II, E-3), and also to Nubia (Cush, II, E-4),
where gold had been discovered. Later Egyptians looked back upon
this period as a golden age. Not only was a high degree of prosperity attained; it was an age of great literature as well, the style of
which formed the model for succeeding periods. An interesting by-
product of Egyptian activity at this time was the invention, or at least
development, of an alphabet. Northwestern Semites working for the
Egyptians in Sinai were able to write the consonants of their own
language by using some of the Egyptian signs together with others
newly invented. Their inscriptions at Sinai are the first known examples of the alphabetic writing subsequently developed by the
Canaanites and borrowed by Israel (see further, p. 33).

THE HEBREW PATRIARCHS

Thus far no contemporary record of Abraham has been found outside the Bible. Yet the background of the narratives about him and
his descendants has been considerably illumined. Genesis 11:31 informs us that his family migrated from Ur of the Chaldees (II, F-3)
to Haran (II, F-2). Ur was a great Sumerian city before the days of
Abraham, and it continued to be an important place for centuries.
Yet the reference here is obscure both textually and historically. In
any event there is no reliable information which indicates any influence of that city on patriarchal life.

With the case of Haran, however, the situation is different. When
Abraham and his family reached Canaan, they continued to keep in
close touch with their relatives there, and apparently looked upon
that area as their homeland (Gen., chs. 24; 29 ff.). Haran was the
chief town of the region called Paddan-aram (Field of Aram) by later
Israel. An earlier name appears to have been Aram of the Two Rivers
(Gen. 24:10, R.V. marg.). This was one of the centers of the new
Amorite settlement, and it is tempting to connect the journeys of the
family of Abraham either directly or indirectly with the Amorite
movement. Several lines of evidence lead to the conclusion that this
can be done.

For one thing, certain of the names of the ancestors and family of
Abraham were also names of towns in the area of Haran: that is,
Peleg, Serug, Nahor, and Terah (Gen. 11:16 ff.). The name of the
city Haran sounds very much like that of one of Abraham's brothers,
though the initial letter in the original language is slightly different.
The identification of one name with an ancient town might be mere
coincidence, but in this case there are at least four in the precise area
from which Abraham came. These names were probably patriarchal
clan names which either were given by the clans to towns they
founded or were taken from the towns which they seized during the
disturbances around 2000 B.C.

Further, the names Abram (in the form *Abamram*) and Jacob (in
the form *Jacob-el*) are known as personal names among the Amorites.
In the Mari archives there is also frequent mention of a tribe of Benjamin which was causing some trouble in the area, though it is to be

FIG. 11. A restoration of Babylon and the Tower of Babel. The tower, properly known as *Etemenanki*, "the House of the Foundation Platform of Heaven and
Earth," was begun in the third millennium B.C. but not completed until Nebuchadnezzar's reign. The tower is an example of the common Mesopotamian *ziqqurat*,
a high, stepped platform surmounted by a temple, in this instance one dedicated
to Marduk who was believed to be the chief god of the land. The structure was
about three hundred feet square at the base and approximately the same in height.
Portions of the enormous city walls built by Nebuchadnezzar c. 600 B.C. are also
shown. In the foreground is the Euphrates River, which flowed along the western
edge of the city.

identified only in name with the later Israelite tribe. Even more interesting is the light thrown on patriarchal customs by the archives
of a later city of northern Mesopotamia named Nuzi (III, D-2). The
customs reflected in these documents explain a number of patriarchal
laws and practices which have been obscure, and they demonstrate
that patriarchal life as described in Genesis is that of the second millennium, and not that of the first millennium, when Israelites were re-
telling the stories and putting them into writing. Thus, the relations
between Jacob and Laban, the hitherto obscure "teraphim" (Gen.
31:19 ff.), Esau's sale of his birthright, patriarchal deathbed blessings,
etc., are now seen in clearer perspective (see further p. 30).

It is also a significant fact that the Hebrew traditions about the
Creation and the Flood (Gen., chs. 1 to 11) contain many resemblances to similar accounts of Mesopotamian people, while they re-
semble nothing in either Egyptian or Canaanite literature. In the case
of the Creation and of the Garden of Eden the resemblances are superficial. Though the views regarding the structure of the world were
essentially similar (the firmament or heavens as a bowl covering the
earth, with waters both above and below, etc.), the refinement produced by the purity of the Israelite faith sets a great gulf between the
Old Testament accounts and the crassly pagan traditions of Babylon.
The same is true regarding the Flood account, but in this case the
parallels with Babylonian documents (which in turn are based upon
Sumerian sources of the third millennium) are so close that a relation
must exist between them. The Babylonian ark, however, grounded
on the Zagros Mountains to the east and north of Babylon (III, E-3),
while according to the Old Testament it rested on the mountains of
Ararat (III, D-1, Armenia; Gen. 8:4)—another indication of the influence of northern Mesopotamia on Israel.

It must be asked, therefore, why it was that the country which was
the farthest from Israel should have had the greatest influence upon
her thinking about the early days of man's life on earth. Today almost
the only possible explanation is that the essential outlines of the accounts of the Creation, the Garden of Eden, the Flood, Nimrod
(Gen. 10:8 ff.), and the Tower of Babel (Gen., ch. 11) were brought
from the homeland in Haran by the Patriarchs themselves. It was

once thought that the Canaanites acted as the intermediaries between Israel and Mesopotamia, but since the recovery of the Ugaritic literature (pp. 30, 36) this view has become increasingly difficult to hold. The story regarding the Tower of Babel must have arisen at a time when Babylon and its great temple-tower were flourishing and well-known: that is, between the eighteenth and sixteenth centuries B.C., before the city was destroyed by the Hittites (see p. 29). The story of the tower, then, gives the approximate age, while the story of the Flood indicates that we are dealing, not with a Babylonian, but with a North Mesopotamian edition.

These and other facts enable us for the first time to answer with confidence the questions as to who the Patriarchs were and whence they came.

Various sources of information also illuminate the life of the Patriarchs in Canaan. The main centers around which they lived (Mamre, Beer-sheba, Bethel, Shechem, Dothan) were all located in the central hill country of Palestine. This region was rather sparsely populated at the time, and therefore particularly suited for pastoral life.

FIG. 12. The Code of Hammurabi. This is a replica of the diorite shaft nearly eight feet in height on which Hammurabi had inscribed his code of laws. This code, the oldest which has come down to us, was compiled by the great king from the ancient laws of his predecessors. At the top of the shaft he is represented as receiving these laws from the enthroned sun-god. At a later time an Elamite conqueror took the shaft as a trophy for his capital at Susa (II, G-3), where it was found during the winter of 1901–1902. At the base of the shaft part of the original text has been erased, probably to make room for another inscription which was never executed.

Dothan, Shechem, and Bethel were all in existence, according to archaeological information. In Num. 13:22 we are informed that Hebron was founded "seven years before Zoan in Egypt." This means that Hebron was established about 1700 B.C., or just before, because the reference here to Zoan (Avaris) refers to its establishment as the Hyksos capital of Egypt (V, C-3, and p. 28). Consequently, Hebron as a city was not in existence in Abraham's day. This accounts for his association with Mamre and the mention of Hebron in an explanatory note to indicate where Mamre was (Gen. 13:18; 23:19). We now have interesting information regarding "the cities of the Plain" and the destruction of Sodom and Gomorrah (Gen. 13:10 ff.; 19:23 ff.). Genesis informs us that the Jordan Valley was thriving and well populated in the days of Abraham, but that subsequently a part of the area that contained Sodom and Gomorrah was destroyed. We know that these cities were situated in the Vale of Siddim (Gen. 14:3), and that this was the area at the southern end of the Dead Sea, now covered with water (X, H-3). Evidence from both archaeological and historical sources outside the Bible supports the tradition of a terrific catastrophe in this area about the time of Abraham (see further, p. 65 f.).

Unfortunately, we lack precise knowledge of the nature of Abraham's religion, but a number of features have been clarified. Particu-

larly important is the apparent fact that the name of the patriarchal family God was "El Shaddai" (Ex. 6:2, 3; Gen. 17:1; etc.). This has been mistranslated "God Almighty"; in reality Shaddai is a Mesopotamian word meaning "The Mountain One"—further evidence of the connection of the Patriarchs with northern Mesopotamia. This was the name of the "God of the Fathers," whom the successive patriarchal generations deliberately chose as their Deity. The relationship between the family and its chosen God was very close, so that he was addressed as "father," "brother," "kinsman," and was considered an actual member of the group. When treaties or covenants were made, he was the third party who sealed the agreement and saw that it was kept (cf. the Mizpah benediction in Gen. 31:49). These factors played a prominent part in the later religion of Israel, in which the same close relationship between God and people continued to exist and was symbolized in the special covenant relationship freely contracted by God and Israel at Mount Sinai (Ex., ch. 24). Thus the patriarchal religion played a most important part in the later religion of Israel and was a central factor in distinguishing it from the degrading, polytheistic nature worship of Canaan.

The above is but a partial list of the results of recent investigation. Archaeology and historical study support the substantial reliability of the stories about Abraham, Isaac, and Jacob—and this is one of the most significant discoveries of the present generation of Old Testament students. Of course, the stories were occasionally modernized by the addition of such references as those to the "Philistines," a people who were not in Palestine until after 1200 B.C. (VI, B-5; see pp. 45 f.). In addition, the narratives were written by later Israelite teachers for the express purpose of teaching about God and his dealings with his chosen people, a fact in which the eternal and abiding significance of this literature resides. Yet the recovery of the life and times of the Patriarchs is a most important achievement, one which has revolutionized our understanding of the book of Genesis and to some extent our whole approach to the historical books of the Old Testament.

THE HEBREW TABLE OF NATIONS
(PLATE II, INSET)

The Inset of Plate II shows the countries and peoples of the world as they were known to the Israelites and listed in Gen., ch. 10. The inhabitants of the world were believed by Israel to have descended from the three sons of Noah: Shem was the father of the Semites; Ham, the father of the African peoples; and Japheth, the father of the Aryan or Indo-European peoples. The list does not include the inhabitants of northern Europe nor of the Far East, because Hebrew life had no contact with them. The area included in the Table of Nations extends from Asia Minor (Turkey) to Abyssinia (Cush or Ethiopia), and from Elam, east of Babylon, to Greece and the distant Tarshish. From the peoples and places mentioned we know immediately that the list in its present form comes from the period between 1000 and 800 B.C. Thus Tarshish, for example, was the name for "smelter" and was used for certain colonies of the Phoenicians in the Mediterranean. One such "tarshish" was on Sardinia and another perhaps in Spain, and we are not sure in this case just which one was meant.

The list is arranged on the whole from a racial point of view, though certain exceptions are to be noted. For example, we know from their language that the Canaanites were a Semitic people, though here they are listed as descendants of Ham (Africa). The reason may be that when Israel entered Canaan, the latter had long been under the control of Egypt (see pp. 34, 35). Thus its inclusion as a Hamitic people is for political and geographical, rather than for racial, reasons. Similarly, Elam is listed as a son of Shem; but we know from the language there spoken that the majority of its people were non-Semitic. Its inclusion under Shem was, therefore, not a matter of race but of historical geography. Apart from such exceptions, however, this division of the peoples of the ancient world into three main groups is very convenient and is still used to some extent by historians and ethnographers.

FIG. 13. The ruins of *Karnak*, a portion of the chief city of ancient Egypt named Thebes (called No or No-amon in the Old Testament). Here the successive Pharaohs spent lavishly of their wealth in the building of magnificent temples and palaces. This picture shows the remains of the chief sanctuary of the city, the imperial temple of the god Amun. The main structure is in the left center. Surrounding the sacred precinct is a massive brick wall, and in the center is the bed of the sacred lake. The view is toward the east, with the Nile River back of the camera. On the west side of the Nile were other temples and the Valley of the Tombs of the Kings, where the tomb of Tutankhamun was found in 1922, untouched by either ancient or modern tomb robbers.

THE GREAT EMPIRES
DURING THE SOJOURN IN EGYPT

PLATE III

THE four centuries which Israel spent in Egypt are a "dark age" in her history. From this entire period little or no information about the Israelites has come down to us. Some record of the beginnings of this era has been preserved in the story of Joseph and the account of Jacob's descent into Egypt. The intervening years are passed over in silence and the narrative of Israel's history does not take up again until it reaches the time of Moses and of the Exodus of Israel from Egypt. If, however, little is known directly of Israel in these centuries, much can be learned by indirection from a study of the great empires which flourished in the Near East during her sojourn in Egypt, especially the empires of the Late Bronze Age (c. 1500–1200 B.C.). These empires, while not the first to appear in history, were the earliest of the great rival empires to contend for conquest and dominion in the Fertile Crescent. The story of this international rivalry and strife is the principal motif in the history of this era. Israel's Sojourn and Exodus were, no doubt, a part of the migrations and upheavals of the age.

For a thorough understanding of this period it is necessary, however, to consider briefly the two centuries just preceding the rise of these empires. Between the Age of the Patriarchs (Plate II) and the

era of the rival empires came two tumultuous centuries. The stability which had been achieved in Egypt by the Egyptian Middle Kingdom (i.e., contemporary with the Age of the Patriarchs) and later in Babylon by the First Dynasty under Hammurabi (p. 24) was interrupted during the seventeenth and sixteenth centuries by foreign invasions. Non-Semitic highlanders poured down into the Mesopotamian plains and brought an end to Semitic rule there, while Semitic rulers from Canaan established themselves in Egypt.

THE HYKSOS PERIOD IN SYRIA-PALESTINE AND EGYPT

Although information about these events in Mesopotamia is very scant, sufficient data are at hand from Syria-Palestine and Egypt to enable us to piece together something of the history of all these countries during this era. About 1720 B.C. Egypt was invaded and conquered by an Asiatic people whom the Egyptians called *Hyksos*, "Rulers of Foreign Lands." The later Egyptian historian Manetho wrote about them as follows:

"There was a king of ours whose name was Timaios, in whose reign it came to pass, I know not why, that God was displeased with us, and there came unexpectedly men of ignoble birth out of the eastern parts, who had

27

FIG. 14. Reproduction of the great Hyksos enclosure at *Tell el-Yehūdiyeh* in Egypt (V, C-3). The Hyksos introduced a new weapon of war, the horse and chariot. Beaten earth embankments of this sort were built by them about 1700 B.C. throughout Syria, Palestine, and the Egyptian Delta as enclosures for the horses.

boldness enough to make an expedition into our country, and easily subdued it by force without a battle. And when they had got our rulers under their power, they afterwards savagely burnt down our cities and demolished the temples of the gods, and used all the inhabitants in a most hostile manner, for they slew some and led the children and wives of others into slavery. At length they made one of themselves king, whose name was Salatis, and he lived at Memphis and made both upper and lower Egypt pay tribute, and left garrisons in places that were most suitable for them . . . and as he found in the Saite nome [county] a city very fit for his purpose (which lay east of the arm of the Nile near Bubastis, and with regard to a certain theological notion was called Avaris), he rebuilt it and made it very strong by the walls he built around it and by a numerous garrison of 240,000 men, whom he put into it to keep it. There Salatis went every summer, partly to gather his corn and pay his soldiers their wages, and partly to train his armed men and so to awe foreigners."

These invaders, whom the Egyptians so despised and hated, built a powerful empire, including Palestine and Syria. Objects belonging to one of their greatest kings have been found in lands as far separated as Crete and Mesopotamia. Recent evidence indicates that most, if not all, of the Hyksos were of western Semitic, i.e., Canaanite, stock. Syria-Palestine, the home of these peoples, enjoyed a period of great prosperity during the period when they were in power. The population increased during one and one half centuries of peace; and great advances can be observed in the arts and crafts. The Hyksos were evidently able to carry out their conquest of Egypt by the introduction of a new weapon of war, the horse and chariot. Great earthwork enclosures were built for chariotry at numerous places in Syria-Palestine and in the Egyptian Delta (Fig. 14). At Shechem and Jericho in Palestine tremendous fortifications were erected, and the country was organized into a feudal city-state system (see pp. 33 ff.). Though Canaan was prosperous, the age was a dark one for Egypt and no extensive writings from it have been recovered.

The Hyksos period is of particular interest to the student of the Old Testament because several lines of evidence suggest that it was during this time, probably not far from 1700 B.C., that Joseph came to power in Egypt. In the Genesis story it is evident that the court of the Pharaoh was not far from Goshen (Gen. 46:28 ff.). This would mean that the Egyptian capital at that time was in the Delta area. This is precisely where it was during the Hyksos period (see Avaris, III, B-4), whereas both before and after the Hyksos the Egyptian Pharaohs used as their capital the city of Thebes in Upper Egypt (Fig. 13 and II, E-3). If, therefore, the family of Jacob entered Egypt either before or after the Hyksos age, we should be at a loss to explain the obvious implication of Genesis concerning the location of the capital, unless, of course, we assume that in this respect the book is mistaken. Further, Ex. 12:40 states that "the time that the children of Israel dwelt in Egypt was four hundred and thirty years." Since it is almost certain that the Exodus from Egypt under Moses took place sometime after 1300 B.C. (see pp. 37 ff.), we are brought back to about 1700 B.C. for the date of Joseph. This and other evidence suggests that the Sojourn of Israel began at a time when Canaanite foreigners were ruling Egypt. Thus the rise to power of a foreigner like Joseph would easily be explained.

It has long been known that the local color of the story of Joseph

is so good that the narratives must have been recounted by those who knew Egypt well. The titles "chief of the butlers" and "chief of the bakers" (Gen. 40:2) are those of palace officials mentioned in Egyptian writings. Dreams were regarded by Egyptians as extremely important. The birthday of Pharaoh was an occasion for feasting, and possibly for the release of prisoners (cf. Gen. 40:20). We know also that magicians were plentiful in Egypt (cf. ch. 41:8), that Asiatic shepherds were indeed "an abomination unto the Egyptians" (chs. 46:34; 43:32), that seven-year famines had occurred in Egypt, that Joseph's life span of 110 years (ch. 50:22) was the traditional length of a happy and prosperous life in Egyptian writings, and that the embalming or mummification of Jacob and Joseph (ch. 50:2, 26) was the customary Egyptian manner of preparing the bodies of important people for burial.

Potiphar made Joseph "overseer over his house" (Gen. 39:4), a title which is a direct translation of an office in the houses of great Egyptian nobles. Pharaoh gave him an office with similar title in the administration of the realm (ch. 41:40), corresponding exactly to the office of prime minister or vizier of Egypt, who was the chief official in the country, second in power to no one but the Pharaoh The Pharaoh's gifts to Joseph upon the latter's induction into office would be quite in keeping with Egyptian custom: "And Pharaoh took off his signet ring from his hand, and put it upon Joseph's hand, and arrayed him in vestures of fine linen, and put a gold chain about his neck; and he made him to ride in the second chariot which he had; and they cried before him, Bow the knee" (ch. 41:42, 43). In Egypt there was also an office of "superintendent of the granaries." This was especially important since the stability of the country lay in its grain. Because of the approaching famine Joseph may have carried on the functions of this office in addition to his duties as prime minister.

As indicated, the Biblical story of the seven years of famine (Gen., ch. 41) is not unusual. Various Egyptian writings speak of famines in the land, and at least two officials, giving laudatory summaries of their good deeds on the walls of their tombs, tell of distributing food to the hungry "in each year of want." One inscription which was written about 100 B.C. tells how Pharaoh Zoser (c. 2700 B.C., one thousand years before Joseph) appealed to one of his gods because of a severe seven-year famine in which the people suffered terrible hardships, robbery became prevalent, and though storehouses had been built their contents were gone.

Joseph's father and brethren were settled in Egypt in the land of *Goshen* (Gen. 46:26 ff.). While this name does not occur outside the Bible, its locality is known to have comprised the area around the

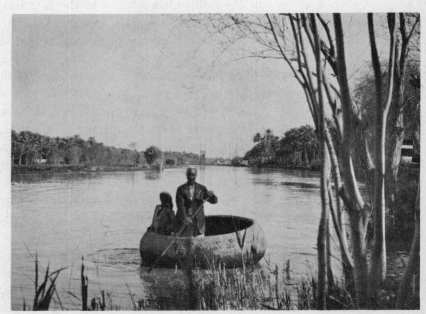

FIG. 15. The Euphrates, the largest river of southwestern Asia and a commercial highway from times immemorial. It rises in the mountains of Armenia and flows south into Syria, where instead of emptying into the Mediterranean Sea it moves southeastward, falling one thousand feet in its seven-hundred-mile journey to the Persian Gulf. In ancient times a network of canals led from it, fertilizing Babylonia and making possible the erection there of a strong state. The modern boat here shown is built of reeds and coated with bitumen, precisely as were the river boats of ancient Babylonia.

Wâdî Tumilât in the eastern part of the Nile Delta (III, B-4; V, C-D 3). This *Wâdî* (the Arabic name for a river bed which is usually dry except in the rainy season) is a narrow valley between thirty and forty miles long connecting the Nile with Lake Timsâh (V, D-3). In both ancient and modern times the area around this valley, especially to the north of it, has been one of the richest sections of Egypt, truly "the best of the land," as it is described in Gen. 47:11.

Two Egyptian writings indicate that it was the customary thing for frontier officials to allow people from Palestine and Sinai to enter this section of Egypt during hard times. One, dating about 1350 B.C., is written from frontier officials to the Pharaoh, telling him that such a group "who knew not how they should live, have come begging a home in the domain of Pharaoh . . ., after the manner of your [the Pharaoh's] fathers' fathers since the beginning . . . ." The family of Jacob was seventy in number (Gen. 46:26, 27). Fig. 9 shows a portion of the Asiatic family of Absha, as it entered Egypt about 1900 B.C. This family was thirty-seven in number; and during the course of the following centuries many such families must have been admitted to the country. It is small wonder, therefore, that no record of Jacob has been preserved in Egyptian writings.

THE ANCIENT WORLD DURING THE FIFTEENTH CENTURY B.C.

Shortly after 1600 B.C. native rulers at Thebes in Upper Egypt (II, E-3) became sufficiently strong to begin the war of liberation against the hated Hyksos. By c. 1550 B.C. the foreigners had been driven from the Delta and a great siege of three years' duration at Sharuhen in southern Canaan (IV, A-6) had been brought to a successful conclusion. The Hyksos' power was now completely broken. During the succeeding decades the Egyptians took over the Hyksos empire in Palestine and Syria. This brought them into direct conflict with the newly formed powers in the north, to which we must now turn.

The highlands of Armenia, Media, and Elam to the northeast and east of the Fertile Crescent were not consolidated into one great power before the sixth century B.C. (Plates XI: B and C). The inhabitants of these upland regions were, however, a constant menace to the civilized world since periodically they poured out of the mountains into the plains.

Babylonian tradition preserves the record of a brief surge to power of the Kingdom of Elam (III, E-3) about 1600 B.C., when a king of that country sacked and burned the cities of lower Babylonia. The First Dynasty of Babylonia, which had attained such illustrious heights under the great administrator Hammurabi (p. 24), was finally brought to an end by highlanders known as the Kassites, causing a dark age in Babylonia similar to the Hyksos period in Egypt. They maintained their control over the country for a period of almost four centuries (c. 1500–1150 B.C.). Under their rule the country remained weak and no effectual effort was made to establish an empire.

Between 1750 and 1600 B.C. non-Semitic Indo-Iranian and Hurrian peoples invaded northern Mesopotamia from the eastern highlands. By 1500 B.C. these invaders had established a powerful kingdom called Mitanni which controlled the whole area between the Mediterranean Sea and the highlands of Media. Their capital was at Washshukanni (III, D-2) on a tributary of the River Habor (*Khabûr*). The royal family and the nobles were the Indo-Iranians (i.e., Aryans). They worshiped Indian gods such as Mithra, Indra, and Varuna. The national sport of these aristocrats was horse racing. Judging from one of their treatises on horse-training which has been preserved in Hittite, far more care was given to the horse than to the average peasant of the time. The Hurrians who came in with the ruling Aryan peoples were of a different, though also non-Semitic, stock. Their language is only just beginning to yield to the efforts of the scholars who are attempting to translate it. In the Old Testament these people are called Horites (see pp. 35 f.). During the fifteenth and fourteenth centuries they spread so widely over the Canaanite lands of Syria-Palestine that one of the Egyptian names for Canaan was

FIG. 16. Foreign captives led before the Egyptian Pharaoh at Thebes. Types of people are clearly shown. On the left is a Libyan from the desert east of lower Egypt. Next to him is a Semite, perhaps from Syria or Palestine (cf. Fig. 10). The third has the typical profile of a Hittite from Asia Minor. The fourth, wearing a feathered headdress, is one of the sea peoples from the Aegean world, among whom were the Philistines. The last is another Semite. (From the temple of Rameses III at *Medinet Habu* in Egypt.)

Khûru, a word derived from the same source as "Hurrian" and "Horite" (see Plate IV).

To the north in central Asia Minor (Turkey) was the Hittite kingdom, centering in the region watered by the Halys River. Its capital was Khattushash (III, B-1), about ninety miles east of the modern Turkish capital, Ankara. By 1600 B.C. strong rulers had consolidated the area into a powerful state. Soon they began to push into northern Syria and Mesopotamia, and even succeeded in devastating Babylon (III, E-3) about 1550 B.C. Pressure from all sides, especially from Mitanni and Egypt, soon called a halt to this advance so that the Hittites do not play an important role until after 1400 B.C.

Plate III shows the extent of the various empires as they existed during the fifteenth century when Egypt had achieved its golden age. The neighbor of Egypt to the northeast was Mitanni, against which she waged continuous but indecisive war. Mitanni itself in this period lay mainly east of the Euphrates, but its territory reached to Lake Van on the north and included Assyria on the east. The Hittites remained quiet in Asia Minor. Babylon was weak under Kassite rulership, while the power and extent of Elam at this time is unknown. The borders as here drawn must not be considered as exact. Not only did they fluctuate constantly, but at no time in this age is our knowledge sufficient to fix them precisely.

THE FATE OF THE EMPIRES

After 1400 B.C. the balance of power achieved in the fifteenth century was broken by two factors: the rise of the Hittite kingdom into a position as the dominant power in the northern part of Western Asia, and the weakening of Egyptian foreign policy under the religious revolutionary, Amenophis IV or Akhnaton (c. 1377–1360 B.C.; Fig. 19). While the Hittites were passive, Egypt and Mitanni had been free to engage in almost continual warfare. When the Hittites began to exert pressure from the north, Mitanni hastened to make peace with Egypt, and the successive kings sent princesses to the Egyptian royal harem to secure the alliance. By about 1370, however, the Hittites had conquered Mitanni, reducing it to the status of a tributary state which acted as a buffer between Asia Minor and Assyria. The Hittites then pushed into Egyptian territory in Syria, and from this time to about 1200 B.C. the border between Egypt and Khatti (the Hittite Empire) lay in the area of Qatna, Kadesh, and Irqata (III, C-3). For the greater part of the fourteenth century the two empires were so occupied with internal affairs that they had little time for disputes with one another. The kings of the Nineteenth Egyptian Dynasty, Sethos I (1319–1301) and Rameses II (1301–1234), however, were vitally concerned with the recovery of the lost portions of their empire, and led their armies through Palestine to Syria. This

FIG. 17. One of the Nuzi tablets. This is an example of the cuneiform (wedge-shaped) method of writing developed in Mesopotamia. A reed or stylus was used to make the signs while the clay was wet. The figures were impressed by a small cylindrical seal, used instead of a signature by the one who had the document prepared. For the Egyptian method of writing with pen and ink on papyrus, see Fig. 9. The latter was the method adopted by Phoenicians and Israelites, passed on to the Greeks and thence to us.

campaign culminated in the great battle at Kadesh (III, C-3) about 1297 B.C., with results that appeared on the whole unfavorable to Egypt, though the Hittites were never able to take advantage of their success. In 1280 B.C. a formal peace, or nonaggression pact, was made, copies of which have been found in Egyptian at Thebes and in Babylonian at Khattushash (III, B-1).

Thus ended the major wars of the fourteenth and thirteenth centuries B.C. Regional conflicts, however, continued. Assyria, relieved of the yoke of Mitanni, began to spread rapidly and by 1250 B.C. had subjugated that country. For the next six hundred years, except for periods of decline in the twelfth and tenth centuries, the Assyrians were the dominant political force in Western Asia (Plate XI: A). The golden ages of Egypt and Khatti were now over. Invading hordes about 1200 B.C. brought an end to the Hittite Empire. After 1150 B.C. the Egyptian Government was controlled by an inept priesthood which made no attempt to interfere in the affairs of Western Asia.

In the Greek world before 1400 B.C. the political and cultural center was the island of Crete (called "Caphtor" in the Old Testament; III, A-2). Here for hundreds of years had flourished the "Minoan" civilization with its capital at Cnossus (or Knossos), where the magnificent palace of the legendary King Minos has been excavated (II, D-2). About 1400 B.C. Crete was overrun by mainlanders from Greece. During the two centuries which followed they controlled the sea trade with Palestine-Syria and Egypt, flooding those countries with products exported in beautiful vases (Mycenaean ware) and establishing colonies in various places, particularly on Alashiya (Cyprus). Because of internal disorders or invasions in Greece this trade appears to have been stopped by about 1225 B.C. and was not revived until the period of Phoenician (Canaanite) commercial expansion into the Mediterranean beginning about the time of Solomon in the tenth century B.C. (see pp. 33, 46).

The period about 1200 B.C. marks the end of an epoch in the history of the ancient world. In the Aegean the golden ages of "Minoan" and "Mycenaean" civilization had come to an end. In Asia Minor the Hittite power had been destroyed. To the south the Mitannian state had been taken over by Assyria. Most of Palestine was in the control of the Israelites (Plate VI and pp. 43 ff.), while Egypt was suffering from an internal weakness from which she was never fully to recover.

WRITTEN DOCUMENTS OF THE PERIOD OF THE SOJOURN

The art of writing had been highly developed and widely cultivated by the time of the Sojourn. Numerous important collections of political, religious, and legal documents have been recovered from this age in a great variety of scripts and languages, some of which cannot yet be translated. For the Biblical student the most important

are the libraries of *Tell el-Amarna* (V, B-6), Ugarit (III, C-2), and Nuzi (III, D-2). The Accadian cuneiform method of writing was that most commonly used. The scribe wrote on clay tablets with a stylus which made wedge-shaped (that is, "cuneiform") characters (see Fig. 17). The *Tell el-Amarna* documents were letters written in this manner by the local kings of Palestine and Syria to the Pharaoh of Egypt about political matters, and they form a most valuable source of information about the Land of Canaan before the Israelite Conquest (see further pp. 34, 35).

The Ugarit texts, dating about 1400 B.C., are largely religious in character and were found in the ruins of a scribal school adjoining a temple. Using a new cuneiform alphabet, the scribes invented a new way of writing the Canaanite language. The dialect employed is closely akin to the Hebrew of the Old Testament, the differences between the two being in part dialectical and in part a matter of respective age. Most significant is the fact that these documents contain a portion of the long-lost Canaanite religious literature and mythology, frequent allusions to which occur in the Old Testament (see further p. 36). Moreover, the texts contain many words and phrases borrowed by Israel, some of which are now explained for the first time. In addition, they provide a store of information about Canaanite poetry, certain forms of which were learned by the Israelites and used in their own psalmody (e.g., in Judg., ch. 5; II Sam. 1:19 ff.; Ps. 29; 68, etc.).

The Nuzi texts are largely concerned with social and business transactions in the small Assyrian city when it was under the control of Mitanni during the fifteenth century B.C. The most significant fact about them is that they throw a flood of light upon social customs of the northern Mesopotamian area in the second millennium B.C., and for the first time illustrate and explain many customs in the stories of Genesis. Such practices as the deathbed blessing or will of the Patriarch (Gen., ch. 27), and the giving of concubines for the purpose of raising family heirs (Gen., chs. 16 and 30), are here seen to be customs of the day. Another custom was for childless people to adopt a son to take care of them as long as they lived and to provide them with proper burial when they died. In return for this service the adopted son was designated as heir of the family's property. This explains the peculiar relation between Eliezer, a man from Damascus, and Abraham. Though a servant he was to be Abraham's heir if no son were born (Gen. 15:1 ff.). The relations between Jacob and Laban are also explained (Gen., chs. 29 to 31). At a time when Laban had no sons Jacob was adopted as son and heir. After a period of service, he was permitted by custom to marry Leah and Rachel, though he could not marry the daughter of any other family (Gen. 31:50). Complications appear to have arisen when sons were born to Laban (first mentioned in Gen. 31:1). The Nuzi law provided that if a son were born after the adoption had taken place, that son and the adopted son were to share the inheritance, but only the son was privileged to take the household idols or "gods," possession of which implied leadership of the family. In Gen. 31:19, 34, 35 the idols of the family are called "teraphim" (compare vs. 30-32). Apparently Rachel stole them from the house to insure the future position of her husband, though the act was in violation of the law of adoption. These and other Nuzi parallels to Genesis show that the description of Patriarchal society is not distorted, but actually reflects the age which the stories purport to describe (see further p. 25).

Many other important documents of the age have been recovered, among them the Assyrian and Hittite legal codes. These together with the code of Hammurabi (Fig. 12) illustrate the secular law of the ancient Near East, portions of which are to be found adapted to Israelite usage in Ex., chs. 21 to 23. The alphabet (in which the Old Testament was written and which was borrowed by the Greeks and transferred through the Romans to us) was being developed and used in Palestine-Syria during the period of the Sojourn, and a number of inscriptions which employ it have been discovered. In addition, a large number of incidental discoveries fill out our picture of Old Testament lands and peoples of which comparatively little was known until recent years.

PLATE III

THE GREAT EMPIRES DURING
THE SOJOURN IN EGYPT
(c. Fifteenth Century B.C.)
Copyright, The Westminster Press, International Copyright Secured. All Rights Reserved

SCALE OF MILES

THE EGYPTIAN EMPIRE
THE HITTITE EMPIRE
THE MITANNIAN EMPIRE
MAIN COMMUNICATION ROUTES
CITIES AND TOWNS

Sites known to have been occupied at this
period, the names of which appear neither
in contemporary literature nor in the Bible,
are given later or modern names——
Names inserted for Geographical Orientation——
in Italics
in Parentheses

PLATE IV

THE LAND OF
CANAAN
BEFORE THE
ISRAELITE
CONQUEST

Copyright, The Westminster Press
International Copyright Secured. All Rights Reserved

SCALE OF MILES
0   5   10   15   20   25   30

BOUNDARIES
UNCERTAIN
BOUNDARIES
CITIES AND TOWNS   o
ROADS

THE GREAT SEA

Sidon
Zarephath
Ijon?
MT. LEBANON
MT. HERMON
River Abana
Damascus
U B
Ahlab,
Meheleb
Tyre
Kanah
Abel
Laish
Dan
Yano'am
Hammon?
Kedesh
GARU
KINGDOM
Achzib
Abdon
Hazor
Aduru
OF
Accho
Merom
Raphono
Rehob?
Beth-anath?
Enu-anabi
Karnaim
Achshaph?
Neiel
Ashtaroth
OG
Cabul
Kenath,
Nobah,
Qanu
Salmonah?
Chinnereth
Sea
of
Madon
Rakkath?
Chinnereth
Helkath?
Hannathon?
Hammath
Ayyanu
Harosheth?
Adami
Japhia
Gath-hepher
Jokneam
Sarid
+ MT. TABOR
Edrei
Anahareth
Tob?
Bozrah
Dor
Megiddo
Shunem
Hapharaim
Beth-arbel
Aron
Beth-shan
Ham
Ramoth-gilead
Yaham
Taanach
Rehob
Ibleam
Pella
Gath-carmel
Aruboth?
Dothan
Jabesh-gilead
Sochoh
Hammat
Jordan
Bezek
Abel-meholah?
Zaretan
Zaphon?
MT. EBAL
Tirzah
Succoth
MT. GERIZIM +
Shechem
Penuel
River Jabbok
Gilgal
KINGDOM OF AMMON
(founded during the 13th century)
Aphek
Tappuah
Adamah
KINGDOM OF SIHON
(founded during the 13th century)
Joppa
Bene-berak
River
Ono
GIBEONITE OR HIVITE
TETRAPOLIS
Lod
Hadid
Luz
Bethel
Rabbath-ammon
Beth-horon
Lower
Beeroth?
Ai
Gezer
Chephirah
Gibeon
Jericho
Aijalon
Gilgal?
Ekron?
Kirjath-baal,
Kirjath-jearim
Jerusalem
Ashdod
Zorah
Jebus
Beth-shemesh
Bethlehem
Libnah
Azekah
Jarmuth
Ashkelon
Keilah
Gath
Mareshah
Salt
Eglon
Lachish
Sea
Gaza
Kirjath-arba
Beth-eglaim
Hebron
River Arnon
Gerar
Kirjath-sepher
Debir
KINGDOM
Zephath,
Hormah?
OF
Raphia
Sharuhen
Arad
MOAB
Beer-sheba
(founded during the 13th century)
Aroer
Brook Zered
KINGDOM OF
EDOM
Kadesh-barnea?
(founded during the 13th century)

FIG. 18. The Canaanite city of Tunip in Syria being stormed by the Egyptian army. The Egyptian artist shows the Canaanite defenders at the moment of surrender. Around the fortress is a dry moat; but the attackers, protected by the formidable Egyptian bowmen, have succeeded in placing ladders against the battlements and in gaining access to the first parapet, where an Egyptian soldier is blowing a trumpet as a signal that the battle is over. At the top the defenders have laid down their arms and raised their hands beseeching mercy. Note that the Canaanites are distinguished from the Egyptians by their long hair and beards. Such Egyptian battle reliefs indicate the appearance of Canaanite fortresses and the manner in which they were attacked. (From the temple of Rameses III at *Medinet Habu* in Egypt.)

THE LAND OF CANAAN
BEFORE THE ISRAELITE CONQUEST

PLATE IV

"CANAAN" was the name by which the original inhabitants of Syria-Palestine designated their territory. In Gen. 10: 15–19 the name "Canaanite" is defined as including the pre-Israelite inhabitants from Gaza on the south to Arvad and Hamath on the north (Plate III, B-C 3). The accuracy of this definition is vouched for by the Canaanites themselves, who used this name for their land as early as the fourteenth century B.C. It originated from one of the most celebrated industries of ancient times— the Canaanite manufacture of purple dye; for in all probability its original meaning was "Land of the Purple." Good dyes for clothing were difficult to obtain, but Canaanites in Syria discovered the murex shellfish, which was native to the eastern Mediterranean coast, and from it obtained a deep crimson color which became the most famous and coveted textile dye of the ancient world. Since it was very expensive, only the wealthy could purchase it, and robes of this color became a mark of high rank—whence the familiar phrases "born to the purple" and "promoted to the purple." When the Greeks became acquainted with the Canaanites, they called them "Phoenicians" and their land "Phoenicia" from the Greek word meaning "purple." Historically, geographically, and culturally, then, the terms "Canaanite" and "Phoenician" mean precisely the same thing.

THE IMPORTANCE OF THE CANAANITES

From an early time the Canaanites played a very important role in the history of civilization. By 3000 B.C. important cities like Jerusalem (C-5), Ai (C-5), Jericho (C-5), Gezer (B-5), Megiddo (C-3), Beth-shan (C-4), Beth-yerah (XVIII, D-3), Byblos (III, C-3), and Hamath (III, C-3) were already in existence. During the subsequent two thousand years the inhabitants of these and other cities formed the bridge between the great centers of civilization on the Euphrates and the Nile, across which moved not only the currents of war and politics but also ideas,

techniques, literature, art, music, religion, and science. Thus when Greece after the ninth century B.C. began its steady climb to the great age of Socrates and Plato, she found among the Canaanites ready teachers in many rudiments of civilized living. From them she borrowed the alphabet and passed it on to us; and today practically all literate people on the globe (except for the Japanese and Chinese) use some modified form of the Canaanite or Phoenician alphabet. Even our word "Bible" is to be traced back to Canaan, for the Greeks learned so much about writing and writing materials from the Canaanites that their word for "book" (*biblion*, whence "Bible") was derived from the name of the Syrian city, Byblos (III, C-3).

By 1200 B.C. a disaster had overtaken the Canaanites. The Israelites had deprived them of most of Palestine, and shortly thereafter Syrians (Aramaeans) took the hinterland of Syria east of Mt. Lebanon. Now confined to the coast of northern Palestine and southern Syria they took to the sea and became one of the greatest sea-trading people of history, founding commercial colonies on the shores and islands of the Mediterranean as far west as Spain. One of the best descriptions of this activity is to be found in Ezek., ch. 27, in which the extensive trade by sea and also by land is described.

It was inevitable that such an energetic people should exert considerable influence upon Israel. Excavations in Israelite towns show that the Hebrews imitated Canaanite dishes, jugs, cooking pots, weapons, jewelry, and the like. From the Canaanites Israel borrowed the alphabet with which the Old Testament is written. A large part of the Old Testament is in poetry and some of the poetry is in particular styles now known to have been borrowed from the Canaanites. The Canaanites excelled in and were famous for their music, and we now know that Israel borrowed or imitated their instruments and learned from them musical arts which were used in Temple worship. Solomon had a business agreement with Hiram of Tyre and hired from him the services of trained Canaanite artists and architects to direct his great building program, of which the Temple in Jerusalem is the best-known example (I Kings, ch. 5–7). Jezebel, before marrying Ahab of Israel, was a princess of Sidon (I Kings 16:31); and we hear of Israelite housewives selling homemade linen clothes to the Canaanites (Prov. 31:24, R.V. marg.), of Canaanite businessmen in a quarter in Jerusalem (Zeph. 1:11), of the barter of wheat, oil, honey, and balm for Canaanite luxuries (Ezek. 27:17). Even the religious life of Israel was affected by the pagan religion of Canaan, and many of the common people fell into idolatry by this means (Judg., ch. 2; I Kings 19:18; etc.). Canaanite civilization had many bad features, but it also possessed much that was good to which Israel was indebted.

LOCATION OF CANAANITE CITIES

One of the ways in which geography influenced the history of the Canaanites is to be seen in the fact that politically they never were a united people. The country of Palestine and Syria is so cut by mountains, rivers, and valleys that local differences had a tendency to be emphasized, and a strong Canaanite state or empire was never formed. Instead, before the conquest of Palestine by Israel, the country was split up among numerous city-states. Each of the larger cities tried to control as much of the territory around it as possible. Each was ruled by a king, and each king was independent of the others. In The Book of Joshua a number of these city-states and their kings are mentioned (see especially chs. 10 to 12). Five of them banded together against Joshua, but were defeated in the Valley of Aijalon (IX, D-E 5). They were Jerusalem (C-5), Hebron (of which the old name was Kirjath-arba, Josh. 15:13, C-5), Jarmuth (B-5), Lachish (B-5), and Eglon (B-5). Other important city-states were Kirjath-sepher or Debir (B-6), Libnah (B-5), Gezer (B-5), Luz or Bethel (C-5), Jericho (C-5), Shechem (C-4), Dor (B-3), Megiddo (C-3), Beth-shan (C-4), Pella (D-4), Hazor (D 2), Kedesh (D-2), Yano'am (D-2), Tyre (C-2), Sidon (C-1), and Damascus (E-1).

The distribution of these Canaanite royal cities should be noted. Few of them are located in the central hill country. Apart from Kirjath-arba (Hebron), Jerusalem, Luz (Bethel), and Shechem, the most important are located in the Judaean Lowlands or Shephelah (I, B-C 5–6 and p. 19), along the coast, or in the valleys of Jezreel (Plate I, C-3) and the Jordan. In other words, the centers of Canaanite civilization were largely in the plains and not in the hill country. In fact, before the conquest of Canaan by Israel the latter was sparsely populated. In all probability this hill country was thickly wooded with

areas where grazing was possible for cattle, sheep, and goats. The Patriarchs wandered up and down the central ridge with their flocks and herds; and the men of the Joseph tribes (Ephraim and Manasseh) were told by Joshua to make room for themselves by clearing the forest (Josh. 17:15).

It was precisely in this region and in the thinly populated Transjordan that the Hebrews secured their first foothold in Canaanite territory. Unequipped as the Israelite invaders were for siege operations, we are not surprised that at first they were unable to capture such fortified cities as Dor, Megiddo, Beth-shan, and Gezer (Judg. 1:27 ff.). Fighting on foot with no weapons but bows, slings, stones, staves, and a few swords and spears, they would have been weak in pitched battles in the open plains where formidable chariots could maneuver. Thus, we are told, Judah "could not drive out the inhabitants of the valley, because they had chariots of iron" (Judg. 1:19). It is interesting to hear Syrian (Aramean) enemies of Israel at a later period discuss this weakness and strength of Israelite tactics. The God of the Israelites, they said, "is a god of the hills; therefore they are stronger than we: but let us fight against them in the plain, and surely we shall be stronger than they" (I Kings 20:23).

POLITICS IN CANAAN BEFORE THE CONQUEST

From about 1550 to 1225 B.C. Palestine was a province of the Egyptian empire (Plate III), except for occasional brief rebellions. Gaza (A-6) and Joppa (B-4) were two of the main provincial administrative centers. Other cities were governed by the local kings whose work and interests were unmolested by the Egyptian administration as long as they paid their taxes or tribute and provided their share of laborers for Egyptian royal projects. The country was thus governed by a double administration. On the one hand there were the local rulers, called "governors" in correspondence with the Egyptian state department; and on the other there were Egyptian commissioners, called "inspectors." The native rulers were allowed to have armed forces, consisting of chariots, owned and operated by the aristocracy, and footmen drawn from the peasant classes of the society. With these forces the Canaanite kings could war with one another as they wished, provided that such conflicts did not reach proportions of sufficient size to endanger the steady flow of royal taxes to Egypt. The Egyptian commissioners levied and raised the taxes and directed the compulsory labor groups in work on roads, in the Valley of Jezreel (I, C-3) where wheat was grown for the Royal Court, in the forest preserves of Mt. Lebanon, and elsewhere. Troops were at their disposal, composed

FIG. 19. The Pharaoh Amenophis IV or Akhnaton (c. 1377–1360 B. C.), a remarkable personage, who was intensely interested in religion. He was the first clear monotheist of history, worshiping the Aton, the personification of the sun disk. In his palace at Akhetaton (*Tell el-Amarna*) were found a large group of letters which form our most important source of information about politics in Canaan during the period preceding the Israelite Conquest. The Egyptian Pharaohs were believed by their people to be gods; and the greatness of the artist of this statue is to be seen in his portrayal in stone of the quiet, serene nobility which is above and beyond the turmoil of this world.

FIG. 20. A reproduction of the bust of Queen Nofretete, wife of Akhnaton. This remarkable portrait was found in the studio of the royal sculptor at *Tell el-Amarna*, and is one of the best known and most beautiful objects of art found in Egypt. Such works as this and Fig. 19 illustrate the high cultural level and refinement of the Egyptians, and help us to understand the sense of superiority which they bore toward all foreigners, particularly the Asiatics. Cf. Gen. 46:34, "For every shepherd is an abomination unto the Egyptians."

of slaves and mercenaries from Cush (Nubia; II, E-4), the Mediterranean islands (especially Crete), and local Bedouin or nomads, supported by a few Egyptians soldiers. As a result of repeated revolts, Egyptian fortresses were built in various parts of the country, one of which has been excavated at Beth-shan (C-4). It was first erected about 1450 B.C., and was rebuilt several times before the decline of Egyptian power. Unhappily for the country, the Egyptian bureaucracy was notoriously corrupt and the Egyptian troops frequently failed to receive their wages or proper maintenance, with the result that they often plundered the local villages and contributed to the general instability of the age.

Under strong Egyptian Pharaohs this double system of administration probably operated in a satisfactory manner; but under weak rulers, corruption of officials, local rivalry and warfare between the Canaanite kings, and predatory operations of Egyptian troops increased to such an extent that the political situation was little short of chaos. Our most important source of information about Canaan during this age is a portion of the archives of the Egyptian foreign office found in the palace of the Pharaoh Amenophis IV, also named Akhnaton (c. 1377–1360, Fig. 19), at the modern *Tell el-Amarna* in Egypt (v, B-6). This king was far more interested in religious matters (he was the first clear monotheist whom we know in history) than he was in the military and administrative affairs of the empire, and the letters from the Canaanite kings which were found in his archives bear witness to the disorder and confusion existing in Canaan. Numerous kings were actively engaged in extending their domains at the expense of their neighbors. Each accuses others of disloyalty and rebellion; yet those accused write to profess their utter devotion to the crown and denounce their enemies as slanderers. The letters so abound with accusations and counteraccusations that it is difficult to discover when the truth is being told. Indeed, one gets the impression that all parties involved are indulging in an intricate game of political and military maneuvering, each with the express purpose of "feathering his own nest," though moving adroitly so that the Egyptian court may not consider him disloyal.

One of the most reviled of the Canaanite kings of the Palestine area was Lab'aya, who controlled a large section of the hill country from his center at Shechem (C-4). He and his sons for a considerable period of time terrorized their neighbors in every direction. Yet in letters to the Pharaoh he humbly protested his innocence of "sin" and rebellion. His father and his grandfather before him were loyal servants of the king, and so is he! He says further that he had to fight to protect himself against his enemies, and, quoting an old proverb, he adds: "If ants are smitten, they do not receive [the smiting passively], but they bite the hand of the man who smites them!" (Cf. Prov. 6:6; 30:25.) The king of Megiddo (C-3), however, was apparently ordered to capture Lab'aya and send him to Egypt. This he did and turned him over to the king of Accho (C-3), so that the latter could send him to Egypt by sea. Instead, the king of Accho finally freed him after being bribed to do so. Lab'aya was unable to reach home, however, before being murdered by his enemies.

In southern Palestine the main city-states of this period were Gezer (B-5), Lachish (B-5), Jerusalem (C-5), and Hebron-Keilah (C-5); and these four states apparently met at a point near Beth-shemesh or Jarmuth (B-5). Over a hundred years later, when Israelites were engaged in the conquest of this area, the number had increased to nine (Josh., ch. 10); and in addition Jericho, Luz (Bethel), and the four Hivite cities (Gibeon, Beeroth, Chephirah, and Kirjath-baal; C-5) were under separate rulers. Thus between about 1375 and 1250 B.C. an increase in the number of these city-states brought on a decrease in their power—a situation which undoubtedly aided Israel in the conquest.

Among the troublemakers of the early fourteenth century were a people who are called *Khabiru*. Many of them appear to have been mercenary or slave troops in the employ of the Canaanite kings. We are nowhere informed, however, as to precisely who they were. Whenever the term is used, both in the Amarna letters and in other contemporary and earlier writings, it appears to refer to people who belonged

to a lower class. In all probability the name refers more to a social status than to a special race, and it seems likely that it may refer to the unsettled seminomadic peoples that continually haunt the settled communities around the Arabian Desert.

The words *Khabiru* and *Hebrew* seem to come from the same root and are somehow related. It is interesting to note that the great majority of the references to the word *Hebrew* in the Old Testament belong to the period of the Patriarchs and of the Sojourn in Egypt. The term is usually used when an Egyptian speaks of an Israelite, or when

FIG. 21. A bronze figure representing the Canaanite god Baal, found at Ugarit in northern Syria. Idols such as these were the "graven and molten images" of the Old Testament. Most of them were cast in copper or bronze, and then "graven." Frequently their helmets and short skirts were made of gold leaf (cf. Hab. 2:19; Isa. 40:19; Jer. 10:14).

an Israelite identifies himself to an Egyptian (cf. Gen. 39:17; 40:15). It is thus probable that the word *Hebrew* referred originally to a much larger group than Israel alone. The latter were "Hebrews," but many other seminomadic peoples were designated originally by the same name. The term was confined to Israelites at a very much later time. On the other hand, it is quite possible that some of the *Khabiru* mentioned in the Amarna tablets, especially those associated with Lab'aya in the Shechem area, may have been related to the Israelites in Egypt, and later may have become members of the Israelite nation (see p. 39).

THE PEOPLE OF CANAAN

After 1600 B.C. the population of Canaan became increasingly mixed. When Israel entered the country under Joshua, numerous groups were encountered which are mentioned in the Old Testament. Joshua 9:1, for example, mentions the Hittite, the Amorite, the Canaanite, the Perizzite, the Hivite, and the Jebusite. As we have noted, the Canaanites were the original inhabitants of the country. The Jebusites were possibly Canaanites who lived in the City of Jebus, another name for Jerusalem (Josh. 18:28; Judg. 19:10). The Hittites were from Asia Minor where a great state was in existence at this time (Plate III, and pp. 29 f.). The Amorites were survivors of a great invasion of peoples from the Arabian Desert about 2000 B.C. (Plate II and pp. 24 f.). The Hivites were probably the same as the Horites; a large group of the latter appear to have been settled in Edom or Seir (Gen. 36:20; Deut. 2:12). Their homeland was in northern Mesopotamia, in the country of Mitanni which was a powerful state during the fifteenth and fourteenth centuries before it was conquered by the Hittites about 1370 and before its final subjugation by the Assyrians a century later (Plate III and pp. 29 f.). In the days of Joshua the Hivites were in possession of four federated cities northwest of Jerusalem: Gibeon, Beeroth, Chephirah, and Kirjath-baal (C-5; Josh. 9:17). They avoided annihilation by obtaining a treaty or covenant with Joshua through trickery (Josh., ch. 9). The Perizzites were a people about whom we know nothing. The Girgashites (Josh. 3:10; 24:11) are equally obscure.

On Plate IV are to be seen the five kingdoms which Israel found east of the Jordan and the Dead Sea (Num. 20:14 ff.; Deut., chs. 2; 3). To the north was the Kingdom of Og, a giant of a man whose bedstead was on exhibition in Rabbath-ammon (D-5) for a long time after his death (Deut. 3:11). The origin of this state is not known; but the very existence of such kingdoms as these in Transjordan at a time when the city-state system was in vogue in western Palestine suggests that a new type of life and a new people have invaded this area. In the Amarna period, correspondence from the city of Pella (D-4) indicates that about 1375 B.C. the northern area of Transjordan, where the Kingdom of Og was later established, was still organized in city-states. One of Og's capitals, Ashtaroth (E-3; Deut. 1:4; Josh. 12:4), was at that time ruled by a man named Ayyab (an early spelling of the name "Job"). It is thus evident that the kingdom ruled by Og was established sometime after this period. An intensive archaeological survey of Transjordan carried out during the years 1932–1943 has revealed that the cities in the region to the south of the River Jabbok (D-4) in the territory controlled by the Amorite state of King Sihon, and by the kingdoms of Ammon, Moab, and Edom, were founded sometime during the thirteenth century. They thus had barely been established when the Israelites from Egypt appeared in their area (see pp. 39 f.). The latter avoided conflict with Edom, Moab, and Ammon; but in the territory controlled by Sihon and Og, the tribes of Reuben, Gad, and half-Manasseh established themselves (Plate VI). The origin of the Ammonites, Moabites, and Edomites is unknown except that they are related to Israel: Edom through Esau (Gen., ch. 36) and Ammon and Moab through Lot (Gen. 19:30–38).

The establishment of these kingdoms in Transjordan and the gradual weakening of the power of the old city-states in central and southern Palestine might lead us to suppose that the energy and power of Canaanite civilization was dwindling by the thirteenth century, when Israel appeared on the scene from Egypt. Excavations in such cities as Kirjath-sepher (B-6), Lachish (B-5), Beth-shemesh (B-5), Gezer (B-5), Bethel (C-5), Jericho (C-5), Megiddo (C-3), and Beth-shan (C-4) indicate that this was precisely the case. From the sixteenth to the end of the thirteenth century a gradual deterioration in the arts and crafts can be observed. Reasons for this decline are not difficult to discover. Certainly the oppressive Egyptian taxation and corrupt administration made life difficult for the Canaanites. In addition, the system of government which fostered the city-state system, permitting and perhaps even encouraging continual warfare and bickering between the cities, would drain the energy and vitality from any people. The social organization of Canaanite society was likewise unhealthy. It was a feudal system with a king and an aristocracy of partly foreign "chariot-warriors" at the top, while at the bottom was a lower class of serfs and slaves. An independent and energetic middle class was nonexistent. This situation of affairs is illustrated by excavations in Canaanite cities. The chief building in the typical city is the palace of the local king, while around it is a maze of rooms and huts which once housed the lower class. Enclosing the city were great fortification walls, with protecting towers and well-guarded gates. These fortifications are so strong and often so elaborate that they could have been built only by a strongly centralized government which had at its disposal a large supply of inexpensive labor. Jericho, for example, was provided with two fortification walls about 1500 B.C. Both were built of brick; the inner one was twelve feet thick, the outer six feet; and the space between varied between twelve and fifteen feet.

THE RELIGION OF CANAAN

Still another factor which may have hindered the development of Canaanite civilization was the extremely low level of its religion. While it is difficult to tell just what influence Canaanite religion had on community life, its barbarous character should at least be pointed out. As in other countries, many gods were believed to exist. The father of the gods was named El. He was "the father of man" as well as of gods, "the father of years," and "creator of creatures." One of his epithets was "bull," with which he was likened to a bull in a herd of cows and calves. He was believed to have a wife named Asherah (as her name is spelled in the Old Testament; e.g., I Kings 18:19), who was supposed to have borne him a sizable family, composed of some seventy gods and goddesses. Chief among the offspring, as son or grandson, was Hadad, whom the people called familiarly Baal ("Lord"). Baal was the personification of those forces in nature which produce rain and vegetation. He was the lord of heaven and earth, whose kingdom was "eternal, to all generations." In northern Syria his wife was believed to be Anath, though in Palestine later another goddess named Ashtoreth (Greek, Astarte) was his wife. In any event both goddesses were the personifications of love and fertility. Anath was also a goddess who loved war. One of her bloody adventures is described in a Canaanite poem. Deciding on a massacre, she smote and slew from seacoast (west) to sunrise. Filling her temple with men, she barred the doors and hurled at them chairs, tables, and footstools. Soon she waded in blood up to her knees—nay, up to her neck. "Her liver swelled with laughter; her heart was full of joy." She then washed her hands in gore and proceeded to other occupations! Other gods were Mot (Death), Baal's enemy; Resheph, the god of pestilence and lord of the underworld; Shulman or Shalim, the god who brings health; Koshar (or Kothar), the god of arts and crafts including music; et cetera.

The various stories told about these gods and goddesses (i.e., the mythology) were actually means of explaining how the natural forces of the world operate. Chief among them was the saga about Baal (Rain and Vegetation) being murdered each spring by Mot (Death) and coming to life again in the fall. Thus the cycle of climate in Canaan (dry, rainless summers and rainy winters) was explained. The amazing thing about the gods, as they were conceived in Canaan, is that they had no moral character whatsoever. In fact, their conduct was on a much lower level than that of society as a whole, if we can judge from ancient codes of law. Certainly the brutality of the mythology is far worse than anywhere else in the Near East at that time. Worship of these gods carried with it some of the most demoralizing practices then in existence. Among them were child sacrifice, a practice long since discarded in Egypt and Babylonia, sacred prostitution, and snake-worship on a scale unknown among other peoples. It is difficult to see how a religion of such debasing character could have had any stabilizing or vitalizing effect whatsoever upon the civilization. Indeed, one would expect just the opposite to have been the case.

We have thus seen that when Israel under Joshua entered Palestine during the thirteenth century B.C., Canaanite civilization was weak and decaying. It was small loss to the world when in parts of the Palestinian hill country it was virtually annihilated. The purity and righteous holiness of the God of Israel were now to be demonstrated against this background of pagan and immoral religion. The intransigence and hostility of the religious leaders of Israel toward the people and religion of Canaan is thus to be seen in its true perspective. There could be no compromise between Jehovah and Baal.

Fig. 22. Asiatic captives making bricks in an Egyptian brickyard, as the Israelites were forced to do during their oppression. At the top left water is drawn from a pool and in the center the clay is mixed. At the top right a molder shapes the clay in a rectangular mold while an overseer sits watching. Near the pool another man lays the completed bricks out to dry in the sun.

THE EXODUS FROM EGYPT

Plate V

AT THE beginning of Israel's history as a nation there occurred the stirring events of the oppression in Egypt, the Exodus, the organization of the people into a covenant nation at Mount Sinai, and the conquest of Canaan. Years of study, exploration, and excavation have been spent in the attempt to solve the historical and geographical problems which these events present. As a result of the work of the last ten years in particular, it is possible to reconstruct the history and geography involved with more certainty and clarity than ever before.

THE OPPRESSION

The book of Exodus opens near the end of the four-hundred-year sojourn of Israel in Egypt. At that time "there arose a new king over Egypt, who knew not Joseph," and who, no doubt because he desired cheap labor for his elaborate construction plans, forced the Hebrews to work as slaves on two "store-cities," Pithom and Raamses (Ex. 1:11). From a number of references outside the Bible we know that on the borders of every settled country in the Near East were groups of nomads who often worked in various capacities for the wealthy, as servants and slaves, scribes, soldiers, laborers, et cetera. Such a group were the Hebrews in Goshen (Plate v, C-D 3), and the unscrupulous Pharaoh found them an easy prey for exploitation.

After many years of debate, it now appears that the two cities which the Hebrews built under Egyptian coercion and direction have been located. Pithom (v, C-3) is probably to be identified with an ancient site in the valley which connects the Nile and Lake Timsâh. (When first excavated in 1905-1906, it was thought that this site was Raamses, but the latter must now be located elsewhere.) The ruins were found to have been those of an old town which had been beautified and furnished with a temple by the great builder, Rameses II (1301-1234 B.C.). No earlier royal construction was found, so the Israelites probably worked there in his day.

More definite is the evidence from the city of Raamses (or Rameses, Ex. 12:37). This was obviously the same as the great capital of Egypt in the Delta during the Nineteenth Dynasty (c. 1319-1200), named the "House of Rameses." The location of this site is now best

fixed at Tanis (v, C-3), the city chosen also by the Hyksos as their capital (see p. 28). While the attempt has recently been made to fix it at modern *Qantîr* a few miles away (v, C-3), the weight of the evidence still favors Tanis. After the expulsion of the Hyksos and the destruction of Avaris about 1550 B.C., the Pharaohs again made Thebes (II, E-3) in Upper Egypt their capital. Judging from both the excavations and the ancient inscriptions they did no royal building in the Delta. In the story of Moses, however, the court of the Pharaoh is not far from the land of Goshen, where the Hebrews lived. This immediately brings us to the Nineteenth Dynasty when the capital was moved to the Delta, in order that the Royal Court might be in better position to reconquer and control the lost Asiatic Empire. The new city, evidently built in part at least with Hebrew slave labor, was celebrated for its beauty. Court poets sang that "none resembles it in its likeness to Thebes"; and the richness of the country around, known as "the land of Rameses," was a subject of frequent comment (cf. Gen. 47:11, where Israelite writers use the familiar name for the area in which Goshen was located, though it was not called by this name in Joseph's day).

This information, therefore, is important in fixing the approximate time when Moses lived. As will be shown later, Israel was in Palestine by the third quarter of the thirteenth century (1250-1225 B.C.), and if this be so, then the Pharaoh of the Oppression "who knew not Joseph" must have been Seti (or Sethos) I (1319-1301 B.C.), the king who began the work on the city of Rameses, according to a monument found at the site. The Pharaoh of the Exodus would then have been Rameses II (1301-1234 B.C.), a great builder who tried desperately to recover the lost glory of Egypt. After the nonaggression pact with the Hittites in 1280 B.C. (see p. 30), he became less active in Asiatic affairs and more and more concerned with the attempt to immortalize his name in Egypt by the vastness of his architectural enterprises.

We are not to think that the number of the Hebrews involved in the Exodus was so large that it caused a tremendous economic blow to Egypt. Even accounting for the provision of manna (probably a honeylike substance still produced by certain species of tamarisk trees in Sinai), between two and six thousand people would appear to

FIG. 23. The traditional Mount Sinai where Moses received the Law and before which Israel encamped. The mountain in the center is *Râs eṣ-Ṣafṣâf*, the beginning of the range of which *Jebel Mûsā* is the chief peak. The precise spot where Moses received the Law, whether on *Râs eṣ-Ṣafṣâf* itself or on *Jebel Mûsā* is unknown. The small plain of *er-Râḥa* in the foreground is probably to be identified with the "desert of Sinai" in Ex. 19:2 and Num. 33:16.

be a reasonable figure. Numbers, chs. 1 and 26, contains census lists which state that the male population of the Hebrews in the wilderness was over 600,000, a figure which would mean a total of at least two or three million when women and children are included. Most Biblical scholars have assumed that these figures are completely unhistorical, but a saner view which has recently been gaining acceptance holds that they are the misplaced census records of the time of David. II Samuel, ch. 24, describes the one census of united Israel of which we know, and the lists in Numbers represent the population of Israel which we would expect at that time according to calculations from archaeological investigation. Numbers, chs. 1 and 26, might thus represent two different editions of the Davidic lists from which the title pages had been lost and which were later thought to come from the time of Moses. This explanation would avoid treating the figures as forgeries and at the same time would permit us to fix the approximate number involved in the Exodus from other sources of information which require a much more modest figure.

THE ROUTE OF THE EXODUS

After permission was finally secured for the Children of Israel and the "mixed multitude" that joined them (Ex. 12:38) to leave Egypt, the initial stages of the journey are described as follows:

And the children of Israel journeyed from Rameses to Succoth [Ex. 12:37]. . . . And it came to pass, when Pharaoh had let the people go, that God led them not by the way of the land of the Philistines, although that was near. (For God said, Lest the people repent when they see war, and return to Egypt.) But God led the people around by the wilderness of the Reed Sea [not Red Sea; ch. 13:17, 18]. . . . And they set out from Succoth, and encamped in Etham on the edge of the wilderness [v. 20]. . . . And the Lord spake to Moses, saying, Speak to the children of Israel, that they turn back and encamp before Pihahiroth, between Migdol and the sea, before Baal-zephon. Before it ye shall encamp by the sea [ch. 14:1, 2].

At that point the Pharaoh sent a detachment of chariots after them, but they were delivered by the miraculous crossing of the sea when a strong wind backed up the waters.

Can this itinerary be followed on a map? Before the location of Rameses, Biblical geographers were not sure that the account was accurate. Now, however, it appears quite sound (see Plate V). Leaving Rameses-Tanis, the Israelites began their circuitous journey toward Canaan. They did not go by the direct military route, past the great frontier fortress of Zilu (Thel) and then along the "Way of the Land of the Philistines" (V, D-E 2-3). That was the well-traveled and well-guarded route to the Egyptian-Asiatic empire in Palestine and lower Syria. There was yet too much work to be done on morale and organization before the former slaves would have been ready for fighting. Instead, they went southward to Succoth, some thirty-two miles away (modern *Tell el-Maskhûṭah*, formerly mistakenly identified with Pithom), and thence into the wilderness of Sinai along "the way of the wilderness by the Reed Sea."

Etham, Migdol, Pihahiroth, and Baal-zephon unfortunately cannot be identified, though the second and third are mentioned in Egyptian writings. Apparently, the people started to go around the northern edge of the sea, encamping at Etham; but perhaps finding difficulty in getting through the frontier garrison they turned back again and moved behind the sea, only to be caught there by the chariots. Then came the wind and the crossing.

The translators of the Old Testament are probably incorrect in identifying the Hebrew name *Yam Suph* with "Red Sea," for the words actually mean "Reed" or "Marsh Sea." It is most improbable that this sea is the Red Sea or its northwestern arm, the Gulf of Suez. For one thing, there are no reeds in the Red Sea, and for another the Reed Sea in this account is one which forms a barrier between Egyptian soil and the Sinai Wilderness. If the Red Sea were meant, then the Hebrews would have been forced to cross a long expanse of desert in order to get to it. On the contrary, however, the verses imply that the Reed Sea was not far from Succoth (V, D-3).

Since the Suez Canal was dug, the topography of this region has changed somewhat, and at least one lake, Lake Ballah, has disappeared. In the days of the Old Testament the region around Lake Timsâh, between Lake Ballah and the Bitter Lakes, may well have been more marshy than it is at present, and the crossing of the "Reed Sea" may have been in the area around Lake Timsâh or just south of it.

There has been considerable debate as to where the Hebrews went after entering the wilderness, since Mount Sinai or Horeb (it was called by both names) has not been located with certainty. The Sinai peninsula is triangular in shape, 260 miles long and 150 miles wide at the north. Along the Mediterranean there is a sandy belt some 15 miles deep. To the south is a gravel and limestone plateau stretching some 150 miles. Below that is the apex of the peninsula with its mass of granite mountains, the highest of which rise some 8,000 feet above sea level. Among these mountains were the ancient copper and turquoise mines to which the Egyptians sent regular expeditions. Here also is the traditional site of Mount Sinai where Moses received the Law and bound the people together in a joint covenant with Jehovah. The tradition that this is the Mount Sinai of Israel is at least fifteen hundred years old, and it is difficult to see how the tradition could have arisen if it did not have some historical basis. In addition, it is possible to point to several stations along the route to this area which correspond to those mentioned in the Bible, but it is not possible to do this for any other route through the peninsula. Further, if the tradition is correct, we should be able to understand the presence of the Midianites at Sinai, among whom was Moses' father-in-law, Jethro or Reuel (Ex. 2:16 ff.; 18:1 ff.). One Midianite clan was called the "Kenites," meaning "metal smiths" (cf. Num. 10:29 and Judg. 4:11). We may assume, therefore, that one of the occupations of the Midianites was copper mining and smelting, and their interest in the mines of Sinai would be obvious.

The attempt has been made to locate Mount Sinai in Arabia east of the Gulf of Aqabah, the homeland of Midian. Some extinct volcanoes exist there, and the "thunders and lightnings, and a thick cloud upon the mount" in Ex. 19:16 are interpreted as evidence of an active volcano. In this case the Hebrews would have journeyed across Sinai to Ezion-geber along the present Mohammedan pilgrim route to Mecca (v, D-F 4); but the stages of the journey as described in Exodus hardly fit this route.

On Plate v the stations of the Israelite journey which can be identified with the most probability along the traditional route have been designated. The first source of water on the ancient road to the Sinai mines is 'Ain Ḥawârah. This, therefore, is probably Marah, the first station of the Israelite journey which was reached after three waterless days in the wilderness (v, D-4; Ex. 15:22 ff.). The next oasis to the south is in the Wâdî Gharandel, which corresponds to the Biblical Elim where twelve springs and seventy palm trees are said to have existed (v, D-4; Ex. 16:1; Num. 33:9). The next stages of the journey took them along the Red Sea, and thence inland to the Wilderness of Sin and to Dophkah (Num. 33:10-12). The exact route at this point depends upon the location of Dophkah. From its etymological meaning in Hebrew we should judge that this name was probably connected with smelting operations. If so, then the best identification of the site is with the Egyptian mining center of Serâbît el-Khâdim (v, E-5). The Wilderness of Sin would then be the plain along the edge of the Sinai plateau called Debbet er-Ramleh. From this point a series of valleys lead directly to Jebel Mûsâ past Rephidim (Wâdî Refâyid; v, E-5). While various mountains in the neighborhood have been identified with the Biblical Mount Sinai, the most probable location is the range designated at v, F-5 (see Fig. 23), of which the chief peak is called Jebel Mûsâ, "Mountain of Moses."

After spending a year at Mount Sinai, Israel left it and journeyed through the Wilderness of Paran (v, F-4; Num. 10:11, 12). None of the stations along the way which are listed in Num. 33:16-35 can be identified with any degree of certainty except Hazeroth (v, F-5) and Ezion-geber (v, G-4). From the latter the itinerary led to Kadesh-barnea in the Wilderness of Zin (v, F-3). Judging from the implications of the narrative as it now stands, the purpose of the Hebrews was to storm Canaan from the south. The pessimistic report of the spies (Num., ch. 13) and the defeat at Hormah (v, F-2; Num. 14:39 ff.) so weakened their morale, however, that they were forced to live in the area of Kadesh-barnea (for description see pp. 63 f.) until the older generation had been replaced by a new one.

THE CONQUEST OF CANAAN

After considerable time had passed, Moses led the new generation of Israelites from Kadesh-barnea with the purpose of going through Transjordan to storm Canaan from the east instead of from the south (Num. 20:22 ff.). The exact route which was taken is somewhat obscure, partly because the location of Mount Hor is uncertain. Apparently they circled northward in order to descend into the Arabah (v, F-G 3-4). According to Deut. 2:1 ff. they continued south in the Arabah to Ezion-geber (v, G-4) in order to traverse the King's Highway (v, G 2-4, and Fig. 25), though Num., ch. 33, says nothing about this journey. In any event, the king of Edom refused permission for them to traverse the highway, and no attempt was made to force the matter (Num. 20:14 ff.). Instead, Moses led the people northward in the Arabah past the mining center of Punon (v, G-3; Num. 33:42; see p. 65) and the spring at Oboth (v, G-3), crossing eastward at the northern border of Edom along the Brook Zered (v, G-3). Ije-abarim on the border of Moab (Num. 33:44) cannot be located with certainty at present, but there is no doubt that the itinerary as shown on Plate v is at least approximately correct.

Likewise unwilling to join battle with Moab, the people circled its territory to the east, and crossing the River Arnon they found themselves at the border of the Amorite Kingdom of Sihon (v, G 1-2 and IV, D 4-5; Num. 21:10 ff.). The latter was defeated in the battle of Jahaz (IX, I-6), the first great triumph of Israelite arms (Num. 21:21 ff.). Then followed the defeat of the giant king Og, whose kingdom north of the Jabbok had capitals at Edrei and Ashtaroth (IV, E-3; Num. 21:33 ff.) Thus ended the first phase of the conquest, with Israel in possession of the territory of Transjordan between Bashan

and the River Arnon. The kingdoms of Ammon, Moab, and Edom were left unchallenged (cf. Plates IV and VI; for description see pp. 36, 65 f.).

The second phase of the conquest, led by Joshua, is described as beginning with Jericho (Josh., chs. 2 to 6), continuing with the capture of Ai, the Gibeonite alliance (see p. 36), the defeat of the five Judean kings, and the conquest of Judah (Josh., chs. 7 to 10). A third campaign was directed against Galilee in the north, and resulted in the capture of the chief city of that area, Hazor (IV, D-2; Josh., ch. 11).

It is peculiar that not a word is said about a conquest of central Palestine, where the Joseph tribes, Ephraim and Manasseh, settled (see Plate VI). The capital of this region at the time was Shechem (IV, C-4), situated between Mount Ebal and Mount Gerizim, and known from excavations to have been a very strong city. While nothing is said about its capture, yet in Josh., ch. 24, it was the scene of the gathering of all the tribes for the renewal of the covenant. It is possible that friends or relatives of Israel were already in control of this region, so that all Joshua had to do was to make a treaty or covenant with them. Most scholars believe that this was the case. In control of Shechem, it is thought, were Hebrews who had never been in Egypt, or more probably had come out of Egypt at an earlier time, some perhaps at the expulsion of the Hyksos (see p. 29), and some, just possibly, at the burial of Jacob (Gen. 50:7 ff.). The Tell el-Amarna letters of Canaanite kings to the Egyptian court in the early fourteenth century indicate that Shechem and the region around it to the north and south were at that time in control of a rebel who showed by his actions little respect for the Egyptian Pharaoh (see p. 35). It is possible also that the story about Simeon and Levi in Gen., ch. 34, may reflect certain early tribal disputes at Shechem. In any event, the city was an early Israelite center (see Judg., chs. 6 to 9, and Josh., ch. 24), which Joshua did not have to conquer.

The best-known story connected with the conquest is the stirring account of the fall of Jericho (v, G-2; Josh., ch. 6). Yet this story furnishes the major problem in the reconstruction of the history of the Exodus. Excavations at the site (see p. 105) have revealed that the Canaanite city suffered two violent destructions during the final century or century and a half of its existence. The first probably occurred in the fifteenth century and the second in the fourteenth. After the latter the site was abandoned until Israelites rebuilt it during the tenth and ninth centuries (cf. I Kings 16:34). Some scholars have held that on the basis of this evidence from Jericho the entrance of Israel into Canaan must be placed during the late fifteenth or early fourteenth century. Other facts, however, appear to indicate that Moses and Joshua lived in the thirteenth century. In this case Joshua could not have captured Jericho because the city was not then in existence. These facts may be listed as follows: (1) As noted on p. 35, the city-state system of early fourteenth-century Canaan was not the same as

FIG. 24. The small Wâdî Qudeirât in which was possibly located the site of Hazar-addar (Plate v, F-3 and p. 64). This valley is watered by the largest spring in the area of Kadesh-barnea. The neighboring spring, 'Ain Qedeis, where Kadesh-barnea is located on Plate v is very small, and the Israelites during their long stay in this area probably made use of 'Ain Qudeirât as well.

FIG. 25. A section of the King's Highway (Num. 20:17; 21:22) as it runs north along a valley to cross the Brook Zered in the background (Plate v, G 2-4). This was the old road through Transjordan used by the four invading kings in Gen., ch. 14. It is here so clearly marked because it was paved by the Romans and is still used. Today it is being constructed anew by the Government of Transjordan. Note the ruins of an ancient watchtower beside it.

it was in the time of Joshua. The Canaan described in The Book of Joshua is later than the *Tell el-Amarna* period of the early fourteenth century. (2) Explorations in Transjordan have shown that the kingdoms of Edom, Moab, and Ammon were not founded until the thirteenth century. This conclusion is based upon the careful archaeological examination of hundreds of sites in which the people of these kingdoms once lived. Some have argued that the Edomites, Moabites, and Ammonites may well have been in the country about 1400 B.C., though living a nomadic life. Numbers, ch. 21, however, mentions a number of towns in which the people were living when Israel traversed this territory, and this presupposes a period when nomadic life had been abandoned. (3) The Egyptian cities of Pithom and Rameses which Israel built for the Pharaoh must have been constructed after c. 1319 B.C. (see above). (4) Finally, as will be noted below, Joshua's Judean campaign took place after 1250 B.C. according to the archaeological data.

Thus the evidence for Joshua's date in the thirteenth century appears strong, while the evidence for the final fall and abandonment of Jericho in the previous century is conclusive. At the present there is no final solution of this discrepancy, and we must await further study and excavation before indulging in too much speculation. For the moment, however, we are led to the conclusion that Jericho fell, not to Joshua, but to relatives of Israel, perhaps from the Shechem area, during the disturbances of the fourteenth century. According to this view, the conquest was a gradual one, covering a considerable period, though the climax came in the thirteenth century when the army under Joshua entered the country from the east.

Any invaders of the hill country from the Jericho area would first be forced to seize a foothold in the region of Bethel and Ai, rather than around Jerusalem, because the valleys leading from the Jordan give easy access to the former, but not to the latter (cf. IX, G 5-6). Consequently, when Josh., chs. 7; 8, describes the capture of Ai, it is describing the first great victory over the Canaanites in the hill country. From excavations it is known that the city involved was not Ai, but rather Bethel (see p. 105), the ruins of which bear eloquent testi-

mony to a violent destruction sometime during the first half of the thirteenth century.

In the tenth chapter of Joshua the itinerary of the conquest of the southern hill country is described. After the defeat of the five Canaanite kings in the Valley of Aijalon (IX, D-E 5), Joshua turned south into the Shephelah or Lowlands (I, B 5-6), carefully avoiding the strong fortress of Gezer, which did not come into Israelite hands until the time of Solomon (v, F-2; IX, D-5; I Kings 9:16). He first captured Makkedah (Josh. 10:28), a city near Beth-shemesh and Azekah (IX, D-6) but one which cannot be located with certainty. Next, he took Libnah at the head of the Valley of Elah (where David was later to fight Goliath; v, F-2; IX, D-6). A small excavation was made at this site in 1898-1899, and while it was found to have been occupied during this period, the precise date of its fall to Israel was not determined. The next Canaanite royal city to the south of Libnah was Lachish (v, F-2; IX, D-7). From excavations this exceedingly strong fortress is known to have been violently destroyed about 1230 B.C., and the conflagration is certainly to be attributed to Israel (Josh. 10:31 ff.). Joshua then proceeded to Eglon, seven miles southwest of Lachish (v, F-2; IX, C-7). The evidence gained from excavations indicates that this city was also destroyed about the same age, though the date of its conflagration cannot be as precisely determined as that of Lachish.

Now in control of the most important fortresses guarding the passes to the later Judean capital at Hebron, Israel turned upon Hebron itself, presumably following the pass by Mareshah (see the road drawn on Plates IV and VI, B-C 5-6). When Hebron was captured, it was a simple matter to take the remaining frontier fortress of Debir (v, F-2; IX, D-8; Josh. 10:38, 39), the Canaanite name of which was Kirjath-sepher. Excavations at this site show that it too was violently destroyed at approximately the same period as Lachish.

From this evidence two things are to be noted. One is that the campaign was carried out during the third quarter of the thirteenth century (c. 1250-1225 B.C.). That Israel was in Palestine at that time is shown by an Egyptian monument of Pharaoh Merenptah (c. 1235-1227 B.C.) who claims to have defeated "the people of Israel" in Palestine during the fifth year of his reign. This event is not mentioned in the Old Testament; it certainly was of minor significance and without lasting effect, for the Egyptian control of Canaan was then very weak. The reference does show, however, that Israel was already established in its later home by 1230 B.C.

A second feature of Joshua's campaign is the evidence of sound military strategy which it exhibits. In conquering Palestine Israel did not waste its strength on the strongest military fortresses at Jerusalem and Gezer (see pp. 44, 97). The strategy employed was the same as that used by the Assyrians and Babylonians later on. That was to conquer first the string of fortresses in the Shephelah which guarded the approaches to the Judean hill country. After that was accomplished the capture of the hill country was a comparatively simple operation.

In Judg., ch. 1, further information in detail is given which at first glance appears to conflict with that of Josh., ch. 10. There we are told that Othniel took Debir (Judg. 1:11 ff.) and Caleb, Hebron (v. 20). The implication is that instead of one great campaign the various tribal groups completed the conquest unaided by others. After the days of Joshua, this was certainly true (see pp. 43 ff.); but these passages are not necessarily in direct conflict with each other if it is assumed that the original plan was Joshua's.

By way of conclusion it should be stated, however, that these chronological problems must not obscure the central facts: namely, that at least some Israelites suffered slavery in Egypt, that they were freed in a wonderful deliverance, and that they were led victoriously into the Promised Land after years of murmuring and faintheartedness. In these remarkable events the Israelites saw the hand of their God, a gracious God who had taken pity on their afflictions, and saved them for his providential purpose.

PLATE V

THE EXODUS FROM EGYPT
(Thirteenth Century B. C.)
Copyright, The Westminster Press
International Copyright Secured. All Rights Reserved
SCALE OF MILES

BOUNDARY OF EGYPTIAN EMPIRE
ROADS
PROBABLE ROUTE OF THE EXODUS
AND MAIN PHASE OF THE CONQUEST
CITIES AND TOWNS

Plate VI

PALESTINE
DURING THE PERIOD
OF THE JUDGES

Copyright, The Westminster Press
International Copyright Secured. All Rights Reserved

SCALE OF MILES

0 5 10 15 20 25 30

KNOWN BOUNDARIES
SOLID, THUS

PROBABLE BOUNDARIES
NOTCHED, THUS

CITIES AND TOWNS   o

ROADS

PALESTINE DURING THE PERIOD OF THE JUDGES

(C. 1200–1020 B.C.)

PLATE VI

THE settlement of the Israelite tribes in their newly won territory is described in Josh., chs. 13 to 19. Israelite society was patriarchal in structure; that is, it was composed of families, each headed by a patriarchal head or father. A number of related families made up a clan, and a varying number of clans made up a tribe. During and at the conclusion of the conquest, the country was parceled out among the eleven tribes, while the tribe of Levi, which was to attend to religious matters, was distributed among the others by the allotment to it of specific towns (Josh., ch. 21). In each tribal area the land was further subdivided among the clans and families. The process by which the distribution east of the Jordan was effected is described as a drawing by lot. Reuben, Gad, and one half of Manasseh (of which the chief clan was Machir) were given the territory of Sihon and Og (Num., ch. 32; Josh., ch. 13). West of the Jordan the house of Joseph, composed of Ephraim and Manasseh, was settled first (Josh., chs. 16; 17), after which the rest of the country was divided at an assembly in Shiloh (Plate VI, C-4). The land thus allotted became the ancestral property of each family, and laws were made to protect the inheritance. The well-known story of Ahab and Naboth's vineyard makes it plain that not even the later kings of Israel had the right to confiscate family property. Naboth was quite within his legal rights when he exclaimed to King Ahab: "The Lord forbid it me, that I should give the inheritance of my fathers unto thee" (I Kings 21:3).

In recent years a great advance has been made in the accuracy with which the tribal boundaries can be traced. This is due primarily to the work of archaeologists in locating the places where the ancient towns once stood (see pp. 13, 14). On Plate VI the tribal districts are shown as they can now be located.

THE SETTLEMENT OF TRANSJORDAN

South, east, and northeast of the Dead Sea were the kingdoms of Edom, Moab, and Ammon, which Israel made no attempt to conquer at this time. The plateau of Edom proper lay directly south of the Brook Zered (VI, D-7; see X, H-J 5-7), although the Arabah (X, G-H 5-6) and some of the wilderness west of it were probably also under Edomite control. Moab at this time was confined between the Brook Zered and the River Arnon, while Ammon lay east of the River Jabbok as the latter turned in a wide loop southward to the capital at Rabbath-ammon (VI, D-5). The tribes of Reuben and Gad were situated in the territory formerly ruled by King Sihon (cf. Plates IV and VI, D 4-5). The northern boundary of Reuben was the *Wâdī Hesbân*, a valley leading to the Jordan from Heshbon (VI, D-5). To the south Reuben bordered on Moab at the River Arnon. Gad extended from the *Wâdī Hesbân* to a point north of the River Jabbok near Mahanaim (VI, D-4), but we cannot establish the boundary precisely. These two tribes were located in a precarious position, since Moab and Ammon were always a threat to their independence. During the ninth century Moab took over all of Reuben's territory, and that tribe disappeared from history (see Plate VII:C). Similarly, Gad was pressed by the Ammonites, who as early as the eleventh century were in position to threaten the Israelite territory as far west as Jabesh-gilead (VI, D-4; I Sam., ch. 11).

To the north the half tribe of Manasseh occupied the kingdom of Og (cf. IV and VI, D-E 3-4) with its strong cities of Ramoth-gilead, Edrei, Ashtaroth, and Karnaim (VI, E-3). The northern boundary is not shown on Plate VI because it cannot be precisely located, but Argob (VI, E-3), Nobah (VI, F-3), and Salcah (VII:A, D-4) were included (Num. 32:42; Deut. 3:14; Josh. 13:11 ff.). During the ninth and eighth centuries this region became a battleground between Israel and the Aramean kingdom of Damascus, while the Ammonites pressed against it on the southeast (see Plate VII:B). King Ahab was mortally wounded in battle at Ramoth-gilead (I Kings 22:29 ff.; VI, E-3).

THE SETTLEMENT OF WESTERN PALESTINE

For the tribal settlement of the country west of the Jordan more information is available, and the core of the documentary lists in Josh., chs. 15 to 19, is very old. Thus among the towns of Simeon, Sharuhen (VI, A-6) is listed (Josh. 19:6). We know from the excavations at the site that it was destroyed shortly after 900 B.C. and not reoccupied for four centuries. Consequently, a list of villages containing this town must date before 900 B.C. Similarly, we are told that the tribe of Ephraim did not drive out "the Canaanites that dwelt in

FIG. 26. The pass of Megiddo, on the main highway from the Plain of Sharon across Mount Carmel to the Valley of Jezreel (Esdraelon). This highway is the main road between Syria and Egypt. Along it armies and caravans have moved for millennia. This view, looking toward the southwest, is taken at the point where a side road branches off at the left to Taanach (VI, C-3).

FIG. 27. The small plain of Lebonah (modern *Lubban*) in the hill country of Ephraim near Shiloh (VI, C-4). The road shown is the highway from Jerusalem through the hill country to Nazareth in Galilee. In the background at the foot of the hill is the modern village on the approximate site of ancient Lebonah (Judg. 21:19).

Gezer [VI, B-5]: but the Canaanites dwell in the midst of Ephraim unto this day, and are become servants to do taskwork" (Josh. 16:10). This verse must certainly have been written in the time of David or Solomon in the tenth century. Not only did Gezer first come under Israelite control at that time (I Kings 9:16), but it was only then that Israel was strong enough to place the Canaanites in labor battalions as slaves (I Kings 9:21). Gezer was destroyed and abandoned at the end of the tenth century and the verse must date, therefore, before that period. We may be confident from these and similar reasons that we are dealing here with old lists upon which much reliance can be placed.

At first glance Plate VI would indicate that during the period of the Judges (c. 1200-1020 B.C.) the Israelites were in control of the whole country. Yet a careful reading of Joshua and Judg., ch. 1, indicates that this was not the case. While the tribal lists divided up the land and Israel laid claim to all of it, there were portions which could not be subdued. As mentioned above, Gezer was not conquered until the time of Solomon, and Jerusalem was first taken by David (Judg. 1:21; II Sam. 5:6 ff.). Judges 1:19 states that Judah occupied the hill country, but "he could not drive out the inhabitants of the valley, because they had chariots of iron." This refers primarily to the coastal plain from Gaza to Ekron and extending inland as far as Gath (VI, A-B 5-6). Similarly, the tribe of Manasseh failed to subdue a string of Canaanite fortresses along its northern boundary, and these separated it from the tribes in Galilee (Judg. 1:27). Chief among them were Beth-shan, Ibleam, Taanach, Megiddo, and Dor (VI, B-C 3-4). From the excavations it appears likely that Megiddo, a strong city guarding the main pass from the Plain of Sharon (Plate I, and VI, B-C 3-4) to the north (see Figs. 5 and 26) fell to Israel at least temporarily either c. 1150 or 1100 B.C. After each of the destructions at these dates, the town was deserted for a period of years. During one of the periods of desertion the battle between the forces of Barak and Sisera as described in the Song of Deborah (Judg., ch. 5) probably took place. The location of the battle was "in Taanach by the waters of Megiddo" (v. 19). These waters are those of the River Kishon (VI, C-3), the sources of which were at Megiddo. Since, however, the town which is mentioned to give the general location was not Megiddo but Taanach some distance away, we may infer that the former was not in existence at that time. Beth-shan (see Fig. 75) continued in Canaanite and Philistine hands and was not destroyed until the time of David, judging from the evidence found in the ruins (cf. also I Sam. 31:10; the temple there mentioned has been excavated).

It is evident, therefore, that the Israelites during the period of the Judges were not in possession of the whole country but chiefly of the central ridge, while Canaanites continued to live around them—a situation that was little altered until the great conquests of David.

THE "JUDGES" OF ISRAEL

There was a striking difference between the political organization of Israel and that of the surrounding peoples during this period. The latter were highly organized. Edom, Moab, and Ammon to the east and southeast were monarchies, controlling numerous cities and with capitals at Sela (see Fig. 46) or Teman (VI, C-D 8), Kir-hareseth (VI, D-6), and Rabbath-ammon (VI, D-5) respectively. The Canaanites continued their old city-state organization (see pp. 34 ff.), each major city possessing its own ruler (for example, Jerusalem, Gezer, Megiddo, Beth-shan, Dor, Sidon, etc.). There was no great power to interfere in the local struggles; effective Egyptian control was at an end (see pp. 29, 30), and the Assyrian Empire had not yet extended its power this far. Assyria, about 1100 B.C., conquered northern Syria, but the success was ephemeral and scarcely affected Palestine.

In contrast to her strongly organized neighbors, Israel was only a loose federation of tribes. These were held together, not by a central political figure who exercised dictatorial control, but solely by a common tradition and a religious bond or "covenant." The visible symbol of the bond was the "Ark of the Covenant," which during most of the period of the Judges rested in the central sanctuary at Shiloh (VI, C-4). With no central government we should expect the tribes to be in constant danger of attack from raiders and "oppressors" on every hand, unless the Israelite sense of religious unity were kept so strong that danger to one tribe would immediately cause all tribes to come to its defense. But according to The Book of Judges the people in settling down to an agricultural life succumbed in large measure to the seductive nature worship which was the religion of Canaan (see p. 36). Whenever they did this, we are told, God sent "oppressors" to afflict them (Judg., ch. 2). In other words, the more paganism they adopted, the weaker the covenant bond between them became, and the more each tribe tended to live by and for itself, isolated from the other tribes. This disunity made subjugation and oppression by outsiders relatively easy.

Several of these oppressors are mentioned: Moabites (Judg. 3:12 ff.), Canaanites (Judg., chs. 4; 5), Midianites from Arabia (Judg., chs. 6; 7; V, G 4-5), Ammonites (Judg., ch. 11), and Philistines (Judg. 3:31; chs. 13 ff.; I Sam., chs. 4 ff.). As previously indicated, the Moabites and Ammonites were peoples of Transjordan whom Israel had not conquered. During this period they took advantage of the separatist tendencies of the tribes and tried to gain control over Transjordan. Apart from the Philistine oppression (see below) the most dangerous threats to Israel were from the Canaanites and Midianites. A formidable Canaanite army was assembled in the Valley of Jezreel (I, C-3) under the leadership of one Sisera from the village of Harosheth (IV, C-3). A call to arms was issued to the tribes of Israel by the prophetess Deborah. Six of the tribes responded and an army was assembled at Mount Tabor (VI, C-3) under the leadership of Barak from Kedesh-naphtali (VI, D-2; Judg. 4:6 ff.). The subsequent defeat of the Canaanites in a battle near Megiddo (VI, C-3) was celebrated by the remarkable poem, composed by an eyewitness, which is preserved in Judg., ch. 5. The Midianite oppression was also exceedingly serious, since it was an invasion from the Arabian Desert of Bedouins who for the first time were using domesticated camels on a large scale. This use of the camel made the Midianites dangerous; they could travel long distances with comparative rapidity without concern for water supply. The story of their defeat by Gideon in the valley leading from Jezreel to the Jordan, between Mount Gilboa and the Hill of Moreh (VI, C-3), is well known.

Complete disaster for Israel in these crises was avoided by spontaneous leaders who were called "judges." These figures have been called "charismatic" leaders, because they were believed to possess some special gift of God's grace. They were set apart from others by special abilities, such as military prowess, wisdom, honesty, and natural capacities for leadership. In disputes between individuals and families, it was only natural that the cases be taken before such leaders for decision. In this way the name "judges" was given them, though for the most part in the stories about them they appear as military leaders. The charismatic nature of the leadership during this period is a remarkable feature of Israel, and distinguishes its history sharply from that of the surrounding peoples.

ARCHAEOLOGY AND THE PERIOD OF THE JUDGES

During the period of the Judges considerable difference can be observed between the material civilization and wealth of Israelite towns and those of the neighbors who were not driven out. Canaanite cities which have been excavated, such as Beth-shan (VI, C-4), Megiddo (VI, C-3), and Salmonah (the probable name of modern *Tell Abū Hawâm*, IV, C-3), show a considerable degree of wealth. Houses were well built, and their contents indicate that an active trade with Syria and Cyprus was carried on. Occasionally objects of art from Egypt are found. At Beth-shan, after Egyptian control came to an end, the temples of the Canaanite deities Dagon and Ashtaroth were built (I Sam. 31:10; I Chron. 10:10); and in their precincts were placed numerous coveted objects, including three Egyptian stelae (monumental stones) set up by the Pharaohs Seti I and Rameses II some two hundred years before.

At Megiddo during the early twelfth century was an elaborate palace of the local king, in all probability as large as the palace which Solomon later built for himself in Jerusalem. In its basement was the treasure room which had been looted of its finest objects when the city was destroyed by some enemy about 1150 B.C. Left on the floor in a confused mass were a large number of gold, ivory, and alabaster objects, which while unimportant to the looters are of great value to us, since they so vividly illustrate the wealth and culture of the Canaanite king (Figs. 28, 29).

In contrast to the wealth of these Canaanite towns the Israelites were extremely poor. Between 1200 and 1000 B.C. the hill country, for the first time, became dotted with towns, indicating an increase in the population and witnessing to the Israelite settlement. Several of these towns have been excavated (see Plate XVIII), and their ruins testify to a civilization very different from that of the Canaanites. Everywhere there is evidence of poverty. House walls are crude and ill-planned. Art is exceedingly primitive. Before about 1050 B.C. there is no evidence of trade with foreign peoples other than with the immediate neighbors. City fortifications, when constructed, were poorly built and scarcely capable of withstanding serious attack. All this was to change during the period of David and Solomon after 1000 B.C., when strong government and military success brought an economic revolution to Israel.

THE PHILISTINES

Shortly after 1200 B.C. there appeared in the southern coastal plain a people called "Philistines" (VI, B-5), from whom the name "Palestine" was later derived. The Philistines were one group of a large number of sea peoples from the Greek islands and particularly from Crete (Caphtor; see Amos 9:7). This we know, not only from references in the Bible and in Egyptian records, but from the characteristic pottery which they made in Palestine. The shapes of the vessels were quite unlike the traditional forms of Canaan, but were patterned after styles well known in the Greek world whence the people came.

While attempting to invade Egypt the sea peoples suffered a severe defeat at the hands of Pharaoh Rameses III (c. 1195-1164 B.C.), and some at least fell back on Palestine (see Fig. 16). One group settled at Dor in the Plain of Sharon (VI, B-3), though we hear about them, not from the Old Testament, but from the Egyptian story of a certain Wenamon, an Egyptian emissary who stopped there on his way to

FIG. 28. One of the ivories from the collection of the king of Megiddo, dating c. 1200 B.C. A Canaanite ruler is shown sitting on his throne, drinking from a small bowl. Before him are an official and a musician plucking the strings of a lyre. The latter reminds us of David playing the lyre (not the "harp") before the moody Saul (I Sam. 16:23). The king's throne is supported by winged lions with human heads. These are the imaginary, composite beings which the Israelites called "cherubim" (which were not the small winged children that appear as "cherubs" in modern art). In Solomon's Temple there were two large figures of this type in the Holy of Holies, on which Jehovah was believed to be enthroned, though invisibly, precisely as Canaanite kings such as this were enthroned (see p. 48; cf. I Sam. 4:4).

Syria for cedar. South of Gerar was another group called the "Cher-ethites" (VI, A-6), but we know nothing about them apart from three references in the Old Testament (I Sam. 30:14; Ezek. 25:16; Zeph. 2:5).

By far the most important of the sea peoples in Palestine was the Philistine group, which was organized around five cities: Gaza (VI, A-5), Ashkelon, Ashdod, Ekron, and Gath (VI, B-5). Each city, with the area it controlled, was ruled by a "lord," who, though independent, co-operated with the others in important matters. Thus in political and military affairs the people were able to act as a united group. As a result they proved to be the most serious threat to the independence of Israel during the period of the Judges. Most disastrous was the battle at Eben-ezer and Aphek (VI, B-4) about 1050 B.C., when the Israelite Ark was captured and taken to Ashdod (I Sam., ch. 4). After the trouble it caused in the Temple of Dagon, it was sent to Ekron, and from there up the Valley of Sorek past Beth-shemesh to Kirjath-jearim (VI, C-5; see also IX, C-E 5-6). The primary interest of the writer of this story was to tell about the Ark, and we are left to infer what happened to Israel politically. From archae-ological investigation we know that Israel's central sanctuary, Shiloh (VI, C-4), where the Ark had been kept, was violently de-stroyed at this time, making the reference of Jeremiah to its destruc-tion quite clear (Jer. 7:12 ff.; 26:6 ff.). Later we hear of Philistine garrisons in the hill country itself (I Sam. 13:3), and also in posses-sion of such a far-away city as Beth-shan (VI, C-4), on the wall of which was hung the body of Saul after his defeat at Mount Gilboa (VI, C-4; I Sam., ch. 31). This means that between c. 1050 and 1020 B.C. the Philistines were able to dominate Israel politically, and it is small wonder that the people of Israel came to Samuel demand-ing a king who would organize them and drive off the oppressor.

One direct consequence of the Philistine pressure was the fact that the small tribe of Dan was forced to leave the territory originally assigned to it (Josh. 19:47; Judg., ch. 18). This tribe had been allotted an area from Beth-shemesh, Zorah, and Aijalon (VI, B-5), to Ekron (VI, B-5), Jehud, Bene-berak, and Rakkon (VI, B-4; Josh. 19:40 ff.). Philistine power drove the Danites from the plains, whereupon they traveled to the foot of Mount Hermon and settled there, after taking a Canaanite city called Laish and renaming it for themselves (VI, D-2; Judg. 18:27-29).

The period of the Judges marks the beginning of the Iron Age; that is, the time when iron came into common use. The metal used for tools and weapons since 4000 B.C. had been copper, though since the Hyksos period (pp. 27 f.) it had been common practice to intro-duce tin into the copper to produce a harder product, bronze. Before 1200 B.C. iron appears to have been a magic product in Western Asia, valued almost as much as gold and silver. This was not be-cause of the scarcity of the ore, but because the secrets of the rather complicated smelting process seem to have been jealously guarded by the Hittites.

Throughout the period of the Judges the Israelites, who were poor in material possessions, were thwarted time and again because of their lack of this important metal for agricultural implements, nails, and weapons. They were unable to drive out the Canaanites from the plains because these people owned iron chariots (Josh. 17:16; Judg. 1:19; 4: 2, 3).

From excavations in Philistine territory it has been learned that the Philistines possessed iron weapons and jewelry, while the Israelites appear to have had none. It is very probable, therefore, that the metal was introduced into common use in Palestine by the Philistines who had learned about it in the north. They held a "corner" on the iron market, however, and closely guarded the trade secrets of its produc-tion. This we infer from the excavations and also from the interesting passage in I Sam. 13:19-22.

Once the Philistine power was broken by the first kings of Israel, Saul and David, the secret of the iron-smelting process became pub-lic property, and the metal came into use in Israel. This promptly resulted in an economic revolution and higher standard of living for the common man. The war with the Philistines was one of survival for Israel. Small wonder that it was celebrated in song and story, since it furnished the occasion for great exploits, notably those of Samson (Judg., chs. 13 to 16) and of David against Goliath (I Sam., ch. 17).

ISRAEL'S NORTHERN NEIGHBORS

During the period of the Judges the people of Israel were not troubled by oppressors from Syria. Yet to the north and northeast Phoenician and Aramean states were in process of formation which were to influence greatly the course of events in Palestine.

The coast line of Syria apparently suffered severely in the twelfth century from the depredations of the invading sea peoples. The great city of Ugarit (III, C-2), and probably Tyre (VI, C-2) also, was de-stroyed and abandoned at this time. Yet by the time of David and Solomon in the tenth century the Canaanites in the Tyre-Sidon (VI, C 1-2) area had been united into a strong state with its capital at Tyre. This Phoenician state came into being during the period of the Judges and was apparently quite unique among the world's king-doms. Instead of concentrating its energies on expanding its terri-tory by force of arms, it spread its influence, its raw materials, and its artisans throughout the Mediterranean by trade and treaties. We are unable to trace its boundaries at any one period or to determine how much territory it comprised. The tribe of Asher, following the con-quest, laid claim to the whole coast from Mount Carmel well into Syria (VI, C 2-3), but it is improbable that Israelites ever really con-trolled this area (see Judg. 1: 31, 32). By the time of Solomon the tribe had virtually ceased to exist, having become a dependency of Phoenicia (VII:A, B-C 2-3).

East of the Syrian mountains to the north and south of Damascus new invaders from Arabia were settling down during the period of the Judges. These were the Aramaeans (a name which is translated "Syrians" in the A.V. and R.V.). Towns were founded by them throughout this area as far south as the Yarmuk (I, D-3), so that by the end of the tenth century the whole of Bashan and eastern Syria was under Aramean control (VII: A-B). By 1000 B.C. the Aramean kingdom of Zobah had extended its frontiers to the Euphrates and was conquering Assyrian territory there, but this was stopped by the Davidic conquest of Zobah (p. 47). During the ninth and eighth centuries the Aramaeans were a formidable enemy of Israel. Even after their subjugation by the Assyrians in 733-732 they continued to be great traders who by commercial means became as influential in Western Asia as Phoenicia was in the Mediterranean.

FIG. 29. A Canaanite maiden, as re-stored from a Megiddo ivory. Note the long hair and flowing robe which were characteristic of the Canaanite fashions of the day.

FIG. 30. Esdraelon or Valley of Jezreel as seen from the hills west of Nazareth. In the background is Mount Carmel, a spur of the hill country of Samaria which pushes out to the Mediterranean. North of Carmel, at Haifa, the British have developed a safe though small harbor.

THE POLITICAL HISTORY OF ISRAEL AND JUDAH

PLATE VII

FOLLOWING the golden age of the empire in the time of David, the territory controlled by the Hebrew people was gradually diminished in extent until in the fifth century it was but a tiny province in the Fifth Satrapy of the vast Persian Empire. Excavations in Israelite and Judean towns reveal the progressive weakening and impoverishment of the people, owing to bad politics, bad economics, civil and international war.

Plates VII and XII, supplemented by Plates XI, XIII, and XIV, picture the political fortunes of the Israelite-Jewish people from the time of David to the period of Paul. Plate VII shows the state of affairs in Palestine during the tenth, ninth, eighth, and fifth centuries B.C.

THE EMPIRE OF DAVID AND SOLOMON

A centralized state with a monarchy apparently became a necessity during the period of the Judges to avoid permanent subjection to the Philistines (pp. 45 f.). We gather that there was opposition to it, as we should expect, since human kingship ran counter to Israel's traditional belief that Jehovah was the true King of his people (cf. I Sam., chs. 8 and 12). The problem was partially solved by considering the king the "anointed" (messiah) of the Lord (I Sam., ch. 10), who was to rule his people under the dictates of God's will as it was revealed to him by God's spokesmen. Thus when Saul was anointed as the first king, Samuel was the spokesman who was to make God's will known to him. An innate instability on the part of Saul and an inflexibility on the part of Samuel, however, soon brought a rupture in their relations. This fact, coupled with Saul's largely irrational jealousy of David, weakened his efficiency as king. Yet his reign was Israel's political salvation. The Philistines were expelled from the hill country following the battle of Michmash (IX, F-5), and the Ammonites were thrown back from Jabesh-gilead (IX, H-2; I Sam., chs. 11 and 14 ff.). Saul's fortress at Gibeah (IX, F-6) has been excavated. It was of rustic simplicity in size and construction; yet nevertheless it was evidence of a good beginning in the political and military strengthening of a divided people.

At the death of Saul (c. 1004 B.C.) his kingdom split into its northern and southern parts. David was made king over Judah at Hebron (VII: A, C-5; II Sam. 2:1-4), while Ishbosheth (Ishbaal), Saul's son, reigned over Israel. Seven and one half years later, after the murder of Ishbosheth (II Sam. 5:5), David was made king over the united people and began an illustrious reign, thirty-three years in duration (ending c. 965 B.C.). During that period the centralization of power in the throne was vastly increased and strongly supported by a large standing army of sworn loyalty to the king.

David's first acts exhibited a high degree of political sagacity. Jerusalem, which had never been conquered by Israel, was captured and made the political center of the state (II Sam. 5:6 ff.). Due to its strategic position between the northern and southern groups, its choice prevented charges of favoritism from arising against David. The Ark of the Covenant was then brought to Jerusalem and placed under the royal protection, so that the court became not only the center of political unity but the symbol of religious unity as well (II Sam., ch. 6).

A brief summary of the remarkable conquests of David is found in II Sam., chs. 8; 10; 12:26 ff. First, he confined the Philistines to a small area on the coast (VII:A, B-5) and dominated them economically. The kingdoms of Edom, Moab, and Ammon across the Jordan were next subjugated and their inhabitants made to work on royal projects. The road to the Red Sea and the trade routes between Arabia and Syria were now in David's control. His greatest military triumph, however, was his conquest of Aram ("Syria"; VII:A-B, D-E 2-3). The Arameans in this region (see p. 46) had come to the assistance of the Ammonites during David's siege of their capital at Rabbah (VII:A, D-5), but they had been defeated. Now he seized Damascus and also subdued Zobah (VII:A, D 2-3), the leading Aramean kingdom. Assyrian records indicate that the state of Zobah had become sufficiently powerful to begin the conquest of Assyrian territory along the upper Euphrates. It is part of the irony of history that David's subjugation of this kingdom may have saved Assyria and made it possible for her to rise rapidly to power and during the subsequent centuries to conquer the whole of the Fertile Crescent.

Just where David finally fixed the northern boundary of his empire is not recorded in II Samuel. It is known only that his empire bordered on the state of Hamath (ch. 8:9 ff.; VII:A, D-1). Numbers 34:7 ff. and Ezek., ch. 48, however, describe the ideal northern border of Israel as extending from Hazar-enan and Zedad to "the entrance of Hamath" (in the area of Riblah and Kadesh; VII:A, D-2). From

FIG. 31. A reconstruction of the Temple of Solomon modeled on the specifications given in the Old Testament and on what has been learned through archaeological study of similar edifices. The Temple itself was built according to Phoenician designs and was notable, not for its size, but for its beauty and artistic workmanship.

that point it would have descended the valley along the eastern side of the Lebanons. This description probably reflects the actual northern extent of the Davidic empire. Otherwise we should be at a loss to explain how the tradition could have arisen that this was Israel's true boundary.

After Edom had been subjugated, David had nothing to fear from the south, because Egypt at that time was unable to interfere in Asia. Treaties were made with the states of Hamath and Tyre to the north, so that the borders of the empire were now firmly established and remained so through most of the days of Solomon. The reign of David was thus one of great political and economic prosperity. Population increased; and the introduction of iron into common use after the breaking of the Philistine control over it (see p. 46) brought an economic revolution to the country.

Solomon (c. 965-926 B.C.) did not add to the Davidic conquests, but instead devoted his reign to the cultural and economic development of his empire. Political ties with the smaller countries and with Egypt were strengthened by the addition to his harem of numerous princesses, chief among whom was the daughter of the Egyptian Pharaoh. He set out on a vast building program, remains of which have been recovered in various parts of the country, notably at Megiddo (VI, C-3), Gezer (VI, B-5), and Eglon (VI, B-5; I Kings 9:15 ff.). Most notable were his palace and administrative buildings and the Temple in Jerusalem.

The erection of the Temple is described in I Kings, chs. 6; 7, and additional data are preserved in Ezek., ch. 40 ff. With this information and with a wealth of archaeological data it is possible to reconstruct the building with a fair degree of accuracy, even though remains of it in Jerusalem have never been found (see p. 97). It was a comparatively small building, slightly more than 100 feet long and

c. 30 feet wide in the interior (see Fig. 31). It was probably built entirely with stone but lined on the inside with cedar and highly decorated. In the rear room ("Holy of Holies") were two olivewood cherubim, standing c. 15 feet high and overlaid with gold leaf, under whose outstretched wings the Ark was placed (cf. Fig. 28). In the vacant place above them Jehovah was believed to be invisibly enthroned. In the exterior court were the large altar of burnt offering, the lavers, and the bronze "sea." The latter was a tremendous bronze bowl, c. 15 feet in diameter and 7½ feet high, which was cast in the clay beds of the Jordan Valley at Adamah (VII:A, C-4). The "sea" and the bronze pillars placed in front of the Temple (I Kings 7:15 ff.) were so large that we marvel at the genius of the artisan Hiram who cast them.

To obtain both material and artists for the work Solomon had a trading agreement with the Phoenician, Hiram of Tyre (I Kings, ch. 5). At the end of twenty years Solomon had accumulated a serious deficit and had to cede to Hiram twenty Galilean cities in the vicinity of Cabul (I Kings 9:10 ff.; VII:A, C-4). To finance this elaborate building program and to support his great court Solomon entered into numerous business ventures. With Hiram's aid he built a fleet of ships for the Red Sea trade (I Kings 10:22), with port at Ezion-geber (VII:A, B-7). This site has been excavated, and has revealed a totally new phase of Solomon's activity. Here the king had built a huge smelter, the largest ever found in the ancient Near East, in which to smelt the ores obtained from the Arabah mines (see p. 65). Another phase of his commercial activity is revealed by I Kings 10:28, 29, which though long regarded as untranslatable, can now be rendered as follows: "And Solomon's horses were exported from Cilicia [XI:B, B-2]: the merchants of the king procured them from Cilicia at the current price; and a chariot was exported from Egypt at the rate of 600 shekels of silver and a horse from Cilicia at the rate of 150; and thus [at this rate] they delivered them by their agency to all the kings of the Hittites and the kings of Aram."

Another interesting phase of Solomon's career was his division of Israel into administrative districts for taxation purposes (see I Kings 4:7 ff.). Over each district was placed a governor, for whom were provided (judging from the excavations at Megiddo, Beth-shemesh, and Lachish) a palace and large, thick-walled storehouses in which the grain, oil, et cetera, collected in taxes could be stored. In a general way the provinces followed the old tribal districts (cf. VII:A and VI), though certain exceptions are to be noticed. The Plain of Sharon in the area of Dor was made a separate district; Zebulun had disappeared and in its place was a district of which a chief city was Megiddo; Reuben and Gad were joined as one province, while Manasseh across the Jordan was divided into two. The areas as outlined on Plate VII:A are given numbers which represent the order in which the districts are listed in I Kings 4:7 ff. How the province of Judah was administered is not clear, since little information on the subject is preserved. It is evident, however, that the old tribal system was giving way before the needs of a centralized and commercialized state.

The fame of Solomon spread far beyond the borders of his realm. Yet by the end of his reign the country was rocked by disaffection, caused by the heavy taxes, the forced labor on royal projects, and the traditional jealousy between north and south. A new dynasty, the Twenty-second, had come to power in Egypt, headed by the Libyan Shishak. As a result, the political tie between the two countries was broken, and Egypt now became a haven for political refugees who were able to plot in safety against the Israelite monarch.

THE EARLY DIVIDED MONARCHY

On the death of Solomon the northern and southern groups of his kingdom immediately separated, as they had on the death of Saul. This time, however, they remained permanently separated. Jeroboam, one of the political refugees in Egypt, returned to become king over Israel, while Rehoboam, Solomon's son, retained the throne of Judah. During the fifth year of the latter's reign, Shishak of Egypt raided the country and destroyed numerous cities, not only in Judah, but also in Israel and in Edom (I Kings 14:25). While the purpose of the raid may have been to revive an Egyptian empire in Asia, it achieved no lasting results since no attempt was made to reorganize the country into subject provinces.

In the years which followed, the strength of the two Hebrew kingdoms was weakened by conflict between them. The tribal district of Benjamin and a portion of that originally allotted to Dan (VI, B-C 5) were included in Judah, but the northern boundary was disputed. The tremendously strong fortifications at *Tell en-Naṣbeh* (XVIII, C-5) were erected at this time, and their great size (Fig. 77) illustrates the bitterness with which the civil war was fought.

About 882 B.C. the throne of Israel was seized by an army officer named Omri (I Kings 16:15 ff.), who became one of the most illustrious rulers of Israel, in spite of the fact that he reigned only twelve years. He was so well known that for more than a century the official name for Samaria in the Assyrian records was "House of Omri," even though his dynasty was swept from the throne in the Elijah-Elisha revolution c. 845 B.C. His greatest act was to build a new and powerfully fortified capital at Samaria (VII:B, C-4). This city has been excavated, and the elaborate palace and a portion of the strong fortifications which he built have been recovered (see pp. 104 f.).

Following the policy of David and Solomon, close commercial relations were established between Israel and Phoenicia, and they were strengthened by the political marriage of Ahab, Omri's son, with Jezebel, the daughter of the king of Tyre. Ahab is pictured in I Kings as a weak character, completely dominated by Jezebel. The latter was an extremely forceful person, who attempted to impose her own religion and the totalitarian methods of Tyre upon Israel. The reaction to her was led by the prophets Elijah and Elisha, who did not rest until every vestige of the dynasty of Omri had been swept from the throne and a new dynasty formed under an army leader named Jehu (II Kings, chs. 9; 10).

Plate VII:B shows the state of affairs at this time. Aram or Syria, having secured its independence during the days of Solomon, was now a formidable kingdom with its capital at Damascus. By the time of Ahab this kingdom was Israel's most potent enemy, and a succession of battles was fought as far south as Ramoth-gilead, an Israelite city which was now on the frontier (VII:B, D-4). Israel and Aram composed their differences long enough to unite in defeating the Assyrian king Shalmaneser III in a great battle in Syria in 853 B.C. (see p. 68). However, war between them broke out anew once the danger was past. Israel was aided in this warfare by Jehoshaphat, king of Judah, with whom the dynasty of Omri had made a treaty of mutual assistance, thus ending the state of hostilities between the two kingdoms. By 840 B.C. both Moab and Edom had rebelled against Israel and Judah respectively (II Kings 3:4 ff.; 8: 20 ff.) and become independent. Mesha, the king of Moab, commemorated his triumph by erecting a stele or monumental stone in Dibon (VII:B, C-5; see Fig. 32). The comparative weakness of Israel during the third quarter of the ninth century is further illustrated by the "Black Obelisk" of Shalmaneser III (Fig. 49), on which a large tribute of gold and silver from Jehu is shown as it was presented to the Assyrian monarch.

ISRAEL AND JUDAH DURING THE EIGHTH CENTURY B.C.

The power of Assyria now became the chief political factor which troubled the small kingdoms of Palestine-Syria. Both Israel and Judah were ultimately to come under Assyrian control, but between c. 825 and 745 B.C. internal troubles in Assyria gave the western peoples a breathing space, of which Israel and Judah took full advantage during the long reigns of Jeroboam II in Israel and Uzziah (or Azariah) in Judah. Excavations reveal that Jeroboam refortified Samaria with a double wall, which in the most vulnerable part of the city was nearly 33 feet wide, fortifications so strong that it took the Assyrian army three years to conquer the city in 724-721 B.C. (II Kings 17:5). Most astonishing was Jeroboam's defeat of Aram and the restoration of the northern Davidic border in Syria (II Kings 14:25; cf. Plate VII:A). During the latter part of his reign (c. 760-750), Amos prophesied in Bethel. The prophet denounced vigorously the

false sense of security which these favorable events had caused in Israel and the social iniquities that accompanied them. Judah likewise prospered, having reconquered Edom (II Kings 14:7) and the copper and iron mines which the latter owned, and for the first time subjugated completely the coastal plain of Philistia (II Chron. 26:6 ff.).

As Amos had foreseen, however, this prosperity was only temporary. He with Hosea and Isaiah shared a belief in impending crisis and doom—a belief which events fully justified. In 745 B.C. the Assyrian advance began again when the great king Tiglath-pileser III came to the throne. The latter inaugurated a new policy of conquering small states, deporting their populations, and turning them into Assyrian provinces, usually governed by Assyrian officials. In 733-732 B.C. he conquered Damascus, Gilead, Galilee, and the Plain of Sharon, turning them into six provinces (Sharon ruled from Dor, and Galilee from Megiddo—Plate VII:C; II Kings 15:29 ff.). To throw back the attack, Rezin, king of Damascus, and Pekah, king of Israel, had formed an alliance into which they attempted to force Judah. Judah, however, refused to join it and was attacked by the others, but the approach of the Assyrian army prevented her overthrow (II Kings 16:5 ff.; Isa., ch. 7). As a result of this first Assyrian conquest in Palestine, Israel was confined to a small area in the hill country of Samaria, saved from further reduction only by paying a heavy tribute together with Philistia, Judah, Ammon, Moab, and Edom.

A few years later, however, as a result of refusal to pay tribute, Shalmaneser V, the successor of Tiglath-pileser III, laid siege to Samaria. He died before the city was captured, but Sargon II (722-705 B.C.) completed the task in the first months of 721 B.C. According to his own statement, he carried 27,290 Israelites (presumably all the political leaders, the elders, the artisans, and the well-to-do) into exile, settling them in the region of "Gozan, and in the cities of the Medes" (II Kings 17:6; XI:A, C-2 and D-2). In their place new

FIG. 32. A replica of the stele or monumental stone of Mesha, king of Moab. It was set up by him in Dibon (IX, I-8) to commemorate his victory over Israel shortly after the middle of the ninth century, which for the first time in a century and a half made his country independent.

FIG. 33. A reconstruction of the Judean fortress-city of Lachish (VII: A-D, B-5). Note the double fortification walls, the strongly protected city gate, and the palace of the local Judean governor in the midst of the city—all probably erected by the command of Rehoboam (II Chron. 11:9). A group of letters written by the officer in charge of a near-by outpost to the commandant of Lachish were found in the ruins of the gate. They date from c. 589 or 588 B.C., before Nebuchadnezzar's subjection of Judah in 588–587 B.C.

settlers were brought from Babylonia, Elam, and Syria by Sargon and his successors. Thus, what the prophets had foretold came to pass; the Kingdom of Israel was ended. The central interest of the Biblical story now shifts to Judah.

Plate VII:C shows the state of affairs in Palestine about 700 B.C., several years after the fall of Israel. Judah had barely escaped the fate of Israel in 701 B.C. when Sennacherib had attacked the country (II Kings, chs. 18; 19; Isa., chs. 36; 37). Hezekiah, against the advice of Isaiah, had entered into a defensive alliance with the Philistine cities, after having secured the promise of Egyptian help. Among his preparations for the battle was the digging of the Siloam Tunnel in Jerusalem to insure the water supply in case of siege (see p. 98, and Plate XVII:A). Isaiah denounced these acts in strong terms (chs. 22; 30:1-4; 31:1-3); yet the revolt was carried out. Sennacherib crushed it severely, destroying, he says, forty-six Judean cities, chief among which was Lachish (VII:C, B-5; Fig. 33). Jerusalem was saved by payment of a heavy tribute (II Kings 18:13 ff.). The Kingdom of Judah was thus left in a weak condition, controlling only its hill country, the lowlands (Shephelah), and part of the barren wasteland (Negeb) to the south of Beer-sheba, where the boundary with Edom was not clearly defined because the wilderness contained no natural resources in which either state was interested.

THE LAST DAYS OF JUDAH (c. 700-587 B.C.)

For the better part of the seventh century Judah continued as a vassal of Assyria, paying regular tribute. But new hope welled in the hearts of the subject peoples when, after 625 B.C., the Assyrian Empire began to totter (see p. 68). Josiah was king of Judah at this time, and he was quick to take advantage of the situation, expanding his kingdom northward in the attempt to re-establish a united Israel. In 621 B.C. he carried out a great religious reform (II Kings, chs. 22; 23) under the influence of an old law book (Deuteronomy or some portion of it) found during repair work in the Temple. Worship at the shrines and high places about the country was prohibited by royal decree. Sacrificial offerings could now be made only in Jerusalem where pagan excesses could be kept under control.

Josiah lost his life in 609 B.C. in the attempt to prevent the Egyptian army under Pharaoh Necho from going to the aid of the Assyrians at Haran (II Kings 23:29, 30; the phrasing of this passage gives the impression that Necho was on his way to fight against Assyria; but Mesopotamian records reveal that just the opposite was the case). The hopes that had arisen with the fall of Assyria were soon dashed, for Babylonia now rapidly took over the former empire (Plate XI:B), following much the same policies.

The dominant prophetic figure of this period was Jeremiah, who warned the Judeans against the disaster which would surely come if their current policies were not altered. His advice, however, was unheeded. Thinking themselves strong enough with Egyptian promises of aid, they revolted, only to be promptly subjugated in 598 B.C. by Nebuchadnezzar (II Kings 24:10 ff.), who carried the youthful King

Jehoiachin into exile together with numerous officials and artisans. Yet the lesson was not learned, and nine years later the country revolted again. This time Nebuchadnezzar utterly laid waste every important town of Judah, destroying Jerusalem and the Temple in 587 B.C. after a siege which lasted a year and a half (II Kings, ch. 25; Jer., ch. 39). The devastation was so complete that town after town was never reinhabited, and it was centuries before the country recovered. Lachish (VII:C, B-5; Fig. 33) has evidence of both destructions. In the ruins of the final devastation of the city gate were found a group of letters written by the commander of a neighboring outpost to his superior in the city, revealing the same state of tension and excitement in the country as does The Book of Jeremiah.

Thousands of Judeans were now scattered in the Babylonian Empire, among them Ezekiel. The poor who were left in Judah were prey to the hostile neighbors. Edom in particular was never forgotten because of the cruelty of her raids upon Judah, and because her people rapidly took over complete control of the southern part of the country (cf. Ps. 137:7; Ezek., ch. 35; Obadiah).

POST-EXILIC JUDAH

Immediately after the Persian conquest of the Babylonian Empire (cf. p. 69) permission was given for the exiles to return to Judah (c. 538 B.C.), and over a period of years a considerable company did so (Ezra, ch. 1 ff.). Plate VII:D shows the approximate size of Judah during this age. It was a tiny province in the Fifth Persian Satrapy, extending from Bethel to Beth-zur. To the north and east were the provinces of Samaria and Ammon, whose governors hindered the returned Jews in every way they could. To the south was the province of Idumaea (or Edom), which by the middle of the fifth century was composed largely of Arabian tribes (cf. Neh. 2:19; 6:1) who had invaded the ancient Edom and brought it to an end, as was prophesied in Jer. 49:7 ff. This province appears to have been controlled from Lachish, where the large palace of the Persian official has been excavated.

The first group of those who returned was led by one Sheshbazzar, who immediately laid the foundations for a new Temple on the site of the one which had been destroyed (Ezra 5:16). He was unable to complete it, however, because of the interference of the hostile neighbors and of "the people of the land" (Judeans who had not been in Exile). When Darius I came to the throne in 522 B.C. he appointed Zerubbabel, the grandson of King Jehoiachin (Jechoniah; Matt. 1:12), as governor of the province. Zerubbabel returned from Babylon with a considerable company of priests and Levites (Neh. 12:1), and with the help of the high priest Joshua and with the encouragement of the prophets Haggai and Zechariah completed the Temple between 520 and 516 B.C. The obstacles in the meantime had been partially cleared away by decree of Darius (Ezra, chs. 5; 6).

During the reign of Artaxerxes I (465-424 B.C.) two additional groups of exiles returned to Judah. The first was led by Ezra (c. 458 B.C.), who carried with him a letter from the king, authorizing him to take the leadership in the reform of the religious life of the community. One of his most important acts was the publication of the Pentateuch (Genesis to Deuteronomy) and the organization of the people's life in accordance with the laws it contained. His intense desire to guard the community from contamination with the surrounding people led to a religious exclusivism which alienated many, in particular the people of Samaria. As a result the Samaritan schism was made complete (see pp. 57 f.).

In 445-444 B.C. an additional group returned under the leadership of Nehemiah, who had been appointed governor with permission to rebuild the walls of Jerusalem (Neh., chs. 1 ff.). This task was brought to completion against the strong opposition of the neighbors and even of several of the nobles of Judah. No enlargement of the city was made, since the new fortifications followed the line of those destroyed by the Babylonians (see Plate XVII:A). Thus a century and a half after Jerusalem's destruction, its rebuilding had been completed and it again became the center and focus of the Jewish national and religious life, both in Judah and throughout the Dispersion.

PLATE VII

PLATE VIII

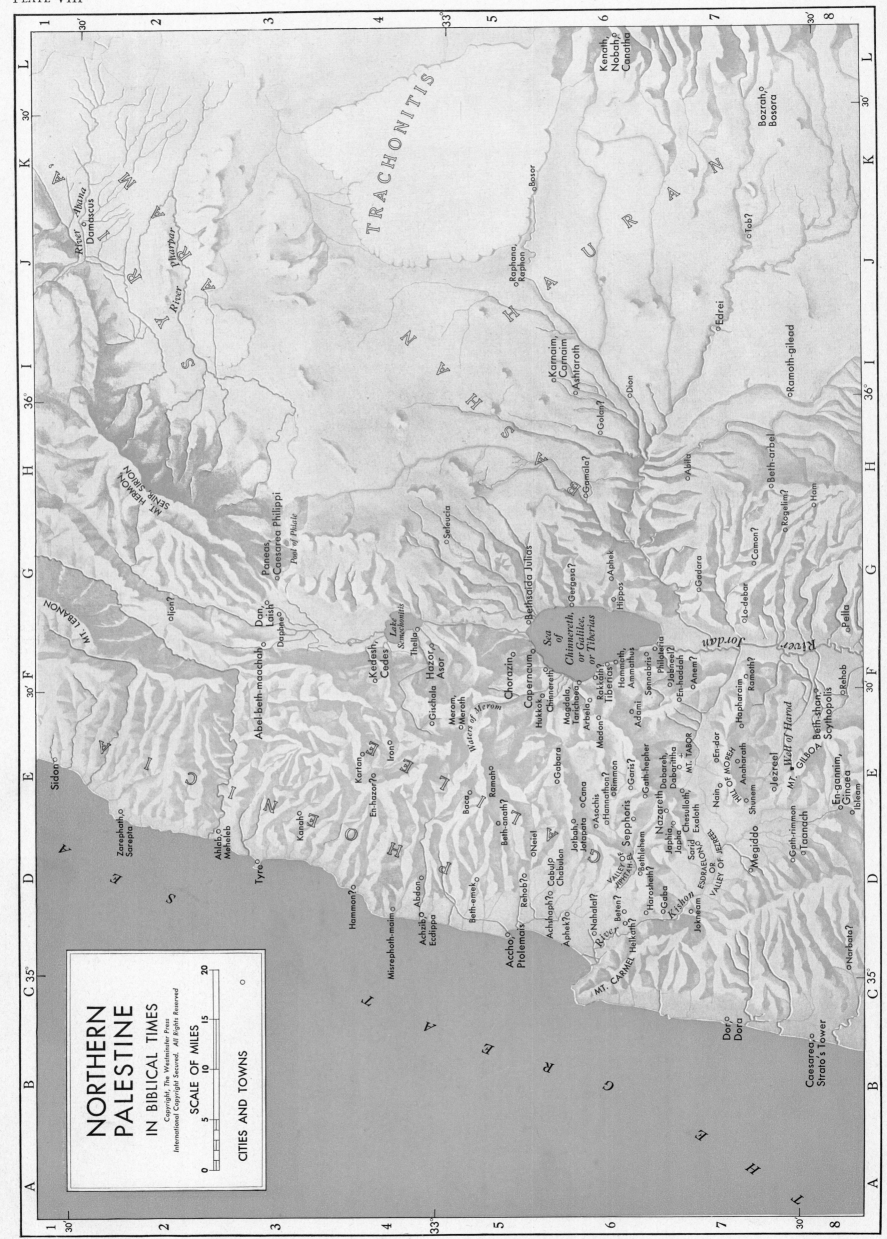

NORTHERN PALESTINE IN BIBLICAL TIMES

NORTHERN PALESTINE IN BIBLICAL TIMES

PLATE VIII

THE center of interest in Northern Palestine is Galilee and Esdraelon (Plate VIII, D-F 4-7). Here, as a survey of the map reveals, the cities and towns were thickest. Here, too, the history of Northern Palestine found its focus. Galilee particularly witnessed religious developments of the greatest significance for both Judaism and Christianity.

THE UNINVITING SEA

In order to understand the history which took place in the Galilean region, it is necessary to make a brief study of the physical features of the surrounding areas and observe how they affected Galilee. Turning first to the west, we note that the seacoast of Palestine proper lacks the broken shore lines and safe harbors which would encourage maritime ventures. South of Mount Carmel (VIII, C-6) the coast offers no harbor; when Herod the Great (40-4 B.C.) rebuilt Strato's Tower and renamed it Caesarea (VIII, B-8), he provided an adequate harbor only by building sea walls out from the shore, a feat which required unusual engineering skill. This Herodian city, however, which later became the residence of the Roman procurator who governed Judaea in the days of Jesus, had its connection with central Palestine rather than with the region north of Carmel.

Mount Carmel itself, an impressive wooded height projecting northwest into the Mediterranean (Fig. 30), never attained great political or military significance. Though famed as the home of an ancient sanctuary of Baal (I Kings 18:19 ff.), it was separated from the main body of Palestine by passes running through the hills on its southeast flank (cf. Fig. 26), and was thus too isolated to be a center of power. Nor did its promontory protect a harbor. Just north of Carmel was a bay which offered partial shelter to shipping. Here Accho, later called Ptolemais (VIII, C-5), was used as a port (Acts 21:7), but it had no adequately protected harbor. There were numerous towns just east of the bay, but they did not face the sea. Their main connection was with the area north and east.

PHOENICIA FACES SEAWARD

Further north, in the district of Phoenicia proper (VIII, D-E 1-4), the situation was entirely different. The closely crowding hills and the lack of an extensive coastal plain made it impossible to support life by agriculture and grazing. Settlers in this section were forced to turn to the sea. Moreover, although there were roads which led from Galilee to the Phoenician ports, they were not the major routes for caravan trade from the east. Therefore no adequate economic basis existed for intimate relations between Phoenicia and Galilee. Accordingly, this stretch of seacoast which developed a seafaring people had no great influence upon the country immediately to the east. The course of history in Galilee and Transjordan was not determined by nearness to the sea.

In full harmony with the physical features of the region, Phoenicia was never part of Israel. Even the golden age of Israelite expansion under David and Solomon saw no attempt to conquer or control this region. Nor did the interest of the city-states of Phoenicia lead them to make any serious attempt to master the country to the east, although they usually controlled the coast as far south as Mount Carmel, and at one time took over certain border villages of Galilee (I Kings 9:11). Phoenicia faced west; her life was centered in sea trade; her expansion was achieved by founding numerous colonies as outposts for her life and commerce (see pp. 33, 34). Most noted of these was Carthage (XIII, B-2).

The chief cities of Phoenicia were Sidon (VIII, E-1) and Tyre (VIII, D-3). The former was more prominent in the second millennium B.C., but the latter, situated in Old Testament times on an island just off the coast, had outstripped her northern neighbor by the time of the Hebrew monarchy. Tyre was a city of unusual strength. Shalmaneser V, Sennacherib, Esarhaddon, Asshurbanapal, and Nebuchadnezzer failed in attempts to capture it. Alexander the Great had to spend seven months before he succeeded in taking it by building a great causeway from the mainland to the island.

By reason of manifold contacts and wide expansion, Phoenicia became the middleman of the ancient world for the distribution of cultural possessions. She is given credit for having carried the alphabet from Asia to Greek lands. She was also famous for her articles of merchandise and extensive trade, so well described in Ezek., ch. 27. Her purple dyes, made from the murex shells found along her shores (see p. 33), were widely known and eagerly sought. Excavation has shown that the famous Phoenician ivory work was used in the Samaria of Ahab (p. 105) as well as in other countries. Both Solomon and Omri made use of her building skill in their temple construction (see pp. 48 f.). Phoenician seamen helped to build and man Solomon's fleet for the purpose of capturing the Arabian and African trade (I Kings 10:22). Solomon's smelter (*tarshîsh*) at Eziongeber (see pp. 48, 65) was probably built from Phoenician models.

In view of these relations between Israel and Phoenicia it is not surprising to read that in a time of famine the Prophet Elijah found refuge in Zarephath (VIII, E-2; cf. I Kings 17:9). But such facts must not be used to argue that Phoenicia and Israel were united in life and interests, even in the Old Testament period. In New Testament times, it is significant that the Elijah incident mentioned above is treated as quite exceptional (Luke 4:26), and the journey of Jesus into "the parts of Tyre and Sidon" (Matt. 15:21) is regarded as a definite withdrawal from the bounds of Israel. Phoenicia was a separate country, and in New Testament times, when the Romans had taken over the entire region of Palestine and Syria, they grouped Phoenicia and the Carmel region with Syria rather than with Palestine.

THE NORTHERN MOUNTAIN BARRIER

The rugged slopes of Mount Lebanon (VIII, F-G 1) and Mount Hermon (VIII, H-2), with the broken surface of the intervening valleys, made travel too difficult and dangerous to encourage regular intercourse between Galilee and the country north of the Lebanons. For this reason Israel rarely attempted to expand in that direction.

FIG. 34. Source of the River Jordan near Caesarea Philippi (VIII, G-3). The water rushes from the southwestern foot of Mount Hermon. This, however, is only one of four sources of the Jordan. Another is just north of Abel-beth-maachah (VIII, F-3); a third on the west slope of Mount Hermon; the fourth in the valley at Dan (VIII, G-3). The sources at Dan and Caesarea Philippi are the largest.

FIG. 35. Mount Tabor. 1,843 feet above sea level. Here met the borders of the tribes of Issachar, Zebulun, and Naphtali. It controlled one of the eastern exits from Esdraelon. From this strategic height Barak started his charge against Sisera (Judg., ch. 4). One Christian tradition locates the scene of Christ's transfiguration on Tabor.

The traditional northern limit was Dan (VIII, G-3; cf. I Sam. 3:20), not far from the sources of the Jordan (see Fig. 34). Only under her strongest rulers did she seek to extend her borders farther north, into the region east of Mount Lebanon; such efforts were crowned with but temporary success.

THE FERTILE REGION OF DAMASCUS

East of Mount Hermon lies a much more inviting area. The rivers Abana and Pharpar (VIII, H-L 1-2), rising on the mountain slopes, flow off to the east. On their way they irrigate a fertile and attractive region, until they break up into many smaller streams and lose themselves in trying to water the thirsty soil. Here was found what might be called an immense oasis. It invited settlers, and offered a center of interest and trade to nomads of the desert.

In this favored spot arose the ancient city of Damascus (VIII, J-1). Her situation guaranteed a permanent life of trade and influence. Nevertheless, her environment set firm limits to her power. To the north and west mountains prevented any direct expansion. On the east the desert offered no great opportunity for development. She might exercise considerable influence upon the rather sparsely settled plateau to the southwest, but Palestine was too far away to be within effective reach of her power.

Thus the region of Damascus, which is what the Old Testament means when it refers to Syria or Aram, had a history somewhat separate from that of Palestine. Strong kings such as Hazael (II Kings 10:32 f.; 12:17 f.) extended their influence across the plateau country into the life of Israel, and there were almost constant trade contacts between the two regions. The famous "Way of the Sea" was one of the trade routes which connected Damascus with Palestine. This ancient caravan route ran southwest to cross the Jordan below Lake Huleh or Semechonitis (VIII, F-G 4), touched the Sea of Galilee on the northwest, passed through Galilee to Esdraelon, and thence either proceeded to the sea or branched off southward to reach points in Palestine or Egypt. Evidence of commercial contact along such roads is given by the Samarian quarter in Damascus and the Damascene quarter in the city of Samaria, in the ninth century B.C. (I Kings 20:34). But direct and effective political control of Palestine was more difficult, and Damascus never achieved this. She usually played the role of a rival power, or of a small kingdom that sought alliance with neighboring rulers against threatened aggression.

At the end of the fourth century B.C. Damascus lost much of her political importance when Antioch on the Orontes River (XI:D, B-2) was founded as the capital of Syria. Even then, however, her importance continued as a center of trade and an outpost on the desert frontier. In New Testament times Damascus had a link southward with the Hellenistic cities of the Decapolis (Plate XIV), which included Scythopolis west of the Jordan (VIII, F-8) as well as Canatha (VIII, L-6), Raphana (VIII, J-5), Dion (VIII, I-6), Hippos (VIII, G-6), Abila (VIII, H-7), Gadara (VIII, G-7), and Pella (VIII, F-8). It is somewhat surprising that a city so far north as Damascus should be a member of this league of Hellenistic cities in Transjordan; her inclusion is a witness to her importance as a trade center and as a bulwark against eastern forces which might threaten this region.

THE ḤAURÂN PLATEAU

South of the Pharpar River lay a broad, high plateau, 2,000 feet above sea level. It was called Bashan in Old Testament times, and Ḥaurân in later centuries (VIII, H-K 4-7). Signs of volcanic action are numerous in this section. The huge mass of hardened lava labeled Trachonitis (VIII, J-L 4-5), and the smaller mass of lava some ten miles northwest, are striking evidence of extensive volcanic activity in prehistoric times. Along the east rim of the Jordan Valley and on the eastern side of the plateau are many extinct volcanoes.

Furthermore, the prevailing limestone of Palestine is here covered with a layer of black basalt, which extends into parts of Galilee. The modern traveler is reminded of these formations when he sees the black basalt ruins of an ancient synagogue at Chorazin (VIII, F-5). The volcanic character of the plateau extends south to the Yarmuk River (I, D-3). In this region the soil is a rich red, and nothing but the limitations of its water supply keep it from being more populous and prosperous. Only to the south of the Yarmuk, however, does water become more plentiful and provide the basis for a considerable population.

The plateau east of the Sea of Galilee was generally affected by the fortunes of Damascus, yet was rarely an integral part of the political and social life of that state. On the other hand, it was little settled by Israelites and seldom mastered by Israelite rulers. Nevertheless, it was too close to the Jordan and Galilee, and too much in contact with the more Israelite section of Gilead south of the Yarmuk, to be entirely independent of the course of events in Palestine. The tribe of Manasseh settled both north and south of the Yarmuk (Deut. 3:13), although the extent of its occupation in Bashan is a question. Solomon taxed this region (I Kings 4:13). In the ninth century B.C., however, Hazael of Syria wrested it from Israelite control.

The later Maccabees gained control of part of the area (Plate XII:A), and later Herod the Great included all of it in his kingdom. His son Philip ruled it as a separate tetrarchy (Luke 3:1). Philip built his capital at Bethsaida Julias (VIII, F-5), which is probably to be located on the shore of the Sea of Galilee rather than two miles north at et-Tell. This location of his capital shows that his tetrarchy was related to Galilee in life and trade; but his territory was not really Jewish. He built also the pagan city of Caesarea Philippi at Paneas (VIII, G-3; cf. Mark 8:27), and the population of this area was predominantly Gentile. It should be noticed that it was only to non-Jewish rulers such as Herod the Great, Philip, Herod Agrippa I (A.D. 37-44; cf. Acts 12:1), and Herod Agrippa II (A.D. 53-c.100; cf. Acts 25:13) that the Romans entrusted the rule of this essentially non-Jewish region (Plates XII:B-D; XIV).

Because Transjordan was constantly threatened from the desert, the Romans were interested in strengthening it. When Rome first took over Palestine, the Nabataeans were constantly pressing on the east and south; Bosora, i.e., Bozrah (VIII, L-7), and *Jebel Haurân*, the mountainous region southeast of Canatha (VIII, L-6), were in Nabataean hands. This desert people also extended its influence further north, and either pressed close to Damascus or occasionally gained temporary control of it. The kingdom of Parthia (XIII, F-G 2-3) also endangered the eastern border of Palestine and Syria. The Romans therefore took steps to make Haurân a secure outpost against such threats, and the Hellenistic cities founded and fostered there were largely intended to fulfill this end. From the time of Trajan (A.D. 98-117) there was a remarkable development of city life and architecture in this region. Christianity made progress, and Bosora became the chief center of Christian life for the area. The Mohammedan conquest in the seventh century, however, marked the end of Christian strength here as elsewhere in the Levant.

GALILEE FACES SOUTH

Thus the regions to the west, north, and east of Galilee do not offer the basis for a large population, nor do their physical features lead naturally to intimate contacts with Galilee. Only to the south does the geographical situation favor more vital ties.

One factor in promoting southern associations is the Jordan Valley (VIII, F 3-8). Its fertile valley and the inviting shores of the Sea of Galilee (VIII, F-G 5-6) tended to turn the attention of inhabitants of the hill country away from the west. On the east side of the Jordan Valley, the steep rise of nearly 2,700 feet from the Sea of Galilee to the Haurân plateau presents a forbidding barrier, and has the effect of binding the Sea of Galilee, including its eastern shore, exclusively to the district of Galilee. Once drawn into living connection with the Jordan Valley, however, and given a focal point in the Sea of Galilee, the people of the hills were naturally connected with the country farther south.

Another factor leading Galilee to face south was the fertile, well-watered plain, Esdraelon. Northern or Upper Galilee, rugged and mountainous, is but the southward extension of the Lebanon range. In Southern or Lower Galilee the foothills drop to more even slopes and offer more level areas, which invite settlement and cultivation. Outstanding in this section is the small but fertile Plain of Gennesaret (XIV, C-D 3), where there is farming throughout the year, and the larger Plain of Asochis (VIII, E-6), on the edge of which were Hannathon and, later, Cana (VIII, E-6). These plains, however, could satisfy only local needs. Esdraelon was wide, well-watered, fertile, and thus inevitably a magnet to draw the interest of Galilee.

Yet the heights of Mount Carmel, and the line of hills which continued southeast and east to Mount Gilboa (VIII, E-8), formed a barrier between Galilee and central Palestine. As a result, Samaria (Plate IX) had a history rather distinct from that of the northern hills. Nevertheless, the pass running southwest from Megiddo (VIII, D-7; see Fig. 26), the road southward from En-gannim (VIII, E-8) into the Samarian hills, together with the route down the Jordan Valley, offered lines of trade and travel, and gave Galilee, in spite of partial isolation, a vital link with central Palestine.

Geography to a considerable extent determines history, and physical features in and around Galilee tell what its life had to be. It would be a meeting place of roads from all directions, and would have some relations with countries on all sides. It could have no secure independence and no completely isolated life. But it could never have intimate unity with the regions to the west, north, and east. It must center about the Sea of Galilee and find its chief contacts in the south. Yet even there it was doomed to have a somewhat loose association.

PRE-ISRAELITE GALILEE AND ESDRAELON

The Biblical student thus comes back to Galilee and Esdraelon as his main center of interest in this region. Galilee has had a long history. As shown by the discussion on p. 106, archaeologists have found there and in valleys south of Carmel some of the most important remains yet discovered of prehistoric man.

At a much later date, but prior to the coming of the Israelites, the

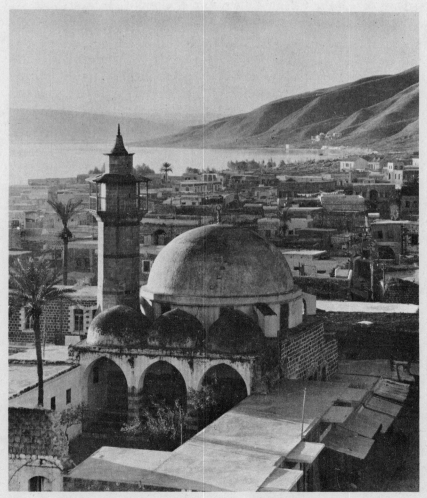

FIG. 36. Tiberias and the Sea of Galilee looking southeast. In the foreground is a Mohammedan mosque; note the tower from which the call to prayer is given. Palm trees indicate mild climate. Observe how the hills enclose the lake on both sides.

FIG. 37. Partially restored ancient synagogue at Capernaum. View from the southwest corner. Steps lead up to entrances on the south. The colonnade of pillars once supported a balcony for women, which ran around the west, north, and east sides; entrance to the balcony was by an outside stairway on the north. It was built about the third century A.D.

Canaanites were strongly established in this region. The chief city was Hazor (VIII, F-4), in Upper Galilee, and still farther north were Kedesh (VIII, F-4) and Yanoʿam (IV, D-2). The Canaanites were also found on all sides of Esdraelon. Among their cities were Madon in Lower Galilee (VIII, F-6), Achshaph (VIII, D-5) not far southeast of Accho, Dor (VIII, C-7) on the coast south of Carmel, Megiddo (VIII, D-7) and Taanach (VIII, D-8) on the southern rim of Esdraelon, and Beth-shan, Rehob, and Pella (VIII, F-8) near the Jordan. The latter group of three cities is mentioned in the Amarna tablets (see p. 30); of them, Beth-shan was by far the most important. From the fifteenth to the middle of the twelfth century B.C. it was a strong Egyptian outpost. It was also a center of Canaanite religious life, as its successive temples bear witness.

THE BIBLICAL PERIOD

The league of Canaanite city-states offered strong opposition to the incoming Israelites. Except for the occupation of the Hill of Moreh (VIII, E-7) by Issachar, the Esdraelon region was not brought under Israelite control until David captured the strongholds there (see p. 44). Prior to this, however, the Galilean hill country had been conquered, and from Mount Tabor, the meeting place of the tribes of Issachar, Zebulun, and Naphtali (VIII, E-7; Fig. 35; cf. Plate VI), Israelite forces made a victorious sally against Sisera, a Canaanite ruler (Judg., ch. 4). Solomon made the plain his fifth Israelite administrative district, with its capital at Megiddo (see p. 48 and Plate VII:A).

From the time of Solomon to that of Jesus the role of Galilee was relatively unimportant. The region was included in the Northern Kingdom, Israel, and in the wars and invasions of subsequent centuries it evidently suffered considerably, since it was situated on the northern border of the kingdom and was always difficult to defend. Its participation in the life of Israel reached the lowest ebb in the early days of the Maccabean revolt, when Simon marched north, rescued all the Jews who wished to remain loyal to the Law, and took them to Judaea (c. 163 B.C.; see p. 73). Not long after this, however, the return of faithful Jews to Galilee must have begun, for by the end of the second century B.C. the Maccabeans were in control of Galilee, a situation which assumes a considerable Jewish group there. Certainly in the first century A.D., while the population was mixed, as it had been through the centuries, the region was predominantly Jewish, dotted with synagogues, and often the scene of fanatical outbursts of zeal for the ancestral faith.

Nevertheless, Gentile population, cities, and influence were present. The two chief centers of such Gentile influence were Sepphoris and Tiberias. Sepphoris (VIII, E-6) was the capital of the tetrarchy of Herod Antipas in the early years of his rule. Some years later he built Tiberias (VIII, F-6; Fig. 36) and made it his capital. South of Tiberias were the hot springs at Ammathus (VIII, F-6), supposed to possess curative properties, and therefore visited then as now by people from distant places. Tarichaea, often sought at the southwest corner of the Sea of Galilee, was probably another name for Magdala (VIII, F-6); it was a center of fishing, fish-packing, and shipbuilding. A hippodrome indicated Gentile influence.

Such facts help us to see why there existed in Jerusalem and southern Palestine a certain contempt for the somewhat suspect Judaism of Galilee. The northern district had been so long a place of mixed population, and so often cut off from normal relations with the "holy city," that the Jewish leaders in the capital regarded it with condescension. When Jesus came from Galilee, and from the obscure village of Nazareth (VIII, E-7), a place not mentioned in any Jewish source of the Biblical period, and presumed not merely to teach in Jerusalem but even to interfere with Temple arrangements (Mark 11:15), it is little wonder that the recognized leaders rose up in resentment. Galilee was inferior; an unauthorized teacher from Galilee could expect no official favor (cf. John 1:46; 7:52).

In such a region, prevailingly Jewish, rather deprecated in Jerusalem, and mixed in population, language, and cultural factors, Jesus grew up. Here he carried on the main part of his ministry. His work centered at Capernaum (VIII, F-5), and he seems to have labored chiefly around the north end of the Sea of Galilee. However, references to Cana (VIII, E-6) and Nain (VIII, E-7), and reports of journeys among the villages to preach and heal (cf. Mark 1:39), show that he must have traveled over most of Galilee (see further p. 86).

POST-BIBLICAL JUDAISM

It is amazing that after the death of Jesus Galilee figures so little in the story of early Christianity. The region is mentioned but once in The Acts, and then in a general way (ch. 9:31). But the obscurity into which Galilee fell in Christian history, until pilgrims began visiting the country to see the Gospel sites, is in sharp contrast with the new importance which this section assumed for Judaism after the fall of Jerusalem (A.D. 70). The continuing Jewish faith found a new center in Galilee. Such cities as Sepphoris and Tiberias became centers of Jewish learning; here the rabbinic tradition was preserved and elaborated.

The vigor and extent of Galilean Judaism in the next few centuries are clear from the many ruins of synagogues discovered and excavated in this region (see p. 106). A decisive majority of the Palestinian synagogues known to belong to this period are located in northern Palestine. Among the most interesting of such synagogues for Christian students, though built definitely later than the days of Jesus, is the one at Capernaum (see Fig. 37). A striking structure is the black basalt synagogue at Chorazin (VIII, F-5). Here, as in the synagogue at Hammath (VIII, F-6), south of Tiberias, an example has been found of the "Seat of Moses" (cf. Matt. 23:2), the seat of honor reserved for the most distinguished elder or visitor, who thus sat facing the congregation. There was noteworthy variety of ornamentation in the synagogues of this period; characteristic features are the seven-branched candlesticks and elaborate floor mosaics. The free use, not only of human figures, but even of the signs of the Zodiac, shows that Judaism then permitted a freedom in ornamentation which in earlier and later days was not tolerated.

Another striking evidence of the prominent place of Galilee in the Judaism of this period has been found at *Sheikh Abreiq* (XVIII, C-3). In addition to synagogue ruins at this site, extensive catacombs have been discovered.

Such significant discoveries throw much light on post-Biblical Judaism. It is still highly desirable, however, for excavators to seek further evidence of first-century Judaism, in order to illuminate that period of Jewish life and reveal the setting of the ministry of Jesus.

CENTRAL PALESTINE IN BIBLICAL TIMES

PLATE IX

FIG. 38. The Dead Sea. About 1,275 feet below sea level. In its deepest portion it is at least 1,300 feet deep. From its shores steep slopes rise to the upland heights of Judah and Transjordan.

BIBLICAL history, apart from the ministry of Jesus in Galilee, has its focus in central Palestine. This area begins on the north at the border of Esdraelon or Valley of Jezreel (Plate VIII, D-7), and extends southward below Hebron (IX, E-8) to the beginning of the Negeb (see pp. 63 f.). It is about eighty miles long and has between the Mediterranean and the Jordan an average width of fifty miles. Its total area is thus approximately 4,000 square miles.

The district was thickly populated. Judging from the exceptionally large number of inhabited places in so small an area, one might conclude that ancient Palestine was largely urban rather than agricultural. The country, however, was and still is largely agricultural and pastoral. The basic foods were wheat, barley, vegetables, grapes, figs, and olives; in modern times the coastal plain has also proved ideal for citrus fruits. The grain ripens during the early spring rains and is harvested in May and June. From April to November there is little rain. Certain varieties of vegetables, however, thrive during the summer months; they are sustained by the early morning dew, which appears regularly, except in occasional hot spells caused by the country's chief climatic curse, the hot wind (sirocco) from the Arabian Desert.

In ancient times, however, farmers found it necessary, as they still do, to live in towns for protection. They did not build their houses in the midst of their fields. Instead, they lived in towns and journeyed daily to their work. Each main city of Old Testament times was located on an easily fortified hill, near a spring or springs. It was surrounded by strong walls and protected by gates, so that it could withstand siege (cf. Fig. 33). Around it were numerous unfortified villages. The farmers lived in them, but when war came they sought safety within the city's fortifications. During the times when a strong government, such as Rome, preserved peace, the number of unwalled villages increased greatly, as did the population. In troubled times, however, both villages and population diminished greatly in number.

In spite of such fluctuations, the general trend showed an increase of population through Old and New Testament times and down to the Byzantine period (fourth to sixth centuries A.D.). In the reign of David, the first time stability of government had been achieved, the population of Palestine was probably less than one million. The most densely inhabited areas were the southern coastal plain (Philistia) and the hill country north and south of Jerusalem (IX, F-6). During the Roman rule, when the country reached the greatest degree of agricultural and commercial development which it attained in ancient times, it probably contained between one million and a half and two million people. The population is about the same today, but this is due to a recent increase; the number of inhabitants has doubled during two decades of British government.

The map indicates where population was most dense. The district between Jerusalem and Bethel (IX, F-5), once occupied by the tribe of Benjamin (cf. Plate VI), contained the largest number of villages. Here were Gibeah (IX, F-6), which Saul made his capital; Anathoth (IX, F-6), the home of Jeremiah; Michmash (IX, F-5), famous as the scene of a battle with the Philistines (I Sam., chs. 13; 14); and Gibeon (IX, F-5), where Solomon in prayer chose wisdom instead of riches (I Kings 3:4 ff.).

JUDAEAN AND SAMARITAN RIVALRY

In this territory of Benjamin lay the border between Samaria and Judah. One of the peculiar facts about the history of ancient Palestine was the rivalry which existed between Judah (IX, D-G 5-8) and Samaria (IX, E-G 2-5). It is not explained by geography. Judah and Samaria form a continuous geographical and economic unit; there is no natural boundary between them. This is shown by the fact that the border, which in an earlier day lay just south of Bethel (IX, F-5), was placed in New Testament times north of Borcaeus (IX, F-4). Yet, in spite of the geographical unity of these districts, the people of the two areas were more or less hostile to one another from the early days of Israelite settlement through the New Testament period.

The cause of this tension goes back to the time of the conquest, when different groups took possession of these two continuous sections of Palestine. Though temporarily united by Saul against a common danger, the two were led by their traditional rivalry to fall apart after his death; Judah anointed David as king, while Israel accepted Ishbosheth (Ishbaal).

When David became king of Israel on the death of Ishbosheth, he was faced with the problem of where to locate his capital. Gibeah, Saul's home, was too small. Hebron, important in Judah, was too far south; its choice would have provoked renewed jealousy in Israel. On the other hand, any Israelite town would have alienated Judah. David chose the Canaanite (Jebusite) city of Jerusalem, which lay on the border between the two areas but belonged to neither. It was claimed by Benjamin, whose border ascended the Valley of Achor (IX, G-6) from the Jordan and circled Jerusalem by the Hinnom Valley (Josh. 18:15 ff.; Plates VI and XVII:A); but this tribe had never subjugated the city. David did, and the city owned by him (the "City of David") proved the ideal choice for the capital (see p. 47).

On the death of Solomon, the two districts again separated, into rival kingdoms, which periodically waged war with each other (see p. 48 f.). The border between them lay in the old tribal area of Benjamin, which became disputed territory, though Bethel, where Jeroboam erected the royal sanctuary of Israel as a rival to the Jerusalem Temple (I Kings 12:28 f.; Amos 7:10-13), was always on or near the southern border of Israel (see Plate VII:B).

When Israel fell in 721 B.C., some twenty-seven thousand of the intellectual and well-to-do classes were deported, and eastern foreigners were settled in their place. Israel became a province of Assyria, Babylonia, and Persia in turn (see p. 49 f.). The presence of foreigners intensified the traditional hostility, and when Judah was reconstituted as a religious state under Ezra and Nehemiah, the northern neighbors, now called Samaritans after their chief city, Samaria (IX, F-3), were excluded from the Temple at Jerusalem.

Thus began the Jewish-Samaritan schism which existed in the time of Jesus (cf. John 4:9). It led to the building of a rival Temple on Mount Gerizim (IX, F-3). During the second century B.C. it found expression in the hostility of the Samaritans to the Jews during the Maccabean struggle for religious and political independence. When, about 128 B.C., John Hyrcanus ravaged Samaria and extended Maccabean control northward from Judaea, he destroyed the Samaritan sanctuary, and it was never rebuilt. This, however, did not stop the use of Mount Gerizim for Samaritan worship. Indeed, such use continued through New Testament times (John 4:20), and even today the small Samaritan sect, centered in *Nâblus*, still celebrates the Passover on the top of Gerizim.

This persistent division of central Palestine cannot be explained by geographical and economic factors. It was rooted in historical and cultural rivalries and jealousies.

PHILISTIA AND JUDAH

In the area south of Jerusalem four vertical zones can be distinguished. Along the coast is the fertile, rolling plain where the Philistines once lived. Their chief cities were Gaza (IX, A-8), Ashkelon (IX, B-7), Ashdod (IX, C-6), Ekron (IX, C-6), and Gath (IX, C-7). This plain was rarely under Israelite or Jewish control. The Philistines early made a determined effort to subdue the whole of Palestine. They were checked only when Saul and David united Israel to resist the danger (see p. 45 f.). During the reigns of David and Solomon, Israel dominated Philistia economically, but did not subjugate it (see Plate VII:A). Uzziah is said to have conquered the plain during the first half of the eighth century B.C. (II Chron. 26:6); the conquest, however, had no lasting effect.

Control of Philistia was important for political reasons; it was the outpost of Palestine and Syria facing Egypt on the south. Economic reasons also were involved; Philistia not only dominated the best land route between Egypt and the north countries, but also in Gaza

FIG. 39. Coastal plain near Ramleh, looking toward Lydda. In the foreground appear olive trees, scattered through the fields.

possessed the natural western terminus for trade from the eastern desert. Hence with the weakening of the Kingdom of Judah, it was inevitable that the region should become a scene of conflict. After the fall of Jerusalem in 587 B.C., the Persians held control until the coming of Alexander the Great in 332 B.C. At this time Gaza felt strong enough to resist, and held out for two months. Its fall meant that Hellenistic influence gained the ascendancy in the Philistine plain. After a century under Egypt, Philistia came under the control of Syria. A few decades later the Maccabees brought the district into their kingdom, but they did not succeed in making it Jewish. Ascalon became an independent city and a center of Hellenistic culture. Gaza, a strong trade center, at times was free from Palestinian control and under the protection of the Roman governor of Syria. Other cities, such as Azotus and Jamnia, were given as sources of revenue and prestige to favorites of the Herods or the Romans.

After the destruction of Jerusalem in A.D. 70, Jamnia (IX, C-5) became a center of rabbinic studies, but in general Galilee proved more important in the rabbinic movement than either Philistia or Judaea (see p. 56). In the first five centuries A.D. Philistia was the scene of vigorous Christian activity, one phase of which, a strong monastic movement, spread eastward into the hill country and flourished about Eleutheropolis (XVIII, B-5).

Between the plain and the Judaean upland is a series of foothills, partially separated from the highland by longitudinal valleys. This is called the Shephelah ("Lowland"; see p. 19 and I, B-5). A series of valleys run across it westward to the plain. The northernmost is the Valley of Aijalon, protected by the two Beth-horons (IX, D-E 5). Next below it is the Valley of Sorek, along which the modern railroad runs from Joppa to Jerusalem (IX, D-6; XVIII, B-C 5). Ekron and Gezer (IX, D-5) protected its outer reaches in the plain, and Beth-shemesh (IX, D-6) was the chief town within it. This valley was the scene of Samson's exploits; he lived at Zorah, and Delilah at Timnah (IX, D-6; cf. Judg., chs. 13 to 16). Along this valley the Ark passed when sent back to Israel by the Philistines (I Sam. 6:12 ff.). Next on the south is the Valley of Elah, protected by the fortresses of Libnah and Azekah (IX, D-6) and famous as the place where David slew Goliath (I Sam. 17:19 ff.). Below it is the Valley of Zephathah (IX, C-D 7), in which occurred the battle between Asa and the Ethiopians (II Chron. 14:10). Further south are the valleys, unnamed in the Bible, protected by Gath (IX, C-7) and Lachish (IX, D-7), Eglon (IX, C-7) and Debir (IX, D-8).

The Shephelah was a very fertile region. It was filled with towns, only a few of which are shown on the map. It was greatly desired by Judah as a protective frontier, for unless the Shephelah was in the control of Judah the hill country was left exposed. Indeed, the usual strategy of invaders was first to conquer the Shephelah and then attack the heart of Judah.

The third vertical zone in the southern part of Plate IX is the rugged hill country between the Shephelah and the Judaean watershed. The latter extends southward from Jerusalem to Carmel (IX, E-8). It is clearly marked on the map, not merely by the relief, but also by the almost complete absence of towns east of this line. In this third zone was the cultivatable district of Judah. In its northern part, as in the Shephelah, the grape industry was especially prosperous (cf. Num. 13:23). In the south, around Debir and Carmel, the raising of sheep, weaving, and dyeing were more common.

During the Old Testament period the hill country of Judah played an active role in history. Hebron was an ancient and famous center. Bethlehem (IX, F-6), the home of David's family, was widely known. Later, during the Maccabean struggles of the second century B.C., this region was the scene of bitter battles for the control of Palestine. Beth-zur (IX, E-7; Fig. 53) was a strategic military point in this series of campaigns. With the exception, however, of Bethlehem, the birthplace of Jesus, the area south of Jerusalem plays no part in the New Testament story.

East of the Judaean watershed was the forbidding and barren wasteland called Jeshimon or the Wilderness of Judah (IX, F-G 6-8; see pp. 19, 65 and Fig. 42). On its western and northern edges were

Tekoa (IX, F-7), whence Amos came, and Herodium (IX, F-7) and Hyrcania (IX, G-6), two of the many fortresses with which Herod the Great gave strength to his rule of Palestine. The barrenness of this wilderness and the barrier on the east formed by the deep trough of the Dead Sea combined with the uninviting character of the dry Negeb on the south (see p. 63 f.) to force Judah to face west and especially north.

SAMARIA

In contrast to the four vertical zones south of Jerusalem, the region to the north possesses but two: the hills and the plain. The hill country of Samaria is more open to outside influence and more richly endowed than is that of Judah. To the west, north, and east, broad valleys give easy access to the Plain of Sharon (IX, D 1-3), Esdraelon, and the Jordan Valley (IX, G-H 1-6). Between the Plain of Sharon and Samaria there is no protecting Shephelah. Along the Jordan the wilderness is not so forbidding as it is west of the Dead Sea.

Perhaps because outside influences here had easy access to the hills, Israelites in the Old Testament period succumbed more easily than did Judah to the paganism of northern neighbors. However, since Samaria was a richer agricultural country, the resulting economic superiority and greater population meant that for a time a stronger state than Judah could be erected there.

It is no surprise, therefore, to note that before the fall of the Northern Kingdom to Assyria in 721 B.C., the center of interest in the Biblical narrative lay in the north. Elijah and Elisha, concerning whose lives and times nineteen of the forty-seven chapters of the books of the Kings were written, labored here. Queen Jezebel, who rivals Judas for the doubtful distinction of being the most notorious figure of the Bible, lived in Samaria as the wife of King Ahab. A century later, Amos and Hosea prophesied in the area. After the fall of the Israelite kingdom, however, this region was never again so significant in the Biblical story. It has little importance for the New Testament narrative. Perhaps the Aenon of John the Baptist's ministry (John 3:23) was near the Salim in eastern Samaria (IX, F-3), though another possible site is near the Salim south of Scythopolis (IX, H-2). John, ch. 4, mentions a brief contact of Jesus with Samaritans at Jacob's Well and Sychar (IX, F-3), a village near the well and often sought at the modern town of *'Askar* (Fig. 6).

Whereas in the south there was a conflict of interest between Philistia and Judah, in the north no comparable situation occurred, because there was never an intensive settlement in the Plain of Sharon (IX, D 1-3). The latter was probably rather swampy and thickly wooded, and hence largely undeveloped. In the first century B.C., however, Herod the Great, vassal king under Rome, chose the site of Strato's Tower (IX, D-1), renamed it Caesarea in honor of the emperor, and spent twelve years rebuilding it on a grand scale. He thus made the city the chief port and virtual capital of Palestine.

During the Old Testament period, however, the political center of gravity for Samaria was always at or near Mount Ebal and Mount Gerizim. At this point all roads through the hill country met (see Fig. 6, and Plates IV, VI, XVIII). Between the mountains was the earliest chief city of the area, Shechem (IX, F-3). It was a strong Canaanite city, which played an active role in the political affairs of Canaan before the time of Israel (see p. 35). Later an unsuccessful attempt was made here to establish the first Israelite monarchy, with Abimelech, son of Gideon, as king (Judg., ch. 9; see also Gen., ch. 34, which reflects early tribal conflicts in the area).

After the division of the kingdom of Solomon, the first Israelite capital was at Tirzah (IX, F-3; see I Kings 15:21, 33; 16:6, 23; S. of Sol. 6:4). Shechem was not in a well-protected spot for a capital, and Tirzah, situated in a valley leading east and northeast, was not a suitable site for wider contacts. When, therefore, King Omri, about 880 B.C., wished to orient his capital toward the west and north, he chose the site of Samaria (IX, F-3), and built there a magnificent capital, which subsequent builders made so strong that it took the Assyrians three years to take it (see p. 105).

After this disaster, the city of Samaria was never again so impor-

FIG. 40. Shepherds' field near Bethlehem. Traditional site of the appearance of angels to the shepherds on the night of Jesus' birth. Many sturdy olive trees are seen in the center of the picture. Note how stones are taken from the fields and used to build fences.

tant politically. Its situation, on an isolated hill with a good water supply, invited military use, and in the troubled centuries that followed it was repeatedly fortified and destroyed. When Herod the Great received Samaria from the Roman emperor Augustus, he spared no expense to make it an outstanding city of his kingdom. Ruins of the large Temple of Augustus on the hilltop, including a great altar and a fragment of a colossal statue apparently representing the emperor, still reflect clearly Herod's friendship for Rome and his adoption of Hellenistic influences in architecture and religion. There was a thriving Christian community here in later centuries; striking evidence of this is the Church of John the Baptist which has been excavated.

THE JORDAN VALLEY

The western side of the Jordan Valley was for the most part never intensively occupied. A noteworthy exception was in the north, around Beth-shan (IX, G-1). In the Roman period a considerable use of irrigation in the region of Phasaelis and Archelais (IX, G 4-5) resulted in a fruitful section which was given usually to some favorite of the ruling power (see p. 84). At this same time Jericho (IX, G-5) underwent expansion. The city spread to the south and east of the old site, and Herod the Great constructed here a palace, baths, theater, and citadels. The area was then noted for its palm groves, balsam trees, and garden products. .

The eastern side of the valley, however, was and still is a more prosperous area. North of the Jabbok (IX, H-3) are numerous perennial streams, along which lay such towns as Succoth, Zaphon, and Zaretan (IX, H-3), Jabesh-gilead and Pella (IX, H-2). Between the Jabbok and Beth-nimrah (IX, H-5) is an area without streams, though it has been cultivated to some extent by irrigation. Between Beth-nimrah and the Dead Sea were several villages. Here Israel encamped before crossing the Jordan to conquer Canaan; the region was then called "the plains of Moab" (Num. 22:1). Considerable development of this area occurred in the New Testament period; a number of towns were then moved further down the little valleys in which they were situated, and relocated on more level ground. This trend reflects a time of rather stable conditions in the area.

TRANSJORDAN

Ascent up the valleys to the east soon leads one to the hilly plateau of Transjordan. The tribe of Reuben received as its inheritance the territory between Heshbon (IX, I-6) and the River Arnon (IX, H-I 8), but during the ninth century B.C. this region was taken by Moab, and the tribe disappears from the records (pp. 43, 49). To the north was Gilead, occupied by Gad and one half of the tribe of Manasseh (see Plate VI). Subsequently Israel contended for Gilead with both the Aramaeans (Damascus) and the Ammonites.

Ammon proper was a semiarid region between Gilead and the desert. Its border was the River Jabbok as it turned in a large semicircle southward (Deut. 3:16). Rabbah or Rabbath-ammon, the chief city of the kingdom (IX, J-5), was a naturally strong place, possessed by Israel only for a short time after its capture by David (II Sam. 12:26 ff.). In the succeeding period Ammon pressed westward, enlarging its territory in proportion to Israel's weakness.

During the period of the divided monarchy both Judah and Israel made attempts to hold the borders of the Davidic empire (see Plate VII: A-B). It was Israel, however, which laid claim to the whole Jordan Valley and Transjordan, including Moab, as far south as the Brook Zered (X, H-I 3-4; VII:B). The reason was that the valleys from the district of Samaria led easily across the Jordan, while the one route from Jerusalem to the Jordan was winding, steep, and difficult (Fig. 61). Hence, of the districts of Transjordan once conquered by David, Judah laid claim to Edom alone.

Yet the intervening Jordan Valley made it impossible for Transjordan ever to become integrally united with Samaria. The later history of the eastern plateau was rather more strongly affected by the proximity of the desert. It may have been with the thought of protecting the region from possible attack by desert peoples that Greek cities were founded and encouraged in this region from the time of Alexander the Great. At some time not later than the first century B.C., ten of these, including Scythopolis (IX, G-1), Pella (IX, H-2), Gerasa (IX, J-3), and Philadelphia (IX, J-5), banded together to form the Decapolis (XIV, D-F 1-5), a league of Hellenistic cities. The later Maccabees were able for a time to control almost the entire area, including the eastern side of the Dead Sea. But the Nabataeans, centered in Petra, were extending their control north as well as west, and in the days of the Herods, Machaerus (IX, H-7) was the southernmost fortress under Herodian control. The problem of how to deal with the Nabataeans and their threat to the Roman outposts was not solved effectively until the early second century A.D., when Rome was able to organize the Nabatean territory into the Roman province of Arabia (A.D. 106).

While the region of Transjordan was never the center of Israelite life, it figured continually in the Biblical history. The tribes of Israel came from the east to cross the Jordan and invade Palestine. Balaam viewed the hosts of Israel from Mount Pisgah (IX, I-6; Num. 23:14), and the death of Moses is reported to have occurred there or on Mount Nebo (IX, I-6; cf. Deut. 32:49; 34:1). Two and a half tribes settled in Transjordan, and through the centuries Israel fought with only intermittent success to hold these eastern regions. In the New Testament period, Peraea (XIV, D 4-5), a name which means the land "across" the Jordan, was combined with Galilee and placed under the rule of Herod Antipas. John the Baptist evidently preached and baptized on the east side of the Jordan; his work at Bethany beyond Jordan is mentioned (XIV, D-5; cf. John 1:28), and he was taken prisoner by Antipas, who had no jurisdiction on the west bank. John was imprisoned and executed at Machaerus, according to Josephus. Jesus, to judge by popular Galilean custom, probably traveled through Peraea on some of his trips to Jerusalem. When the early Christian group left Jerusalem at the outbreak of the Jewish rebellion against Rome (A.D. 66-70), they went to Pella. Christianity had a great expansion in Transjordan in the early centuries. Prominent in this period were Gerasa, where the ruins of many splendid churches have been excavated and studied, and Medeba (IX, I-6), where a marvelous mosaic map of Palestine has been found in the floor of an ancient church.

Modern political arrangements have illustrated anew both the partial independence of Transjordan from the region west of the Jordan, and the close relation of the eastern plateau to the desert. After the First World War Great Britain received a mandate over Palestine, including the Transjordan portion. She found it advisable, however, to organize Transjordan as a separate unit of administration, in which Arab leaders were given a prominent place.

FIG. 41. Jerash, site of the ancient Gerasa. In the foreground a semicircle of columns still marks the location of the ancient forum. Running north from the forum was the main north-south street, with columns on either side. Some columns are still in place. Trees mark the course of the stream which runs through the site. Beyond the stream lies the modern village, built mainly with stones taken from the ruins.

PLATE IX

CENTRAL PALESTINE
IN BIBLICAL TIMES

SCALE OF MILES

0   5   10   15   20

○ CITIES AND TOWNS

THE GREAT SEA

PLAIN OF SHARON

PHILISTIA

WILDERNESS OF JUDAH

ASCENT OF ZIZ

Salt Sea, Lake Asphaltitis

MTS. OF ABARIM

River Jordan

River Jabbok

LAND OF ZUPH

VALLEY OF AIJALON

VALLEY OF SOREK

VALLEY OF ELAH

VALLEY OF ZEPHATHAH

VALLEY OF BERACHAH

Caesarea, Strato's Tower
Apollonia
Joppa
Jehud
Beth-dagon?
Ono
Lod, Lydda
Bene-berak
Gath-rimmon?
Pegae, Antipatris
Aphek
Eben-ezer?
Ramathaim-zophim, Arimathaea?
Hadid, Adida
Neballat
Modein
Narbata?
Socoh
Gilgal?
River Kanah
Borceus, Lebonah
Tappuah
Acrabetta
Pirathon?
Samaria, Sebaste
En-gannim, Ginaea
Aruboth?
Dothan
Ibleam
Taanach
Gath-rimmon?
Thebez
Tirzah?
Neapolis MT. EBAL
MT. GERIZIM
Shechem, Sychar?
Sychar Jacob's Well
Shalem, Salim?
Janoah
Shiloh
Zeredah
Timnah-serah, Thamna
+MT. GAASH
Bethel, Luz, Bethela?
Gophna
Ophrah, Ephraim?
Ai
Beth-aven
Michmash, Machmas
Geba
Rock Rimmon
Baal-hazor
Corea?
Ataroth
Phasaelis
Archelais
Alexandrium
Naarath
Dok?
Jericho (N. T.)
Jericho (O. T.) Gilgal?
Paroh Beth-arabah
Almon
Anathoth
Beth-hoglah?
Stone of Bohan?
Hyrcania
En-gedi, Engaddi
Abel-meholah?
Bezek
Jabesh-gilead
Pella
Beth-shan, Scythopolis
Rehob
Salim?
Mt. GILBOA
Well of Harod
Rogelim?
Ham
Mahanaim?
Tishbeh?
Tabbah
Zaretan?
Zaphon?
Amathus
Ragaba
Penuel
Succoth
Adamah
Betonim
Beth-nimrah
Gerasa
Jogbehah
Rabbath-ammon, Philadelphia
Mephaath?
Bethennabris
Abila
Abel-shittim
Beth-haran, Livias
Jordan? Julias, Livias
Bethany Beyond
Beth-jeshimoth
Besimoth
+MT. NEBO
+MT. PISGAH
Heshbon, Essebon
Elealeh
Samaga
Medeba
Johaz?
Jahaz?
Baal-meon
Almon-diblathaim?
Kedemoth?
Mattanah?
Libba, Lemba
Ataroth?
Kirjathaim
Nobah?
Machaerus
Callirhoe
Zareth-shahar, Nahaliel
Dibon
Aroer
Beth-gamul
City of Moab?
River Arnon
Ramoth-gilead
Jericho
Hebron
Mamre
Beth-anoth
Cain
Ziph
Juttah
Carmel
Maon
Zior
Gedor
Giloh
Keilah
Beth-zur,
Bethsura
Halhul
Aetam
Bethzacharia
Netophah
Herodium
Tekoa,
Thekoue
Bethlehem
Bethbassi
Bether
Bethphage?
En-shemesh
Bethany
Anathoth
Gabath Saul
Gabath
Emmaus Nicopolis
Emmaus Nephtoah
Manahath?
Jerusalem
Chesalon
Zorah
Eshtaol?
Beth-shemesh
Zanoah
Socoh
Azekah
Jarmuth
Adullam
Gederah
Kirjath-jearim
Chephirah Mizpah?
Gibeon, Gabao
Ramah
Adasa
Adida?
Azmaveth
Ataroth?
Elasa
Beeroth, Beroa?
Caphar-salama?
Shaalabbin
Beth-horon Lower
Beth-horon Upper
Gezer,
Gazara
Gibbethon
Jarmuth
Timnah?
Libnah?
Moresheth-gath?
Mareshah, Marisa
Nezib?
Saphir?
Lachish
Eglon
Debir, Kirjath-sepher?
Adoraim, Adora
Dumah
Arab?
Socoh
Anab
Shamir?
Ziklag?
Hormah, Zephath?
Beth-eglaim?
Gaza
Anthedon
Ashkelon, Ascalon
Ashdod, Azotus
Ekron, Accaron?
Cedron?
Gath?
Ether
MT. SEIR
Ellekeh?
Gath
Jabneel, Jamnia
Beth-tappuah
Adoraim
Ziph
Ether
Gath-rimmon?
Eshtemoa
Aphek
Alurus
Gedor

AMMON

GILEAD

EPHRAIM

MANASSEH

DAN

ISSACHAR

JUDAH

BENJAMIN

61

PLATE X

SOUTHERN
PALESTINE
IN BIBLICAL TIMES

Copyright, The Westminster Press
International Copyright Secured. All Rights Reserved

SCALE OF MILES

CITIES AND TOWNS

FIG. 42. Jeshimon or the Wilderness of Judah, the barren wasteland to the east of the Judean watershed. The high plateau or Moab rises abruptly from the Dead Sea in the background. The bleakness of the area is forbidding, but the visitor to Palestine never tires of watching the ever-changing pastel shades of color in a view such as this.

SOUTHERN PALESTINE IN BIBLICAL TIMES

PLATE X

BELOW Hebron and Kirjath-sepher the hills of Judah drop down abruptly into relatively level plains, becoming drier as one goes south. This bleak, forbidding region, cut by countless dry valleys or wadis and dotted with sand dunes, was known in Biblical times as the *Negeb* (see p. 19), a word usually translated as "the south," though it originally meant "dry" or "parched." Through this sparsely populated desert wilderness ran Judah's traditional southern border, along the so-called "River of Egypt" (Plate X, A-6, and V, F-3) and the range of mountains lying between the Wilderness of Paran and the Wilderness of Zin, then into the Valley of the Arabah (X, G-H 4-8). Beyond the latter lay the ancient lands of Moab and Edom. The River of Egypt is not properly a river but one of the numerous dry valleys which carry off the excess water during the winter rains.

Leaving Hebron in Judah (IX, E-8), the traveler finds the hills descending rapidly to Beer-sheba, where evidence of intensive occupation in Biblical times immediately ceases. To the south the watershed lies in the region of Aroer (X, F-3). To the west of this watershed is an inhospitable desert of shifting sand dunes and soft, chalk-like limestone seamed with red flint. As the limestone crumbles, the flint is washed out so that it sometimes covers the surface of the ground for miles. Occasionally there is a small spring-watered valley or plain where the soil is sufficiently good to be cultivated. The few

Arab Bedouin who live here depend on the brief winter rains for their small crops. These rains, however, are so uncertain that frequently the grain is parched before it ripens to maturity, and rarely do the springs supply sufficient water for irrigation. In the summer the weather is extremely hot, and made the more unpleasant by the fine sand blown across the landscape by the wind. In the winter the cold is penetrating and made worse by winds which find nothing to check them in the rolling plains.

East of the watershed, the country is even more uninviting. This region is more arid and is filled with mountain ranges and deep valleys. The Ascent of Akrabbim (Num. 34:4; Josh. 15:3; Judg. 1:36), or "Pass of Scorpions," leading up from the Arabah to the plateau of Ziph and Aroer (X, F-4 and F-3) is an important landmark of this area.

Though the Negeb was very sparsely inhabited in Biblical times, astonishing efforts were made between the fourth and the seventh centuries A.D. to occupy and cultivate it. Most remarkable are the ruins of numerous Christian churches and monasteries, especially those at Alusa (X, D-3), Oryba ('*Abda*, X, D-5), Subaita (XVIII, B-7), '*Aujā el-Hafir* (XVIII, A-7), and *Kurnub* near Ziph (X, F-4). During the winter of 1935-1936 excavators at work on the churches of '*Aujā el-Hafir* discovered a mass of papyrus documents, the first ever found in Palestine. They were written in Greek and Arabic, and dated

FIG. 43. An erosion dam at *Kurnub* (near Ziph; x, F-4), built by the Byzantine inhabitants as part of their energetic attempts at water and soil conservation.

in the sixth and seventh centuries A.D. Among them were deeds, contracts, receipts, letters, a list of Latin words and phrases from Virgil's *Aeneid* with their Greek equivalents (the work of some student who was laboriously trying to read Virgil), Christian legends, and fragments of the New Testament. While forts had been built in this region by the Romans to protect the trade route between Gaza and Arabia, the primary reason for the occupation here in the Byzantine period was undoubtedly religious. Christians who wished to withdraw from the active world found here a quiet place to practice the devotional life without interference from worldly interests. And here they stayed until the Mohammedan conquests.

It has been thought by some that there must have been much more rainfall here in ancient times than at present; otherwise existence would have been impossible. Exploration has revealed that this was not the case, but that extraordinary care was taken for the conservation of water. Innumerable dams, reservoirs, and cisterns were constructed, in which the winter rain was collected and from which a supply of water for the months of dryness was obtained. These energetic efforts in water conservation are the most remarkable feature of the ruins of the Negeb (see Fig. 43).

THE NEGEB DURING THE BIBLICAL PERIOD

The Negeb is first mentioned in the Biblical story during the journeys of Abraham and Isaac. Abraham lived here for a time (Gen. 13:1; 20:1), and passed through it on his way to and from Egypt. The main military and trade route lay along the coast, and was called in Ex. 13:17 "the way of the land of the Philistines" (Plate v). An inner route still used by nomads follows a series of springs from Beer-sheba to Rehoboth to Azmon, and then westward to Egypt (Plates IV and v). It was probably along this latter route that Abraham, and later the family of Jacob, journeyed to Egypt.

Both Abraham and Isaac are said to have had controversies with the king of Gerar (x, B-1) and to have dug a number of wells in "the valley of Gerar" (Gen. 26:15 ff.). This valley is the modern *Wâdi Ghazzeh*, possibly to be identified also with "the brook Besor" of I Sam. 30:9, 10, 21 (x, B-C 2-3). Only two of the places where these wells were dug can be identified, Rehoboth (x, C-4) and Beer-sheba (x, E-2). The water level along this particular valley is not far below the surface of the ground and wells are comparatively easy to dig.

The most famous Biblical town in the area is Beer-sheba (x, E-2). "From Dan to Beer-sheba" was the common phrase describing the northern and southern limits respectively of Israelite territory. Like Dan, Beer-sheba was noted not merely as a geographical limit, and as an abode of the Patriarchs, but also as a holy place. Here Abraham planted a tamarisk tree and called on the name of his God (Gen. 21:33); here the sons of Samuel judged (I Sam. 8:2); here Elijah fled (I Kings 19:3); and here both Israel and Judah fell into pagan practices denounced by Amos (Amos 5:5 ff.; 8:14). The town is not mentioned in the New Testament, but later Christian writers say that it

was a very large village, with a Roman garrison, and that it was the seat of a Christian bishopric. This Christian town was called Bersabee (x, E-2) and was located on the site of the modern Arab village. Nothing older than the Roman period has been found here, however, and it is probable that the Old Testament town was on the site of the mound of *Tell es-Seba'*, 2½ miles to the east.

After the Patriarchal period, the Negeb next played an important role during the period of the wandering in the wilderness. At this time the most important place in the narrative was Kadesh, or Kadesh-barnea (x, C-7). To this region the wanderers came from Sinai intending to obtain entrance to Canaan from the south (Plate v). The discouraging report of the spies and defeat at Hormah (x, D-1) so weakened the people's morale, however, that they were forced to spend a generation in the area (Num., chs. 13 ff.; Deut. 1:19 ff.). Here Korah rebelled (Num., ch. 16) and Miriam died (ch. 20:1). Somewhere in this region north of Kadesh was Mount Hor, where Aaron died (vs. 22 ff.). The identity of this particular peak has been lost, however, among the many mountains in the area.

The ancient name of Kadesh is still preserved at a small spring called *'Ain Qedeis* (probably also the En-mishpat, "Spring of Judgment," of Gen. 14:7). The amount of water supplied by this spring is so limited, however, that few Israelites could have existed on its supply alone. About four miles northwest is the most copious spring of the whole area, *'Ain el-Qudeirât*, situated in a little valley made fertile by the spring's waters (Fig. 24). Between the tenth and eighth centuries B.C. a Judean fortress was built here; and some scholars have maintained that if any one site is to be identified with Kadesh, this must be the one. Yet in Josh. 15:3, 4 the southern border of Judah is described as running from the Salt Sea to the Maaleh-acrabbim (Ascent of Akrabbim, x, F-4), passing along the Wilderness of Zin to Kadesh-barnea, to Hazar-addar (to be read thus and not "Hezron" and "Adar"), turning to Karkaa, and thence to Azmon (x, B-6) and to the River of Egypt, following the latter to the Sea (cf. Plate VI). The three main springs in the area are *'Ain Qedeis*, *'Ain el-Qudeirât*, and *'Ain Qoseimeh*. It seems probable, therefore, that Kadesh was actually located at the first, Hazar-addar at the second, and Azmon at the third, with Karkaa perhaps lying at the junction of the valleys between Hazar-addar and Azmon. The simplest solution to the problem would be that the Israelites stayed, not merely at Kadesh, but in the general area, using all three of the springs.

Among the roving tribes who frequently appeared in the Negeb were the Amalekites, a people who occasioned repeated trouble for Israel (e.g., Num. 13:29; Judg. 6:3; I Sam. 15:1 ff.; 30:1ff.; Ps. 83:7). Tribes which were friendly to Judah were the Kenites and Jerah-meelites who lived near Arad (x, F-2) and Beer-sheba and were later absorbed into the tribe of Judah (vi, B-C 5; and I Sam. 27:10). Also absorbed by Judah were the tribes of Simeon and Caleb. Caleb was in possession of Hebron and the area south of it (Judg. 1:12 ff.; Josh., ch. 14), while Simeon occupied a group of villages, in the area of Beer-sheba, Ziklag (x, E-1), Hormah (x, D-1), and Sharuhen (x, C-2): see Josh. 19:1-9 and Plate VI.

During the course of David's life as an outlaw, fleeing from the jealous Saul, he spent most of his time in the northern portion of the

FIG. 44. The entrance to *Umm el-'Amad*, an ancient mine of Edom.

FIG. 45. *Qaṣr Abū el-Kharaq*, the best preserved of the ancient Moabite border fortresses. It is located just south of the probable site of the "City of Moab" (x, K-1).

Negeb. For a time he lived in the Judean wasteland southeast of Hebron. He spared Saul's life when he could have killed him at En-gedi (x, H-1) and again at Ziph (x, F-1; I Sam., chs. 24; 26). Nabal, of Maon, who had possessions at Carmel (x, F-1) refused to aid him and was saved from attack only by the intervention of Abigail (I Sam., ch. 25). Subsequently, David made Ziklag (x, E-1) his base for raiding the tribes of the Negeb (I Sam., chs. 27; 30).

The area east of the Judean watershed and extending northward the length of the Dead Sea was Jeshimon, the Wilderness of Judah (see also IX, F-G 7-8). It was an ideal place for a refuge, and has continued so to modern times. Few towns were situated in it because there was very little water. It was a barren, rugged wasteland, cut by numerous deep and jagged valleys leading down to the Dead Sea (Fig. 42). Masada (x, H-2) was the finest of the many natural fortresses in this region. It is an isolated, flat-topped hill along the cliffs of the Dead Sea, and inaccessible except by winding paths in two places. Here Herod the Great (see p. 75) fled with his bride Mariamme in 42 B.C. when Jerusalem was taken by the Parthians. In A.D. 70 it was the last refuge of an army of Jewish patriots who fled there after Jerusalem had fallen to the Romans (p. 76).

During the sixth-fifth centuries B.C. the Negeb was occupied by the Edomites, who were pushed out of their former territory by Arab tribes. Thus began Idumaea, the Greek name for the new "Edom." Eventually even Hebron became an Edomite city (see p. 50 and Plates VII:D, XII:A-D).

SOUTHERN TRANSJORDAN DURING THE BIBLICAL PERIOD

While southern Transjordan is far more plentifully supplied with water and thus more fertile than the Negeb, it is more of a pastoral than an agricultural country. The writer of II Kings 3:4 calls Mesha, one of its kings in the ninth century B.C. (see Fig. 32), a "sheep-master," whose yearly tribute to Israel was 100,000 lambs and 100,000 rams with the wool (R. V. marg.). The country is a plateau, deeply cut along the Dead Sea by east-west valleys which carry the winter rains down into the deep basin of the Sea. Chief of the valleys are the River Arnon and the Brook Zered. Below the Dead Sea the valleys run in a northwesterly direction into the Arabah, the continuation of the Jordan-Dead Sea cleft (see Plates V, X). The towns and villages appear in a narrow north-south belt, scarcely twenty-five miles wide. To the east the country gradually slips away into the vast expanse of Arabian desert without clearly marked boundary.

In Palestine generally, and in most of Transjordan, the rock underlying the thin topsoil and cropping out on every hillside is a soft, crumbling limestone. Along the eastern border of the Arabah, however, the valleys cut down through this limestone into an older, soft, colorful sandstone. This sandstone formation, one of the most important physical features of the country south of the Brook Zered, is the same as that of the region about Mount Sinai (V, E-F 5) and bears the same metallic ores. Recent exploration has shown that the Edomite ore contained both copper and iron in large amounts; and this

explains the economic importance of the country. Small wonder, then, that its possession was so coveted by David, Solomon, and subsequent Judaean kings that they were willing to risk large armies in an exceedingly difficult battlefield. Some of the ancient mines have been discovered (Fig. 44), and also a number of the mining camps and villages (for example Punon, X, H-6). The latter are usually surrounded with slag from which the metal has been extracted. Numerous small furnaces, once used for the preliminary smelting of the ore, are also found, though now in ruins.

Recent explorations reveal that Solomon was a most energetic exploiter of this ore, though the fact is not mentioned in the Bible. Great walled camps were built for the slave labor which was sent to work the mines; and a large smelter, employing some of the principles of the modern blast furnace, was constructed at Ezion-geber (V, G-4) to refine the metal. These discoveries at last explain the hitherto mysterious reference in Deuteronomy to the Promised Land as one "whose stones are iron, and out of whose hills thou mayest dig copper" (ch. 8:9).

The present sparse population of this region might give the impression that it was no more intensively occupied in Biblical times than was the Negeb. However, hundreds of ruined villages dot the country today, indicating that it was once thickly settled. The ancient names of these villages are not known; hence they do not appear on Biblical maps. The occupational history of the country as determined by recent exploration falls into three main periods: (1) c. 2300-1900 B.C.; (2) c. 1200-700 B.C.; and (3) c. 100 B.C. to A.D. 700.

During the first period an advanced civilization flourished for a time, and this may furnish the background for the invasion of the four kings described in Gen., ch. 14, though the matter is very uncertain. Centuries later the main highway through Transjordan (Plates IV and VI) was still called "The King's Highway" (see Fig. 25).

Several lines of evidence show that the cities of Sodom and Gomorrah were located somewhere in the southern part of the Jordan-Dead Sea basin. Study and exploration now indicate that they were at the southern end of the Dead Sea. The Vale of Siddim (Gen. 14:3) was located in all probability in what is now the basin of the sea below "the Tongue" which protrudes opposite Masada (x, H 2-3). This is the shallowest part of the sea today. In Roman times it was even shallower, for it was then possible to cross from the Tongue to the western shore. The level of the sea has been steadily rising, and is considerably higher today than it was a century ago. The clearest indications of this fact are the submerged forests still visible along the southern shore.

FIG. 46. *Umm el-Bayyârah*, site of Sela ("The Rock"), the virtually impregnable mountain-fortress of Edom.

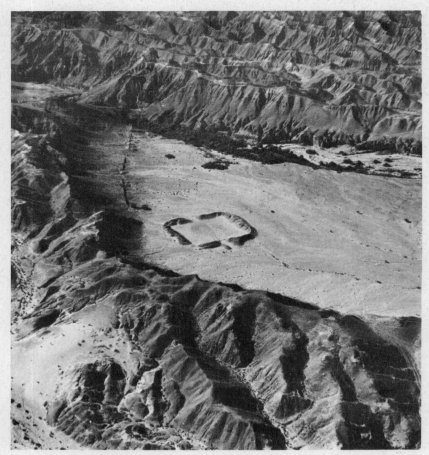

FIG. 47. A Nabataean-Roman site, eight miles south of the Dead Sea, in the Edomite hills along the Arabah, illustrating Nabataean ability to wrest a living from bleak and marginal lands. Note the remains of the aqueduct which once led water to the enclosure.

Ruins of the Christian and medieval Zoar have been discovered in the area (x, H-3), and there is little doubt that the ruins of the Old Testament town, together with those of Sodom and Gomorrah, are now covered by the waters of the sea. That this region was once fertile and well-settled is indicated by the Biblical story of Abraham and Lot. When their herdsmen had quarreled the two families were separated. Lot chose the Plain of the Jordan which "was well watered every where, before the Lord destroyed Sodom and Gomorrah, even as the garden of the Lord [Eden], like the land of Egypt, as thou comest unto Zoar" (Gen. 13:10, A.V.). Lot then moved to Sodom, which with the other "cities of the Plain" (Gomorrah, Admah, Zeboiim, and Zoar) was located in the Vale of Siddim.

On some occasion in ancient times this vale with its cities was overwhelmed by a great conflagration, the memory of which is preserved not only in the Bible (Gen. 19:23-28), but also in later Greek and Latin writings. "The vale of Siddim was full of slime [asphalt] pits" according to a Biblical writer (Gen. 14:10), and petroleum deposits are still to be found in the region. Ancient writers also tell of the presence of gases which, though not observable today, were probably those commonly found in conjunction with petroleum deposits. The entire region is on the long fault line which formed the Jordan Valley, the Dead Sea, and the Arabah. Throughout history it has been the scene of frequent earthquakes. Geological activity, therefore, may well have been responsible for the settling of the valley's floor and for the disastrous petroleum, asphalt, and gaseous fires which accompanied the earthquakes. This would explain the "brimstone and fire" and the smoke which "went up as the smoke of a furnace" (Gen. 19:24, 28). The story of Lot's wife becoming a pillar of salt is certainly associated with the great salt mass in the valley, *Jebel Usdum* ("Mountain of Sodom"), a hill, some five miles long and three miles wide, stretching in a north-south direction at the southwestern end of the Dead Sea (the ridge west of the name Zoar, x, H-3).

The kingdoms of Moab and Edom (Plates IV-VI and p. 36) flourished during Transjordan's second period of intensive inhabitation and cultivation (1200-700 B.C.). During the six centuries prior to the founding of these kingdoms the inhabitants had reverted to a nomadic life. In the thirteenth century, however, people began to settle in villages once more. The kingdoms established were strongly fortified with walled cities and blockhouses along the borders and within the interior (Fig. 45). After the eighth century B.C. rapid disintegration set in once more and the power of the countries declined, probably because of prolonged warfare with Israel and Judah and aggression from Assyrian and Babylonian armies (see pp. 67 ff.).

The chief city of Moab was Kir-hareseth (x, I-3), located on a high and easily fortified hill. In the time of Elisha, Israelite and Judaean armies laid waste the country of Moab and besieged Kir, to which King Mesha had retired, but were unable to take it. When Mesha sacrificed his eldest son on the walls, the siege was broken (II Kings 3:25-27).

Teman (x, I-8) was one of the chief cities of Edom. Amos in his prophecy against Edom said: "Thus saith the Lord; For three transgressions of Edom, and for four, I will not turn away the punishment thereof . . .: but I will send a fire upon Teman, which shall devour the palaces of Bozrah" (ch. 1:11, 12, A.V.). Teman was the southernmost large city of Edom, and Bozrah the northernmost (x, I-6). The country was noted for its great wise men, many of whom lived in Teman (Jer. 49:7; Obad. 8, 9). One of them, Eliphaz, was the leader of the three friends of Job (ch. 2:11). While Teman was probably the actual capital of the country, the citadel to which the people fled in time of siege was Sela, "The Rock" (x, H-8). This was a virtually impregnable, flat-topped mountain (Fig. 46). The sense of security which it gave the Edomites is well described by Obad. 3: "The pride of thy heart hath deceived thee, O thou that dwellest in the clefts of Sela [R.V. marg.], whose habitation is high; that saith in his heart, Who shall bring me down to the ground?"

THE NABATAEANS

The civilization of southern Transjordan reached its peak during the third period of the country's history (100 B.C. to A.D. 100). This was the age of the Nabataeans, one of the most gifted and energetic peoples of ancient times. They were Arabs who invaded Edom between the sixth and fourth centuries, and gradually rose to a position of great wealth and power, controlling the rich trade routes between Arabia and Syria (see Plate XII:A-D). Their kingdom was highly organized and intensively populated. They took over the methods of defense which the Edomites and Moabites had worked out before them, but improved them and enlarged their scope. Villages and fortresses dotted the country. They pushed the border of arable land much farther into the desert than any people either before or since through remarkable efforts at water conservation. Cisterns and reservoirs were built wherever needed. Dry river beds were dammed in order to catch the heavy winter rains. Even aqueducts were constructed where needed (Fig. 47). Their pottery dishes represent a high point in ceramic art—highly decorated, of almost an eggshell thinness, delicately and beautifully worked.

The capital of Nabataea was Petra, a Greek translation of the Old Testament Sela (x, H-8). Part of it was literally carved out of rock, and is one of the most spectacular sights of modern Palestine. Houses, temples, and tombs were cut in the soft, multicolored sandstone cliffs. Flights of stairways, also hewn from the rock, lead up every hill. Free standing pillars before temples and tombs look as though they had been placed in position, and not hewn from the solid stone (Fig. 52). Beautiful murals still adorn some of the interiors. Petra was a resplendent and well-protected capital, on which heavily laden caravans converged from all directions. In the New Testament only one of its kings is mentioned, namely Aretas IV (9 B.C. to A.D. 40), who controlled Damascus at the time of Paul's conversion (II Cor. 11:32), and who also soundly defeated Herod Antipas of Galilee (called "that fox" by Jesus, Luke 13:32) when the latter divorced his first wife, Aretas' daughter.

The Nabataeans were conquered by the Roman emperor Trajan in A.D. 106, after which their civilization soon disappeared. During the next centuries Roman roads (Fig. 25) and fortresses were constructed in strategic places, so that the lucrative trade routes could now be under Roman control. Never again, however, did the country attain the prosperity which it had reached during the time of Jesus.

FIG. 48. One of the Cilician Gates (XI:D, B-2). These "gates" are a series of sharp defiles which cut through the Taurus Mountains in a space of some ten miles. Through them runs the main highway into Asia Minor from Cilicia, Syria, and Mesopotamia. For over four thousand years this highway has been a well-traveled trade and military route. Hittite, Assyrian, Greek, and Roman armies have passed through the mountain gap shown in this photograph.

THE GREAT EMPIRES OF ISRAELITE TIMES

PLATE XI

THE story of man's oft-repeated attempt to dominate his world by the use of totalitarian power is a fascinating account. It is the story of ambitious men who consolidate their power over a people, and turn the total resources of that people toward world conquest. Strangely enough, the conquest has not always been an unmixed evil. The organizing energy required often stirred creative powers to such an extent that great prosperity resulted and achievements in science and art were phenomenal.

Yet conquest was more often a dreadful thing, draining the resources of subject peoples and keeping them in a state of poverty, terror, and seething hatred. The mounds which dot the ancient Near East are filled with the evidence of this state of affairs. In Palestine and Syria especially the average city was frequently destroyed in war. Small wonder that Israel was so concerned with death and judgment and salvation! Small wonder that the psalms are filled with the pleading of tortured men that they may be delivered from the hands of their enemies!

The period of the Old and New Testaments was the first great epoch of empire-building, and in its maelstrom of tragedy and triumph the Hebrew people were inevitably caught. The Egyptian Empire of the fifteenth century B.C. was the greatest which the world had seen (Plate III). Yet it was dwarfed by the achievements which followed. During the eighth and seventh centuries the Assyrian Empire was formed, including in its scope the whole of Mesopotamia, Palestine-Syria, southern Asia Minor (Plate XI:A), and even for a time Egypt. By 600 B.C. Assyria had fallen and Babylonia had taken its place, ruling over substantially the same territory (Plate XI:B). Babylonia soon fell, however, to the Medes and the Persians, and by 500 B.C. the Persian Empire included in its scope the whole of Western Asia, Egypt, and Thrace in Europe; and its armies were threatening Greece (Plate XI:C). By 330 B.C. Alexander the Great had mastered Greece and the Persian Empire. After his death three great Hellenistic empires divided his domain (Plate XI:D). Then in the

first century before Christ, the Romans, with a military power and organizing genius unparalleled in antiquity, conquered and unified the entire Mediterranean world (Plate XIII).

Such was the procession of empires in which the small country of Palestine was caught. Geographical situation decreed that political independence could be achieved in that country only during the brief periods when the procession had temporarily halted. And as it was then, so it is also in modern times.

THE EMPIRE OF ASSYRIA

The country of Assyria lay along the upper Tigris River, and in the early period of its history Assur (or Asshur) was its chief city (XI:A, C-2). As early as 1900 B.C. the people of this small region were prosperous traders. One of their trading colonies was as far away as Kanish in Asia Minor, where an active interest in the silver mines of the area was one of the chief concerns (II, E-2; III, C-2).

In the thirteenth century Assyrian armies had crossed the Euphrates, and about 1100 B.C. an Assyrian monarch led his troops to the shores of the Mediterranean Sea. These conquests, however, were of a temporary nature. During the second half of the tenth century there began a series of rulers whose conquests during the subsequent century give evidence of a planned program of empire-building. This program was carried out with extraordinary vigor and determination. After securing the back door to Assyria in the high-land regions to the north and east, and after subduing Babylon, the kings pushed westward.

The middle Euphrates region around Gozan (XI:A, C-2) and Haran (XI:A, B-2), and the area east of the watershed in Syria from Hamath to Damascus (XI:A, B 2-3), were in the hands of Aramean invaders, who were destined to flood the whole area with traders and settlers, and after 500 B.C. to make their language its official tongue. During the ninth century Assyria pushed her way through these people to the Mediterranean Sea. The greatest Assyrian em-

67

peror of that century was Shalmaneser III (859-824 B.C.), by whose time the conquering armies were ready to turn southward toward Palestine. In 853 B.C. he met in Syria a great coalition headed by Hadadezer (Ben-hadad) of Damascus. While this battle is not mentioned in the Old Testament, the emperor tells us that next to Damascus the strongest contingents were those of Hamath and of Ahab in Israel, the latter furnishing 2,000 chariots and 10,000 infantry. The Assyrian monarch claimed the victory, but nevertheless was unable to follow up such advantage as he may have gained.

As a result of the religious revolution in Israel, which under Elijah and Elisha not only swept the dynasty of Ahab from the throne but also deposed Ben-hadad of Damascus, the coalition was broken up (II Kings 8:7-15; chs. 9; 10). Shalmaneser was quick to take advantage of this fact, and in 841 B.C. pictured the embassy of Jehu, the new king of Israel, bringing tribute to him (Fig. 49). While he did not capture Damascus, he so weakened that city as to make it a minor power.

But suddenly Assyrian victories were brought to a halt by internal difficulties, and Palestine and Syria had a breathing space of nearly a century's duration. Then another series of vigorous monarchs started anew the relentless push of conquest. Tiglath-pileser III (745-727 B.C.), after consolidating his borders to the east and north, led his armies westward. His policy was to divide the west into subject provinces, each with its own governor, though leaving the native kings on the thrones of certain outlying areas, provided they paid a regular tribute (see Plate VII:C). He also instituted a policy of exchanging large sections of the populations of conquered territories, to break up nationalistic feeling and to make the population less united and more pliable. In 733-732 B.C. he conquered Philistia, took Galilee and Transjordan away from Israel, and destroyed Damascus. The much-reduced Israel, as well as Judah, Ammon, Moab, and Edom, he left under their native rulers, whom he required to pay tribute (cf. II Kings 15:27 ff.; 16:5 ff.; Isa., ch. 7). In 721 B.C. Samaria was destroyed by Sargon II (722-705 B.C.) for rebellion, and 27,290 of its people were exiled, some of them to "the [Valley of the] Habor, the river of Gozan" (II Kings 17:6; III, D-2; XI:A, C-2). In the

FIG. 49. A cast of the Black Obelisk of the Assyrian monarch Shalmaneser III (859–824 B. C.). On this stone the king gave a brief account of his wars, and pictured various nations bringing tribute to him. In the second scene from the top the embassy of Israel is humbly offering to his majesty "the tribute of Jehu," consisting chiefly of silver, gold, and lead vessels and bars. Either Jehu himself or his ambassador is shown kissing the ground at Shalmaneser's feet.

years which followed, people deported from Babylonia, Elam, and Syria were forced to live in Samaria.

In the next century the Assyrian emperors were desperately engaged in a continuous struggle to hold their gains. Repeated threats had to be met from Babylon and Elam on the south (XI:A, C-D 3), from a medley of peoples, including the Medes, on the north and northeast (XI:A, C-D 2-3), from the rising power of Phrygia on the northwest (XI:A, B-2), and from Egyptian intrigue in Palestine on the southwest (XI:A, B 3-4). In 701-700 B.C. Judah barely escaped complete subjugation at the hands of Sennacherib (II Kings 18:13 ff.). As it was, the king claims to have reduced 46 fortified Judean cities, and to have shut up Hezekiah "like a caged bird in Jerusalem." Jerusalem (XI:A, B-3) was saved by payment of a huge tribute. Chief among the Judean strongholds was Lachish, the siege and capture of which was portrayed on a palace relief in Nineveh (XI:A, C-2). In the subsequent reigns of Esarhaddon (681-669 B.C.) and Asshurbanapal (669-626 B.C.; the "Osnappar" of Ezra 4:10), Manasseh of Judah continued to pay tribute, except for a brief rebellion (II Chron. 33:10-13). Nevertheless, the Assyrians, apart from the conquest of Egypt, which they held for a few years only, now found their energies completely absorbed in defensive warfare against southern, eastern, and northern powers. The golden age of the empire was drawing to a close.

The remarkably detailed knowledge which we have about the Assyrians comes largely from vast palaces and imposing temple-towers built by the kings along the Tigris, especially from *Dur Sharrukin* ("Sargonburg"), Nineveh, and Calah (XI:A, C-2). The first was a magnificent royal residence erected by Sargon II on a grander scale than the ancient world had yet seen. It was abandoned, however, by his son Sennacherib, who made Nineveh his capital. This city then became renowned the world over as the symbol of Assyrian power and aggression. It extended some two and a half miles along the Tigris, and the circumference of the inner walls was about eight miles. The palace was a tremendous structure. In one place the excavators cleared seventy-one halls, lined with stone reliefs, nearly two miles in total length, depicting various activities of the king and his armies.

Asshurbanapal also made Nineveh his capital, and the reliefs in his palace represent the finest examples of Assyrian art. This king was much interested in intellectual matters, and took pride in his mastery of the art of writing. One of the greatest discoveries ever made by archaeologists occurred in the unearthing at Nineveh of his great library, composed of some 22,000 clay tablets. Here the king had systematically collected the religious, scientific, and literary works of the past. They represent our chief source of knowledge regarding life and thought in ancient Mesopotamia.

THE BABYLONIAN EMPIRE

On the death of Asshurbanapal in 626 B.C. the great empire of Assyria rapidly fell to pieces. For centuries the Chaldeans, Semitic nomads, had been slowly moving into Babylonia. They now gained control of that country, and began the conquest of Assyria proper. In this they were joined by the Medes, who in 614 B.C. captured Asshur. Forming an alliance, the two then attacked Nineveh, which fell in 612 B.C. This was a momentous date in ancient history. The greatest power which the world had yet known had fallen, and from all the subject peoples arose a chorus of hatred, gratitude, and new hope. To this sternly exultant mood the Hebrew prophet Nahum gives most vivid expression.

The Assyrian army fell back on Haran (XI:B, B-2), and in 609 B.C. the Babylonians attacked. Meanwhile Pharaoh Necho of Egypt marched north through Palestine to aid the Assyrians. King Josiah attempted to halt him at Megiddo, but was killed in the attempt (II Kings 23:29 ff.). The Assyrians were defeated at Haran, and Necho took over their territory in Syria-Palestine. The new Egyptian empire in Asia was short-lived, however, for in 605 B.C. the vigorous Nebuchadnezzar arrived in Syria with a Babylonian army, administered a crushing defeat to the Egyptians at Carchemish (XI:B, B-2), and took over the whole of the west to the border of Egypt. The new hopes which the fall of Assyria had raised among the subject peoples were dashed. Babylon was substituted for Nineveh.

We do not possess detailed information about the conquests of Nebuchadnezzar, because he followed the Babylonian tradition of writing chiefly about his religious and architectural activity, rather than about military exploits. Yet he was certainly the central figure of his time. Syria and Palestine remained vassal territory because there was no great leader to establish a coalition against him. Only Jehoiakim of Judah, with Egyptian encouragement, offered trouble. Judah was promptly besieged in 598 B.C., and the young king Jehoiachin, who had just succeeded his father, was carried into captivity (II Kings, ch. 24). A decade later Judah again rebelled, in spite of strong protests by Jeremiah. This time the country was utterly devastated, and Jerusalem with the Temple was destroyed (II Kings, ch. 25).

Meanwhile most people in Judah still considered the captive Jehoiachin as their legitimate king, and expected his return at any time (Jer. 28:1-4). Documents found at Babylon in the basement of the Palace of Nebuchadnezzar list Jehoiachin, his five sons, and numerous other Judeans, along with people from Philistia, Egypt, and Phoenicia, as receiving regular provisions from the royal storehouse.

Apart from his wars, the chief work of Nebuchadnezzar was the enlargement and beautification of Babylon, which now surpassed Nineveh in architectural glory. He repaired the great Temple of Marduk, the Tower of Babel (see Fig. 11, and p. 24), and erected a vast imperial palace, on top of which, rising terrace upon terrace, was a garden. This place was called "The House at Which Men Marvel," and the "Hanging Gardens" were listed by the Greeks among the Seven Wonders of the World (Figs. 50 and 51).

Commerce, literature, art, and science flourished during this age. The Chaldeans were the founders of astronomy as a science. Careful astronomical observations were continuously kept for over 360 years, and these calculations form the longest series ever made. One great Chaldean astronomer, living shortly after the completion of this period of observation, was able to calculate the length of the year as 365 days, 6 hrs., 15 mins., and 41 secs.—a measurement which the modern telescope has shown to be only 26 mins., 26 secs. too long! His calculations on the diameter of the face of the moon were far more accurate than those of Copernicus. Certain measurements of celestial motions by another Chaldean astronomer actually surpass in accuracy the figures long in practical use among modern astronomers.

THE PERSIAN EMPIRE

During the days of Nebuchadnezzar two powerful empires, the Median and Lydian, existed to the east, north, and northwest of Babylon. By a treaty the boundary between them had been fixed at the Halys River in Asia Minor (Plate XI:B). The Medes, who had captured Asshur in 614 B.C. and assisted the Babylonians in destroying Nineveh in 612 B.C., had their capital at Achmetha (Ecbatana; XI:C, C-2). By 549 B.C. a Persian named Cyrus had united the people of his land and defeated the Median king. The attention of the west was now focused on the career of this extraordinary individual. A Judean prophet rightly interpreted the signs of the times, and saw in Cyrus one anointed of the Lord, who "giveth nations before him, and maketh him rule over kings" (Isa. 41:2; 44:28; 45:1). By 546 B.C. Sepharad or Sardis, the capital of Lydia (XI:C, A-2), had fallen to Cyrus, and Croesus, its king, was a prisoner. Cyrus was then ready to strike at Babylonia; in 539 B.C. he easily defeated the Chaldean army (led by the crown prince Belshazzar? Cf. Dan., ch. 5) and entered Babylon without opposition.

Thus just seventy years after the final Assyrian defeat at Haran in 609 B.C., the days of the Semitic empires were past. The Persian, Greek, and Roman empires were ruled by Indo-Europeans or Aryans. In 525 B.C. Egypt was added to the Persian Empire by Cyrus' son. In the space of twenty-five years the whole civilized east as far as India was brought under the firm control of Persia (Plate XI:C). Repeated

FIG. 50. Ruins of the Ishtar Gate of Babylon. The animals shown were made of highly colored glazed tile. For a reconstruction see Fig. 51.

attempts were made to add Greece (XI:C, A-2) to this empire. One was led by Darius the Great, who was defeated by the Greeks at Marathon in 490 B.C.; another, ten years later, was led by Xerxes, who was defeated in a naval battle off Salamis. Unable to subdue Greece, the Persians nevertheless held a firm hold over Asia for almost two centuries.

The organization of the great empire was a colossal task, brought to completion by Darius the Great (522-486 B.C.). While ruling Egypt and Babylonia directly as actual king, he divided the rest of the empire into twenty "satrapies" or provinces, each under a governor or "satrap"—a development of the earlier Assyrian provincial system. Aramaic, the language of Aramean ("Syrian") traders, which by this time had become the commercial tongue of the Fertile Crescent, was made the official language of government. Stamped coinage, an idea borrowed from Greece, was introduced throughout the empire as a convenience for business and government alike. A fleet was organized, and to provide a sea route from Egypt to Persia, a canal was dug between the Nile and the Red Sea.

Babylon and Susa (Shushan; XI:C, C-3) were used as royal residences. Cyrus had built a palace at Pasargadae, and there he was buried (XI:C, D-3). Darius, however, erected a magnificent palace with attendant buildings at Persepolis (XI:C, D-3), structures which surpassed in grandeur even the work of Nebuchadnezzar in Babylon. It is most unfortunate that Alexander the Great saw fit in 330 B.C. to burn them, leaving only the ruins for the modern excavator to uncover (Fig. 3).

The Assyrian and Babylonian policy of deporting subject peoples was reversed by the Persians, whose enlightened policies won a measure of gratitude from subject peoples. The exiled Jews benefited from this policy, and quite a large number of them returned to the area of Jerusalem, building a new Temple between 520 and 516 B.C. (Ezra, chs. 5; 6), and rebuilding the walls of Jerusalem under Nehemiah's leadership after 445 B.C. (Neh., chs. 2 to 6).

The best of the Persian monarchs felt obligated to rule justly and righteously. Their acts and words set them apart from Assyrian kings

FIG. 51. A reconstruction of ancient Babylon in the time of Nebuchadnezzar, showing a royal procession passing through the Ishtar Gate on its way to the palace. The latter had on its roof the famous "Hanging Gardens," shown in the upper right. In the distant background is the Tower of Babel (see Fig. 11).

in this regard, and the reason is probably to be sought in their religion. Darius and his immediate successors, at least, were followers of Zoroaster, a Median religious reformer who lived about 600 B.C. Zoroaster saw life as a ceaseless struggle between the forces of good and evil. The good, the light, he believed, was a supreme being, named Ahura Mazda. Opposed to him and the helpers he created were the evil spirits; but the good Ahura Mazda would ultimately prevail over them. Zoroaster called men to take their stand on the side of the good, and worship "the righteous Master of Righteousness." The influence of this religion spread widely, and even Judaism by the second century B.C. had borrowed certain conceptions from it.

THE HELLENISTIC EMPIRES

In the fourth century B.C. the center of political power moved westward and Greek culture made a strong though largely futile attempt to penetrate eastward. Culturally, Greece had long been important. Its brilliant cluster of city-states had generated a vitality and originality still unsurpassed. Particularly at Athens (XI:D, A-2) political vigor, expressed in civic interest, extensive sea power, and outreaching colonies, had joined with intellectual and artistic genius to create a permanently stimulating heritage.

An eastward movement of Greek influence may appear strange. Greek colonies and trade had previously been limited to the Mediterranean and the Black Sea (Plate XI:B). Two factors, however, directed attention eastward. The Greek cities in Asia Minor were inevitably bound up with trends farther east. Moreover, the competing city-states of Greece recognized that Persia, which at Marathon and Salamis had tried to conquer the Greeks, was still a threat.

These divided city-states found unity and protection, but only through unwilling subjection to Macedonia (XI:D, A 1-2). Philip of Macedon (359-336 B.C.), whose capital was at Pella (XI:D, A-1), extended his power southward until a decisive battle in 338 B.C. gave him control of all Greece except Sparta (XI:D, A-2).

It fell to Philip's son, Alexander the Great (336-323 B.C.), to carry

out the war Philip had planned against Persia. This brilliant pupil of Aristotle, a provincial governor at sixteen, able general at eighteen, and king at twenty, swiftly won loyalty in Macedonia and Greece. In 334 B.C. he crossed the Hellespont into Asia Minor to challenge Persia. A victory at the River Granicus (XI:D, A-2) opened Asia Minor to conquest. The next spring, he passed through the Cilician Gates (XI:D, B-2; Fig. 48) and decisively defeated the Persian army of Darius at Issus (XI:D, B-2). Turning south, he subdued Syria, Palestine, and Egypt (XI:D, B 2-4). At the western mouth of the Nile he founded the famous city of Alexandria (XI:D, A-3). Returning northward, he crossed the Euphrates at Thapsacus (XI:D, B-2), moved east, and in 331 B.C., at Gaugamela, near Arbela (XI:D, C-2), he crushed the remaining forces of Darius and was master of the Persian Empire.

Alexander continued eastward. His route took him through Babylon (XI:D, C-3), Susa (XI:D, C-3), Persepolis (XI:D, D-3), Ecbatana (XI:D, C-2), and Zadracarta (XI:D, D-2). At Prophthasia, in Drangiana (XI:D, E-3), when it had become apparent that he wanted to unite East and West in one great brotherhood, revolt was brewing among his followers, but he crushed it, and moved on into Bactria (XI:D, E-1), Sogdiana (XI:D, E-1), and India. There his troops mutinied and refused to go further. He returned westward, moving his troops partly by sea and partly by a land route through Gedrosia (XI:D, E-3) and Carmania (XI:D, D-3). At Babylon death ended his plan to create a world brotherhood with a culture prevailingly Greek (323 B.C.). He had proved a military genius; he had planted Greek cities and Greek influence in a wide area. But he made no deep and lasting imprint on the eastern regions which he had conquered. His work and the later Roman conquest did, however, determine the direction in which Judaism and Christianity were later to spread.

At his death there was no logical successor to hold the empire intact, and Alexander's generals fell to fighting among themselves. One of the many rivals, Ptolemy Lagi, emerged with secure possession of Egypt. Seleucus, another general, was able in 312 B.C. to establish the Seleucid dynasty in Syria and the east. The battle of Ipsus (XI:D, B-2) in 301 B.C. finally excluded from Asia the Antigonid dynasty, which henceforth contented itself with Macedonia. By 275 B.C. the situation shown on Plate XI:D had resulted. Three great empires existed, and they continued in essentially the same form until the eastern expansion of Rome absorbed them one by one. In Macedonia, Antigonus Gonatas ruled (283-239 B.C.). He was not able, however, to bring Greece under his control. In Egypt the Ptolemaic dynasty was firmly established, and Ptolemy II Philadelphus (285-246 B.C.) ruled also Cyrene, the southern part of the Aegean Sea, Lycia, Cyprus, and Palestine.

The dry climate of Egypt has permitted the survival of thousands of papyri, and from these records much of our knowledge of ancient life and history is derived. Tradition dates the translation of the Pentateuch from Hebrew into Greek in the reign of Ptolemy Philadelphus. The number of Greek-speaking Jews in Egypt, especially in Alexandria, was increasing, and they needed a Greek translation of their Scriptures.

The greater part of Alexander's empire, however, was in the hand of the Seleucid Antiochus I (280-262 B.C.), whose capital was at Antioch in Syria (XI:D, B-2). Northern Asia Minor, including Bithynia under Nicomedes (XI:D, B-1), Pontus under Mithridates (XI:D, B-1), and Galatia (XI:D, B-2), where the invading Gauls had just settled, was outside his control. But his empire extended from Thrace in Europe to the borders of India, although the effectiveness of his control over the eastern provinces is open to doubt. These eastern areas were soon to be lost, and Parthia (XI:D, D-2) was soon to begin its rise to power.

At this time Palestine was fulfilling its usual role of border region. Ptolemy Lagi had obtained control of it when Alexander's empire began to break up, and Ptolemaic control, though challenged more than once by the Seleucids, continued until 198 B.C., when Antiochus III added Palestine to the Seleucid empire. From that time until the coming of the Romans in 63 B.C. the history of Palestine was closely linked with that of Syria (see pp. 73 ff.).

PLATE XI

PLATE XII

A

PALESTINE
IN THE
MACCABEAN PERIOD
(168-63 B.C.)

Copyright, The Westminster Press
International Copyright Secured. All Rights Reserved

SCALE OF MILES
0 5 10 20 30

BOUNDARY LINE SHOWS MAXIMUM
EXTENT OF MACCABEAN KINGDOM
UNDER ALEXANDER JANNAEUS
(103-76 B.C.)

KINGDOM OF
ALEXANDER JANNAEUS

FREE CITY

CITIES AND TOWNS

B

PALESTINE
UNDER
HEROD THE GREAT
(40-4 B.C.)

Copyright, The Westminster Press
International Copyright Secured. All Rights Reserved

SCALE OF MILES
0 5 10 20 30

KINGDOM OF
HEROD THE GREAT

DECAPOLIS

FREE CITY

CITIES AND TOWNS

C

PALESTINE
UNDER
HEROD AGRIPPA I
(41-44 A.D.)

Copyright, The Westminster Press
International Copyright Secured. All Rights Reserved

SCALE OF MILES
0 5 10 20 30

KINGDOM OF HEROD AGRIPPA I

DECAPOLIS

FREE CITY

CITIES AND TOWNS

D

PALESTINE
IN THE TIME OF
HEROD AGRIPPA II
AND THE
ROMAN PROCURATORS
(54-66 A.D.)

Copyright, The Westminster Press
International Copyright Secured. All Rights Reserved

SCALE OF MILES
0 5 10 20 30

RULED BY
ROMAN PROCURATOR

DECAPOLIS

KINGDOM OF
HEROD AGRIPPA II

FREE CITY

CITIES AND TOWNS

MACCABEAN AND HERODIAN PALESTINE

PLATE XII

TO GRASP the importance of studying the history of Maccabean and Herodian Palestine, one need only review the outstanding religious developments of the period. At least one Old Testament book, Daniel, was written. Formation of the Hebrew canon of the Old Testament was practically completed. The Pharisee sect arose, and the rabbis developed much of the oral tradition which still gives orthodox Judaism its basic character. Above all, the Christian movement appeared and entered upon its missionary career. Obviously neither Judaism nor Christianity can be understood without careful study of the history of this significant period.

PALESTINE UNDER SYRIA

During the decades preceding the Maccabean period, the struggle between Syria and Egypt for the control of Palestine came to a decisive issue (see p. 70). For over a century after Alexander the Great's empire had been divided among his generals, Egypt dominated Palestine. Syria, however, was constantly seeking to extend its power southward, and under Antiochus III (223-187 B.C.) finally succeeded. His first effort, to be sure, was thwarted when in 217 B.C. he was beaten in battle at Raphia (Plate XII:A, A-6). In 198 B.C., however, he defeated the Egyptian forces at Paneas (XII:B, D-2) and became master of Palestine.

The policy of the Syrian rulers was to promote the influences which would effect unity of culture in their territory. Hence they looked with disapproval upon the strangely different Jewish religion, and were ready to further any steps which would strengthen Hellenistic culture in Palestine. In this effort they found many allies among the Jewish people themselves. Even some of the younger priests at Jerusalem took up the Greek language, athletic sports, and manner of dress. The Jews were split over the issue.

THE MACCABEAN REVOLT

This was the situation when Antiochus IV, called Epiphanes or "(God-) Manifest" (175-163 B.C.), became impatient with the stubborn opponents of his policy and determined to stamp out the Jewish religion. In 168 or 167 B.C. he desecrated the Jewish Temple at Jerusalem, prohibited the sacrifices, and made possession of a copy of the Law, keeping of the Sabbath, and the practice of circumcision crimes for which the penalty was death. Representatives of the king erected heathen altars in various places and tested the loyalty of the Jews by requiring them to offer pagan sacrifice.

Obviously this was a life-and-death struggle for Judaism, and resistance soon appeared. The revolt began at the little town of Modein (XII:A, C-5), in the hill country northwest of Jerusalem. Here lived the aged Mattathias, a priest of the Hasmonean house. When summoned to sacrifice he refused, killed a Jew who was willing to abandon his ancestral faith, and also slew the Syrian officer. Then, with his five sons, he fled into the hills, where he was joined by many who were ready to die rather than give up their faith.

Such loyal Jews were in a difficult position. They faced civil war with other Jews, and they were in revolt against the king. Mattathias was too old to lead the movement; on his deathbed, shortly after the revolt began, he appointed his son Judas to captain the rebel forces. From the title given Judas comes the name Maccabean; Judas was called Maccabaeus, which is usually explained to mean "Hammerer" and to refer to his sudden, heavy blows against the enemy. But it would be quite wrong to think of Judas as the general of a large and disciplined army. The Syrian forces controlled most of Palestine, and Judas depended much upon sudden thrusts and brilliant surprise attacks. Yet the desperation of the Jews, who were fighting not only

for their lives but also for their faith, made them the equal of an army many times their number.

The campaign of Judas took place mainly in the region of Judaea. Employing the methods of guerrilla warfare, he won victories at Beth-horon, Emmaus (XII:D, C-5), and Bethsura (XII:A, C-5). When the Syrian leaders withdrew to Antioch to prepare greater forces for the war, Judas led his forces to Jerusalem, and although the Syrians still held the Citadel, he cleansed the Temple of pagan objects, rebuilt the altar, and resumed the sacrifices in December, 164 B.C. Since that time the Jews have observed the Feast of Dedication, or Hanukkah, in memory of this occasion. The profanation of the Temple and the struggle of the Maccabeans to rescue it from the control of the Gentiles is the background of The Book of Daniel (c. 166 B.C.).

Judas and his brothers next made expeditions to Gilead, Galilee, and Idumaea to rescue loyal Jews. In other words, for a brief time the band of loyal Jews was limited to the central part of Judaea, and did not constitute the whole of the population even in that small area. Judas, however, after bringing to safety Jews in other regions who were in danger from the Gentiles or more often from their own countrymen, had to meet the armies of the Syrian king, who was now determined to crush the growing rebellion. His general, Lysias, forced Judas to withdraw from battle at Bethzacharia (XII:A, C-5), where Eleazar, the brother of Judas, lost his life. Bethsura (Fig. 53), an important military center which changed hands several times in these decades, had to surrender to the Syrians. Then, however, news of a rival claimant to the rule of Syria forced Lysias to make peace with Judas and grant religious freedom to the Jews.

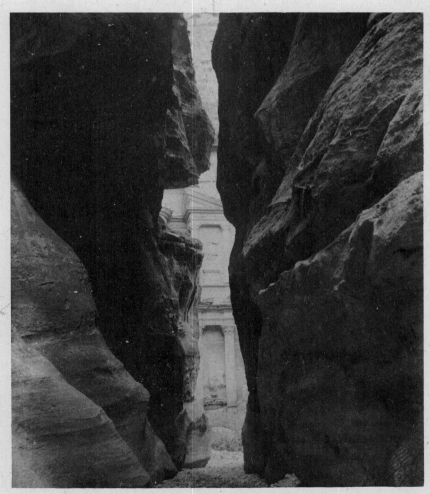

FIG. 52. The *Sîq* and *el-Khazneh* at Petra. The approach to this site of rugged grandeur and great defensive strength is through the *Wâdî Mûsâ*, which for a mile and a quarter forms a narrow gorge, the *Sîq*, with side walls 100 to 160 feet high. At a final turn there comes into view the *Khazneh*, or "Treasury" of Pharaoh, as the Arabs call it. This famous temple, whose front is carved in the red sandstone side of the valley, is over ninety feet high. It is dated in the second century A.D. or earlier.

THE FIGHT FOR POLITICAL FREEDOM

This marked the achievement of the aim with which the revolt began. However, it did not satisfy the Maccabean leaders. They began to work for political independence. One thing which they undertook was to gain support from the Romans; to this end they concluded a league of friendship with the Romans about 161 B.C. This league, however, was of no immediate benefit to the Jews; the Romans did not intervene in Palestine until they were ready to take it over and control it (63 B.C.). The immediate future held in store more conflict with the Syrians, who were called in by the pro-Syrian party of the Jews to fight against Judas. After an indecisive fight at Capharsalama (XII:A, C-5), the Syrians were defeated and their general Nicanor killed at Adasa (XII:A, C-5). But the forces of Judas had been hard hit. When Bacchides came down from Syria with another army and met Judas at Elasa (XII:A, C-5), few Jews rallied to the battle. Judas was killed and his army crushed (160 B.C.).

His brother Jonathan assumed the leadership, but had pitifully few soldiers to support him. He was, indeed, almost a fugitive, and at first could wage only furtive guerrilla warfare. For a time he dwelt at Machmas, i.e., Michmash (XII:A, C-5). His first successes were due not so much to Jewish military prowess as to Syria's internal troubles, which so occupied the Syrians that Jonathan was able to get control of all Jerusalem except the Citadel. Hard-pressed by their troubles at home, the Syrians also evacuated many of their strongholds in Judaea, although they did not give up the important fortress at Bethsura. Jonathan took Joppa (XII:A, B-4), won a victory near Azotus (XII:A, B-5), and was given Accaron, i.e., Ekron (XII:A, B-5). In an attempt to strengthen his political position, he renewed the alliance of the Jews with Rome.

Emboldened by success, Jonathan went to meet the Syrian general Trypho at Scythopolis (XII:A, D-4). Trypho, however, avoided battle; instead he enticed Jonathan to a parley at Ptolemais (XII:A, C-3), and treacherously took him prisoner. He then began to move against Jerusalem, using his captive as a hostage. Jonathan's brother Simon, however, assumed command of the Jews, and Trypho, finding himself balked, finally put Jonathan to death (142 B.C.).

Simon gained from one of the rival claimants to the Syrian throne the grant of political freedom (142 B.C.), and the Jews dated a new era from this year. Nevertheless, as soon as Syria's internal affairs permitted, her leaders resumed attempts to subjugate the Jews. In the meantime, however, Simon won noteworthy successes. He finally forced the Syrian garrison out of the Citadel at Jerusalem. He took Gazara (XII:A, B-5), Joppa, and Bethsura, and is said to have made Joppa a port for Jewish use. At Joppa he defeated the Syrian general Cendebaeus, who attempted to re-establish the Syrian rule of

Palestine. His successful career was soon cut short (134 B.C.) by the treachery of his son-in-law Ptolemy, who murdered Simon and two of his sons at Dok (XII:A, C-5), near Jericho, and sent agents to murder Simon's other son, John Hyrcanus, who was at Gazara. John, however, learned of the plot, and by hastening to Jerusalem gained control of that city before Ptolemy's supporters reached it. He was promptly recognized as the rightful successor of his father, and became both ruler and high priest.

THE PERIOD OF TERRITORIAL EXPANSION

John Hyrcanus had a long and successful reign (134-104 B.C.). In its early years he was forced to admit the control of the Syrian king for a time, but he later renounced this control and extended the range of Jewish power. For instance, he gained the mastery of Medeba (XII:A, D-5), east of the Jordan. He broke the resistance of the region of Samaria, and captured Sichem (XII:A, C-4). After seizing the Samaritan temple on Mount Gerizim, he destroyed this bitter rival of the Temple in Jerusalem (cf. John 4:20). He took the city of Samaria (XII:A, C-4) and razed it He also captured Scythopolis and successfully asserted control over the Plain of Jezreel.

His son and successor Aristobulus I ruled but a year (104-103 B.C.). He extended Jewish control northward to Galilee, which Judas had abandoned to the Gentiles. Josephus states that Aristobulus was the first Maccabean to assume the title of king.

In the reign of Alexander Jannaeus (103-76 B.C.) the territory under Maccabean control reached its maximum extent, approximately that shown on Plate XII:A. His reign was by no means without its conflicts. When he attacked Ptolemais, that city appealed to Ptolemy of Egypt for help. Ptolemy saw a chance to extend his power to the north, and undertook against Alexander Jannaeus a futile campaign which included battles at Asochis (XII:A, C-3) in Galilee and Asophon (XII:A, D-4) in the Jordan Valley. Alexander was able to take Gadara (XII:A, D-3) and Amathus (XII:A, D-4) on the east side of the Jordan. In the southwestern corner of Judaea he took Raphia, Anthedon, and Gaza (XII:A, A 5-6). By this time, however, the worldly character of Maccabean ambitions and methods had grown until Alexander was using foreign mercenary soldiers to aid him in his warfare. The movement which started out to protect religious freedom had become so secular and nationalistic that many of his devout countrymen supported the Syrian ruler against him. He almost lost his power in a battle with the Syrian Demetrius at Sichem, but was saved by last-minute support from some Jews who at first fought against him.

Further difficulty for Alexander arose when the Syrian ruler came boldly into Palestine to meet Aretas, the Nabatean king, in battle. The latter defeated and killed the Syrian king, and later overcame

FIG. 53. Beth-zur (Bethsura). Air view while the 1931 excavation was in progress. Particularly during the Maccabean period this isolated hill was an important military stronghold. Note the hilly character of the Judean upland, and the way the rocks are cleared from the field and used in soil conservation.

Alexander in battle at Adida (XII:D, B-5), a town near Lydda in Judaea. By some concession Alexander induced Aretas to withdraw, and continued his attempt at further conquest until on a campaign against Ragaba (XII:A, D-4), east of the Jordan, he died.

His widow Alexandra succeeded him (76-67 B.C.). Upon her death her two sons fought for the rule; Hyrcanus II was defeated near Jericho (XII:A, C-5) and Aristobulus II gained the throne. At this point a decisive change occurred. The Idumaean Antipater took the side of Hyrcanus. He saw that he could gain power for himself by championing the cause of Hyrcanus, and enlisted Aretas III of the Nabatean Kingdom in an attempt to put Hyrcanus on the Jewish throne. Thus backed, Hyrcanus brought forces to Jerusalem and sought to gain control of that city. At this juncture both Aristobulus and Hyrcanus appealed to Pompey, the Roman general who at the time was in Syria. He came to Jerusalem and took control of it for the Romans. This was in 63 B.C. The Jews never had even the semblance of independence after that date.

ROME TAKES CONTROL

Pompey removed from Jewish control the coastal cities, Samaria, and the non-Jewish cities on the east of the Jordan. However, he left Judaea, Idumaea, Galilee, and Peraea under Jewish rule. The entire region was put under the supervision of the Roman representative in Syria. Thus the link with Syria, which had continued to a greater or lesser extent since 198 B.C., continued in a new form under Roman control.

Rome was entering upon the series of internal struggles which finally resulted in the establishment of the empire. Pompey was defeated by Julius Caesar, who made Hyrcanus II the ethnarch of the Jews. Caesar recognized, however, that the brains behind Hyrcanus were those of Antipater, and he therefore made Antipater procurator of Judaea. He also gave Joppa back to the Jews (47 B.C.). Antipater used his sons Phasael and Herod in the administration of his territory; Herod showed special skill and energy in suppressing brigands in Galilee.

Caesar was assassinated, however, in 44 B.C., and Palestine again suffered from uncertainty. Cassius demanded seven hundred talents from Judaea, which Antipater raised and paid. Shortly thereafter (43 B.C.) Antipater was murdered, and Antigonus, son of Aristobulus II, tried to gain control of Judaea. To further his purpose he called upon the Parthians, who at the time were trying to expand westward into Syria, and the Parthians helped him to gain control of Jerusalem (40 B.C.). This temporary success proved his undoing. The Parthians were not able to maintain their westward thrust, and the Romans naturally did not want a Parthian ally in control of Judaea. Herod sought the help of Rome, and in 40 B.C. was declared king of Judaea; the term Judaea was here used in its wider sense, practically equivalent to Palestine. It was three years, however, before he was able, with the help of Roman forces supplied from Syria, to establish effective rule over all his realm. Thus he held his kingdom by the grant and power of Rome.

THE REIGN OF HEROD THE GREAT

The reign of Herod the Great lasted until his death in 4 B.C. It is notable in history as the reign under which Jesus was born (Matt. 2:1). The early years of his rule were not easy. The Roman Antony gave Cleopatra the coastal cities of Palestine and the commercially lucrative balsam groves near Jericho.

When Octavian, later known as Augustus, defeated Antony and became ruler of Rome (31 B.C.), he confirmed Herod's position as king of Judaea. After the death of Cleopatra in 30 B.C. Herod also received the cities which Antony had given her. He further received a number of other cities—Gadara, Hippos (XII:B, D-3), Samaria, Gaza, Anthedon, Joppa, and Strato's Tower (XII:B, B-4). These cities, which had been taken from the Jews in order to protect their Gentile population and culture, could be given to Herod because, while he sought to keep on good terms with the Jews, he also was eager to promote Hellenistic culture and loyalty to Rome. A short time later,

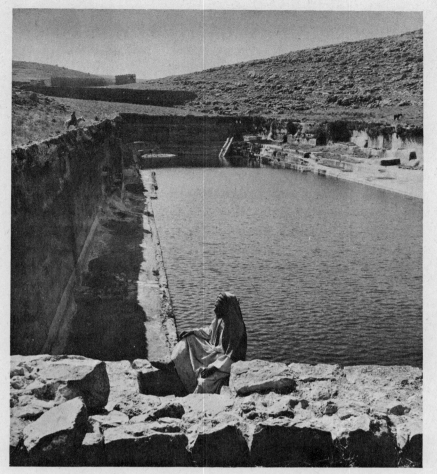

FIG. 54. One of "Solomon's Pools," so called under the influence of Eccl. 2: 6. Two aqueducts were built to carry the water from the three pools to Jerusalem, seven miles distant. The date of pools and aqueducts is uncertain, but the pools were probably built not later than the second century B. C. It appears that Pontius Pilate built or repaired one of the aqueducts.

for helping the Romans, Herod was given Trachonitis, Batanaea, and Auranitis (XII:B, D-F 2-3). In 20 B.C., it seems, he was given that part of the former lands of Zenodorus which lay between Galilee and northern Trachonitis. His kingdom thus took on the wide extent shown in Plate XII:B.

Indeed, Herod seemed on the verge of becoming even more widely influential. Augustus appointed him procurator of all Syria. However, his effective power was exercised in Palestine and the wider extension of it did not materialize. To add distinction to his rule and to promote Hellenistic influences, Herod undertook numerous ambitious building projects. He rebuilt Samaria and named it Sebaste, a name it still holds. He rebuilt Strato's Tower on a grand scale, and named it Caesarea in honor of the emperor. Antipatris (XII:B, B-4) in the Coastal Plain and Phasaelis (XII:B, C-4) in the Jordan Valley he laid out and named after his father and brother, respectively. He improved Anthedon and renamed it Agrippias or Agrippium, but the name soon fell into disuse. He constructed many fortresses for the defense of his territory—Alexandrium (XII:B, C-4), Hyrcania (XII:B, C-5), Herodium (XII:B, C-5), Masada (XII:B, C-6), and Machaerus (XII:B, D-5); at the first two of these he built palaces.

One of his most ambitious projects, never finished in his lifetime, was the rebuilding of the Temple in Jerusalem. This was begun in 20-19 B.C. The main building was soon finished, but the outlying structures were not completed until A.D. 64, only a few years before the whole was destroyed (A.D. 70). Herod was not content, however, to build magnificent cities and buildings in Palestine. With the taxes from his burdened subjects he constructed buildings and made gifts not only in many cities near Palestine, such as Damascus (XII:B, E-2), Tyre (XII:B, C-2), and Sidon (XII:B, C-1), but also in places as far away as Rhodes and Athens. He thus sought to make his zeal for Hellenistic architecture and culture widely known and recognized.

THE KINGDOM OF HEROD AGRIPPA I

The terms of Herod's will are described in the discussion which accompanies Plate XIV (see p. 84). His son Archelaus was deposed from the rule of Judaea, Samaria, and Idumaea after ten years, and from A.D. 6 to 41 Roman procurators ruled this area. Herod Antipas governed Galilee and Peraea as tetrarch from 4 B.C. until exiled in A.D. 39. A third son of Herod the Great, Philip, was tetrarch of the region east and northeast of the Sea of Galilee from 4 B.C. until his death in A.D. 34. Plate XIV depicts the situation in the time of Jesus' ministry. We here resume the story with the rule of Herod Agrippa I (A.D. 41-44).

Agrippa, extravagant and impoverished grandson of Herod the Great, held ambitions which long seemed doomed to disappointment. Indeed, in Rome he was once imprisoned by the Emperor Tiberius for remarking that he wished Tiberius would die, so that Caligula could succeed him. When Caligula did become emperor in 37 B.C., he released Agrippa and made him king of both the former tetrarchy of Philip and the region Lysanias had ruled in Abilene (XII:C, E-1). This aroused the jealousy of Herodias (Mark 6:17), who urged her husband, Herod Antipas, to go to Rome and ask for the title of king instead of tetrarch. Upon arrival there, however, he was accused of plotting against the emperor, was deposed and banished to Gaul. Galilee and Peraea were added to Agrippa's realm.

Agrippa had little zeal to prove a good ruler, and spent much time in Rome. He was there in the last days of Caligula's life, and induced the emperor, who had decreed that his statue must be set up in the Temple at Jerusalem, to revoke the order. When Claudius succeeded Caligula (A.D. 41), Agrippa was again fortunate in having a friend as emperor. Claudius added to Agrippa's kingdom the territory of Judaea and Samaria. Thus in A.D. 41 Agrippa was king over all the territory which his grandfather, Herod the Great, had ruled; in addition, his kingdom included Abilene. It was this Agrippa who persecuted the Christians and executed James the son of Zebedee and imprisoned Peter (Acts 12:2-4). His reign, however, was short; he died a painful death at Caesarea, according to both The Acts (ch. 12:20-23) and the Jewish historian Josephus.

HEROD AGRIPPA II AND THE ROMAN PROCURATORS

When Herod Agrippa I died in A.D. 44, his son Herod Agrippa II was but seventeen years old. Since it did not seem wise to entrust power to one so young, Palestine was put under a Roman procurator. The young man was not forgotten, however, and in c. A.D. 50 he was made king of Chalcis, a territory just to the north of Abilene. The procurators Cuspius Fadus and Tiberius Alexander seem to have had no great trouble, but under Cumanus (A.D. 48-52) friction led to outbreaks at Jerusalem and Samaria. Felix, under whom Paul was imprisoned at Jerusalem and sent to Caesarea (Acts 21:27 to 24:27), was procurator from A.D. 52 to about A.D. 60.

By this time Agrippa II was coming into prominence (see XII:D). In A.D. 53, he had been transferred by Rome from the kingdom of Chalcis to a kingdom which included not only the former tetrarchy of Philip, east and northeast of the Sea of Galilee, but also Abilene. When Nero became emperor in A.D. 54, he added to Agrippa's kingdom Tarichaea and Tiberias (XII:D, D-3) in Galilee, and in Peraea, Abila and Julias (XII:D, D-5), with the villages round about. Agrippa appears to have retained his power until his death.

Felix was succeeded by Porcius Festus, who was procurator from about A.D. 60 to 62. It was before Festus that Paul made his defense and appealed to Caesar (Acts 25:1-12). The next procurator was Albinus (A.D. 62-64). Before the arrival of Albinus in Palestine the Jewish high priest had instigated the murder of James the brother of the Lord, the leader of the Christian group in Jerusalem. Friction between the Jews and the Romans grew under these final procurators, and under Gessius Florus (A.D. 64-66) it finally flamed into open rebellion.

Neither the power of Florus nor the influence of Herod Agrippa II, who had considerable weight with the Jews, could quiet the people. The Roman legate in Syria attempted to intervene. He took Sepphoris (XII:D, C-3) in Galilee, but was routed at Beth-horon (XII:D, C-5). The Jewish rebels seized Masada (XII:D, C-6) and organized resistance in other parts of the country. Josephus, a young Jerusalem priest, was sent to Galilee to lead activities against the Romans. He competed with John of Gischala (XII:D, C-2) for the Jewish following until captured by the Roman general Vespasian at Jotapata (XII:D, C-3). Josephus then became a champion of the Roman cause, and sought to induce his countrymen to submit. Later at Rome he wrote the history of his people, and thereby provided one of our most important sources concerning ancient Jewish history.

The Romans completed the subjugation of Galilee in A.D. 67. In A.D. 68 Vespasian took Gadara (XII:D, D-3), Antipatris (XII:D, B-4), and Emmaus (XII:D, B-5), overran Idumaea and Samaria, and took Jericho and Adida (XII:D, B-5). In other words, he overcame all organized resistance outside of Jerusalem which might harass him when he took up the siege of the capital city itself. The death of Nero, however, in A.D. 68, interrupted the campaign; Vespasian's troops proclaimed him emperor, and little more was done to quell the Jewish revolt until Vespasian was firmly established as emperor at Rome. The Jews meanwhile quarreled among themselves and became weaker. Titus, Vespasian's son, took up the siege of Jerusalem in A.D. 70, and succeeded in capturing the city after hard fighting. The Temple was destroyed and has never been rebuilt. Upon the occasion of his triumph in Rome the army of Titus carried vessels from the Temple, and the Triumphal Arch of Titus, which still stands in Rome (Fig. 58), pictures the procession and tokens of victory.

The capture of Jerusalem was the decisive victory of the war, which ended with the taking of certain fortresses, such as Herodium, Machaerus, and finally Masada. Roman troops were quartered at Jerusalem. Decades later, under the Emperor Hadrian (A.D. 117-138), another revolt took place about A.D. 132-135. It was led by Bar-Cochba. When it had been crushed, Hadrian carried out the plan he had already conceived, and rebuilt Jerusalem as a Gentile city. He called it Aelia Capitolina, and no Jew was permitted even to enter it. Although this severe exclusion was relaxed in later centuries, the Jewish state remains but a memory—except to some who see it as a luring dream of the future.

FIG. 55. View across Lake Huleh, seven feet above sea level, to Mount Hermon, whose heights, c. 9,100 feet above sea level, are always snow-capped. Note the high land east of Lake Huleh.

THE ROMAN EMPIRE AT THE BIRTH OF JESUS

PLATE XIII

THE rise of Rome to world power made Europe the center of political history. Prior to the emergence of Rome as a rival for empire, Asia had been the home of the most vigorous ruling powers. Alexander the Great transferred the focal point of history to southeastern Europe for a few brief years; but as a result of his attempt to extend his rule east to India the European portion of his empire was overshadowed, and when his territory was divided up after his death, Syria and Egypt became more important than Macedonia. It fell to Rome to effect the long lasting location of political dominance in Europe.

THE RISE OF THE ROMAN EMPIRE

In the early centuries of its history the city of Rome (Roma, Plate XIII, C-2) had little more than local importance. By 338 B.C., however, she had ended the Latin League by imposing her rule on its other members. She was then undisputed mistress of all Latium, the southern part of Etruria, and the northern section of Campania; in other words, she controlled about half of the western portion of the Italian peninsula. At the outbreak of the First Punic War in 264 B.C., when the serious challenge to Roman power by Carthage (Carthago, XIII, B-2) had to be met, almost all of the peninsula of Italy up to the valley of the Po River (Padus, XIII, Inset: F-3) was already firmly under Roman control.

The next two centuries were a time of spectacular expansion. Once Carthage had been defeated and destroyed, no powerful rival existed in the Mediterranean area, and Rome extended her rule in all directions. In 63 B.C. Pompey completed his work of taking over the eastern Mediterranean lands, including Palestine. The Roman power was then acknowledged in a series of provinces, protectorates, and client states which ringed the Mediterranean and made it indeed what the Romans liked to call it, *Mare Nostrum* ("Our Sea").

The empire did not reach its largest extent until A.D. 117, under the Emperor Trajan (A.D. 98-117). He added Dacia (XIII, D 1-2), Armenia (XIII, F-2), Assyria, Mesopotamia (XIII, E-F 2-3), and Arabia, the former Nabataea (XIII, E-3), to the list of Roman provinces. Nevertheless, the essential outlines of the empire were established by the beginning of the Christian era. All of northern Africa was under direct or indirect control. Europe west of the Rhine (Rhenus) and south of the Danube (Danuvius) was subject to the Roman will. Practically all of Asia Minor, as well as Syria and Palestine, was Roman territory. Plate XIII depicts the outreach of Rome at that time. Except for the Parthian Empire on the eastern frontier (XIII, E-H 2-3) and the turbulent tribes of northern Europe east of the Rhine (XIII, Inset, E-F 1-2), there was no serious threat to Roman domination.

THE EMPEROR AUGUSTUS

The development of Rome from city-state to world empire inevitably compelled alteration of her original political structure. In the earliest times the patricians had governed. Generations of determined struggle enabled the plebeians to gain a fair measure of participation in government, and by 366 B.C. their right to hold high office had been established. The machinery of government was that of a city-state. There were a popular assembly and various elective officers, most important of whom were two consuls who held office for a single year. In case of emergency one of the consuls could appoint a dictator. There was a senate, which, since it was composed of leading men and included those who had held high office, contained experienced leaders.

Nevertheless, the system devised for a city-state was not well adapted to efficient imperial administration. With the expansion of Roman control, the administrative problems which the Government faced grew increasingly complex and heavy. As a consequence, the republic fell into difficulties, and by the first century B.C. the situation was acute. Strong men began to emerge and exercise special powers. One of these was Pompey, who in 67 B.C. was entrusted with the task of stamping out piracy in the eastern Mediterranean. He successfully concluded this campaign and extended the power of Rome to the east.

Shortly thereafter Julius Caesar proved to be a leader of outstanding military and governmental talents. After his successful campaign in Gaul and his less fruitful campaigns in Britain, he gained the ascendancy over his chief rival, Pompey, became dictator of Rome, and no doubt would have developed the republic into an empire had

FIG. 56. The Appian Way. This, the oldest of the famous Roman roads, was begun in 312 B.C. It originally ran south from Rome to Capua, but was later extended until it reached Brundisium. In places the ancient road is still in use. In the background, one of the aqueducts by which water was carried into Rome on a line of arches.

not his life been cut short by assassination in 44 B.C. His death led, not to restoration of the republic, but to further intrigues for control of the empire. The republic, for all practical purposes, was already dead. After a time of confusion, in which rival alliances of competing candidates fought for power, Octavian finally crushed his most formidable opponent, Mark Antony, and emerged as virtual emperor.

It is difficult to determine the date which marked the actual beginning of the empire. Octavian's strategy was to maintain the forms of the republic; for example, in 22 B.C., several years after he was in complete control, he refused to accept the position of dictator and consul for life. Nevertheless, the main dates which mark the establishment of his reign are clear. The battle of Actium (XIII, C-2) in 31 B.C. was a decisive defeat for Antony, who committed suicide the next year. Thus in 30 B.C. the last strong rival was removed, and in the same year tribunitian power was conferred on Octavian for life. However, the actual start of imperial rule may be dated in 27 B.C., when, in an Act of Settlement which ostensibly restored the republic and returned the power of rule to the senate, Octavian received control of all the difficult provinces and was given the name Augustus. From this time he carefully kept the control of the empire in his hands, while his cautious and outwardly conservative methods prevented any effective protest against his assumption of permanent supreme control.

Augustus was an able ruler. He organized a permanent standing army and placed its legions where danger was likely to arise. He traveled extensively throughout the empire, organizing the provinces and settling basic problems of administration. Something like eleven years of his reign were spent outside of Rome, a fact which witnesses to the care he devoted to provincial control. He was perhaps too cautious in failing to press a campaign for subjugation of the central European tribes, which were thus left to destroy the empire in a later century; he decided against further efforts to conquer Germania (XIII, Inset: E-F 1-2) after a rather unsuccessful beginning. His deci-

FIG. 57. The Roman Emperor Augustus. Photograph of a statue now in the Vatican in Rome.

sion on this point may be criticized, but he gave peace to a war-weary empire and stability to the Roman government.

THE ARMY

The power of Rome was never based upon its navy. Indeed, after the establishment of the empire there was little need for a strong naval force. Rome controlled the entire Mediterranean area and no naval power existed to challenge her rule of the sea. The army, therefore, was the basis of the Roman empire.

In the days of the republic the army was a citizen's militia, in which the Roman served only temporarily and as needed in emergency. The growth of the empire, however, called for a more permanent military force, and the Roman general Marius, in the war against Jugurtha in 107 B.C., developed what was practically a permanent professional army. During the period of the civil wars in the first century B.C., great numbers of men were brought under arms, but Augustus retired many, with proper provision for their livelihood, and organized his standing army on a much smaller scale.

The policy of Augustus was to station the Roman legions where revolt or invasion was to be feared. A quick survey of their stations shortly before his death in A.D. 14 will show this. In Spain (XIII, A 1-2), which had only recently been completely subjugated and organized, there were three legions. The Rhine front had four in the lower region and four in the upper Rhine district. Along the Danube three were located in Pannonia (XIII, C-1), two in Moesia (XIII, D-2), and two in Illyricum or Dalmatia (XIII, C 1-2). In the east, where Parthia was a constant threat, Syria (XIII, E 2-3) had four legions. Egypt (XIII, D-E 3-4), vital for grain and commerce, had two. The province of Africa (XIII, B-C 2-3) had one. The legions were thus used to guard the frontiers; the location of four in Syria indicates the military danger in that area and suggests the political tension in the region where the Christian movement had its origin.

The legion contained ten cohorts of infantry, each cohort having 480 men; it had also a cavalry company and an artillery unit. It was made up of Italians in the early empire; but auxiliaries enlisted from other regions were attached, so that the total personnel of a legion force amounted to about 10,000 men. Important among the officers of the legion were the centurions. As the name indicates, each commanded a company of a hundred men. It is not surprising that the New Testament always speaks of centurions with respect; they were the key men in the practical functioning of the legion. Rulers of client states, such as Herod Antipas, appear to have organized their forces on the Roman model (cf. Luke 7:2 ff.).

The empire had other police forces, noteworthy among which was the Praetorian Guard at Rome, probably referred to in Phil. 1:13.

ADMINISTRATION OF PROVINCES

Roman influence usually extended much further than the limits of formal organized control. Particularly in the early stages of domination in a border area, the Romans were content with indirect rule, and generally preferred to support a local ruler who was loyal to Rome and acceptable to the native population. The use of the Herods in Palestine is well known; Octavian and the senate designated Herod the Great as king (40 B.C.) and gave him such support as would further Roman interests, while he in return recognized that Rome was his master and must pass on the question of his successor or successors. At the time of the birth of Jesus, Augustus was continuing this policy, which had proved so successful in enabling the Romans to take over territory without resorting to armed conquest. In Africa, Mauretania (XIII, A-B 2) was under Roman influence. In southeastern Europe, Thracia (XIII, D-2) was in a similar situation. On the east side of Asia Minor, the Kingdom of Polemo, Armenia Minor, and Cappadocia (XIII, E-F 2) illustrate the same method.

This procedure was used in certain border states. The basic unit of imperial administration, however, was the province. By the Act of Settlement of 27 B.C. provinces were divided into two classes. Those of normal and stable life were under the Roman senate, which sent out a governor for a single year. Most desirable and remunerative

FIG. 58. Roman Forum and Arch of Titus. In earliest times, this Forum was the center of political and religious assemblies. It was later covered with columns, statues, arches, and other monuments. In the distance, the Arch of Titus, which commemorates Titus' victory over the Jews and destruction of Jerusalem in A. D. 70.

were the governorships of the provinces of Asia (XIII, D-2) and Africa, traditionally assigned to the consuls who had just retired from office. The governors of all provinces under the senate, however, were called proconsuls, so that the New Testament is correct in calling the governors of Cyprus (XIII, E-2; cf. Acts 13:7, R.V.) and Achaia (XIII, C-D 2; cf. Acts 18:12, R.V.) by this title.

The provinces of the other class, known as imperial, were under direct control of the emperor, who delegated his power, usually for several years, to legates (cf. Luke 2:2) and procurators (cf. Matt. 27:2). The original group of imperial provinces included Egypt, Syria, and those in Gaul and Spain; as new provinces were organized, they were added to the imperial class. Moreover, the emperor reserved the right to make changes in the division. When a senatorial province offered an urgent problem he could take it over and control its administration directly. On the other hand, when there was no further need of maintaining personal supervision of a province, he committed its management to the senate. Such changes occurred under later emperors.

One province, however, held a special position. Egypt was so productive in crops and trade, and its grain supply was so vital to the peace of Italy, that Augustus kept it as his personal domain. No Roman senator or other possible political rival visited there without special permission. Rome had a dangerously large proportion of its population (about 200,000) on a free grain allowance; it was dependent on Egypt for a large share of its food supply, and Augustus could not run any risk of having this supply cut off. The Apostle Paul, on his journey to Rome to be tried before the emperor, no doubt traveled on two of the many grain ships operating between Egypt and Rome (Acts 27:6; 28:11).

ROMAN COLONIES AND CITIZENSHIP

The fact that Augustus had to provide a grain allowance for 200,000 persons at Rome suggests the need of a population outlet from the capital city. From an early time the attempt was made to meet this problem by founding colonies, first in Italy, later in remoter parts of the empire. In them were settled Roman citizens, especially veteran soldiers who were ready to retire from active duty. These colonies were often already existing cities, which thus received an added population. Among those founded before or during the reign of Augustus were such widely separated cities as Corduba, Hispalis, and Emerita (XIII, A-2) in Spain; Narbo, Lugdunum, Vienna, and Arelate (XIII, B-1) in Gaul; Carthago in Africa; Corinthus (XIII, D-2) in Achaia; Philippi (XIII, D-2) in Macedonia; and Berytus (XIII, E-3) in Syria. The native residents of such colonies

were granted Roman citizenship and thus enjoyed a favored position in the empire.

The removal of surplus population from Rome was by no means the only object in establishing colonies. Each such city became a center of loyalty to Rome, and promoted political stability in its region. Moreover, because so many of the settlers were veteran soldiers still able to serve in defensive warfare, the Roman colony often became an outpost of Roman military strength and was useful in cowing the inhabitants of a restless area. Furthermore, the network of colonies, stretching across the empire, served to foster trade and promote economic unity.

In addition to colonies marked by the presence of citizens sent out from Rome, other cities possessed citizenship by the grant of the Romans. Certain cities had entered into treaty relationship to Rome and enjoyed certain privileges, including exemption from ordinary taxes and the right to use their own laws; such were Athens (Athenae; XIII, D-2), Rhodes (Rhodus; XIII, D-2), and Tyre (Tyrus; XIII, E-3). In general, the Romans followed the policy of "divide and rule"; to prevent the cities of an area from uniting against Rome, they fostered various forms of direct and privileged relation to the empire. This tended to check any desire which a city might feel to revolt or plot against its benefactor.

The mention of colonies recalls the fact that Roman citizenship was widely held. It was gradually extended not only to the people of Italy but to increasing numbers throughout the empire. A rapid extension of the privilege took place in the first century B.C., when during the Civil Wars the number of citizens rose from 400,000 to 4,000,000. Augustus was cautious in this as in other matters, and during his reign the number increased less than a million. It was not until the time of the Emperor Caracalla that an edict granted full citizenship to practically all free residents of the provinces (A.D. 212).

A special class of citizens were the freedmen. Slaves set free by the emperor or a citizen became citizens of the empire. Many slaves had been acquired by war and purchase, and emancipation became common. This seemed a threat to the stability of Roman life and blood, and Augustus sharply limited the right of masters to free slaves and grant them citizenship.

It should be remembered, however, that the possession of citizenship did not involve such participation in government as we connect with the privilege today. The emperor, and to a minor degree other officials at Rome, guided the course of the empire. Roman citizenship, nevertheless, did give desirable advantages to favored residents of the provinces. They enjoyed not only a certain social prestige, but also added legal rights and definite economic benefits. The Apostle

Paul, who like his father before him was a Roman citizen, was able when unfairly treated by a provincial official to appeal to Caesar and thus transfer his case to the imperial court (Acts 22:28; 25:11).

TRAVEL IN THE EMPIRE

Efficiency of administration, military security, and trade interests demanded the development of easy communication throughout the empire. The Romans made great use of the sea in transporting grain to Rome from Egypt, Africa, and the Black Sea region. In a day of sailing vessels, however, the stormy winter season compelled a general intermission of sea traffic. To stop for the winter at such places as Crete (Creta; XIII, D-2; Acts 27:12) or Malta (Melita; XV, B-4; Acts 28:11) was the common practice of ships which were unable to make harbor in Italy before wintry storms rendered sea travel dangerous. A further disadvantage was that on certain sea lanes the prevailing winds permitted travel in only one direction. This explains why ships sailing from Alexandria to Rome first went north or northeast, to the southern coast of Asia Minor, and then worked their way westward (Acts 27:6).

Many rocky points were danger spots which sailors preferred to avoid. This explains in part the importance of Corinth. Because the southern coast of Achaia was rocky and dangerous, much traffic crossed the Isthmus of Corinth (XIII, D-2), using the two ports near Corinth, Lechaeum on the west side of the isthmus and Cenchreae (Acts 18:18) on the east side. To save the time and expense of unloading, land transport, and reloading, smaller ships were actually hauled over the narrow, low isthmus on a causeway. A few decades after Augustus' reign, Nero (A.D. 54-68) made a futile attempt to dig a canal through the isthmus; the attempt was renewed successfully in modern times, along the same line which Nero marked out (see Fig. 59). In Egypt a canal from the Nile (Nilus; XIII, E 3-4) to the extreme northwest arm of the Arabian Gulf (Sinus Arabicus; XIII, E-F 3-4) was dug long before Roman times and restored by Trajan (A.D. 98-117); it furthered trade with countries east of the empire.

The chief port of Rome was Puteoli (XIII, C-2), at least for grain trade, but Ostia (XIII, C-2) was much closer and continued to retain considerable importance.

The remarkable network of Roman roads, one of the outstanding achievements of Roman administrative and engineering skill, proved more important in many ways than the sea lanes. These justly famous roads provided facilities for land travel not surpassed until the coming of the railroad. Constant use of the highways was made possible by a well-built, well-drained, well-kept system of hard roads, marked by milestones.

In the reign of Augustus, the road network was by no means so large or well-built as it was in the later years of the empire. In newer provinces there had not been time to construct the highways needed for easiest communication and greatest military mobility. For example, in Palestine, which was still under a vassal king, the system of Roman roads, still partially marked out today by the many milestones which have been discovered, was not yet under construction. In older parts of the empire, however, excellent roads were already in existence. Noteworthy examples are the famous Appian Way, along which travelers from Puteoli proceeded on the last part of their land trip to Rome (Acts 28:13, 14; see Fig. 56), and the Egnatian Way, which enabled travelers from Italy to cross over from Brundisium (XIII, C-2) to Dyrrhachium (XIII, C-2) or Apollonia (XIII, C-2) and thence go east by land to Thessalonica (XIII, D-2) and eastern points.

Such excellent roads greatly promoted trade and travel. Free and safe communication between all parts of the empire also did much to develop wider horizons, a more cosmopolitan spirit, and a continuous interchange of intellectual and spiritual treasures.

RELIGION AND CULTURE

The Roman policy concerning religion was to maintain the ancestral worship of the gods of Rome and at the same time show tolerance toward the deities of other peoples in the empire. This was possible because polytheism was basic in Roman religion, and the gods

FIG. 59. Corinth Canal. Finished in 1893. Nearly four miles long, 70 feet wide, 26 feet deep. It follows the line along which Nero attempted to dig a canal about A. D. 67.

of the provincial peoples could either be identified with the ancestral deities at Rome or tolerated as additional objects of worship. Even the Jews, who insisted on a monotheistic faith and would join in no pagan rites, found tolerance, especially from the time of Julius Caesar on, and received special privileges which protected them in the exercise of their worship. New faiths were frowned upon, and cults with obviously degrading features were suppressed, but tolerance was the general practice.

One significant development, the practice of emperor worship, was hardly visible in the time of Augustus. The beginnings, however, were already present. Julius Caesar received suspiciously high honors while still alive and was declared a god after his death. Augustus had taken a name which suggested majesty and perhaps more than human rank. The eastern provinces were used to paying their rulers divine honors. The way was being prepared for the outrageous demand of the mad Caligula (A.D. 37-41) that his statue be set up in the Temple at Jerusalem and for the open claim of Domitian (A.D. 81-96) to be "lord and god."

In the day of Augustus, as in the later days of persecution, many refused to take such claims seriously. They regarded the paying of divine honors as merely the manifestation of patriotism. They doubtless considered religion, especially the state religion, a useful means of fostering and maintaining unity in the empire. Indeed, there was a widespread skepticism about all the old gods of pagan Rome.

The truth is that Rome had neither the spiritual nor the cultural vitality to infuse inner unity and strength into the empire. Not even Greece had the spiritual gift which the empire needed. It took Christianity to provide that. But Greece did have the cultural heritage which was the cohesive factor in the intellectual life of the time. Indeed, at the opening of the Christian era the prevailing culture was not Roman but Hellenistic. The Greek language was so widely spoken that it was the common medium of communication in such widely separated regions as Africa, Spain, Italy, and Asia Minor. It was a rival of Aramaic in Syria and Palestine. Athens, Tarsus, and Alexandria were among the centers of study and learning to which Romans went. Greek culture came to Rome not only from free traveling scholars and teachers but also from well-educated slaves, acquired in war or by purchase. Rome gave stable political unity under which the Christian faith could rise and spread, but it was the heritage of Greece which provided the language and intellectual background which made possible one far-flung Church.

PLATE XIII

THE ROMAN WORLD
AT THE BIRTH OF JESUS
Copyright, The Westminster Press, International Copyright Secured. All Rights Reserved

SCALE OF MILES

0   100   200   300   400   500

ROMAN PROVINCES — Bounded by Color
CLIENT STATES
ROADS
SEA ROUTES
CITIES AND TOWNS — o

NORTHERN GAUL
AND BRITAIN

PLATE XIV

May 1954

PALESTINE
DURING THE
MINISTRY OF JESUS

SCALE OF MILES

0   5   10   15   20   25   30

TETRARCHY OF PHILIP

TETRARCHY OF
HEROD ANTIPAS

UNDER PONTIUS PILATE

DECAPOLIS

AREAS UNDER
SPECIAL CONTROL

CITIES AND TOWNS   o

ROADS

Sidon
Sarepta
Tyre
ABILENE
Damascus
MT. LIBANUS
MT. HERMON
Caesarea Philippi
PANIAS ITURAEA
ULATHA
TRACHONITIS
Gischala Thella
Lake Semechonitis
GAULANITIS
Baca Meroth
Raphana?
Ptolemais
Chorazin
Capernaum Bethsaida
PLAIN OF Julias
GENNESARET
Chabulon
Cana Magdala Sea of
Tarichaea Galilee Gergesa?
Tiberias Hippos AURANITIS Canatha
Sepphoris Nazareth
Gaba Dion
Exaloth, MT. TABOR
Xaloth Gadara
Nain Abila
Caesarea
Scythopolis
Ginaea Pella
Salim?
Gerasa
PLAIN OF SHARON
Samaria
Sebaste
Sichem, Sychem, Sychar?
MT. GERIZIM Salim?
Jacob's Well
Antipatris PERAEA
Borcaeus
Arimathaea? Phasaelis
Joppa Jordan Philadelphia
Lydda Ephraim? Archelais
Jamnia River
Emmaus Jericho Bethany
Azotus Beyond
Jerusalem Bethphage? Jordan?
Ascalon Bethany
Bethlehem
JUDAEA Lake
Gaza Asphaltitis
Hebron Machaerus
Jarda, (Dead
Jorda Sea)
Raphia Masada
IDUMAEA
Petra

MT. CARMEL
PHOENICIA
GALILEE
DECAPOLIS
BATANAEA
SAMARIA
(MEDITERRANEAN SEA)

FIG. 60. Sea of Galilee. View northward along the northwest shore of the lake. Just left of the foreground is the Plain of Gennesaret.

PALESTINE DURING THE MINISTRY OF JESUS

PLATE XIV

TO GAIN an understanding of the geographical background of the ministry of Jesus it is not enough to seek out individual sites. Students of the Gospels must grasp the larger setting of his life and work. This requires first of all an examination of the relation of Palestine to Rome.

During the public ministry of Jesus, Palestine was a border region on the eastern frontier of the Roman Empire. To the south and east stretched the desert area of the Nabatean kingdom, which centered in Petra (Plate XIV, C-8) but extended northwest to the Mediterranean and north to the vicinity of Damascus (XIV, E-1). To the northeast was the Parthian Empire, which in 40 B.C. had attempted to control Palestine and still constituted a threat to Rome's mastery. Since there were thus forces near Palestine which required watching, and rebellious spirits within the country were always plotting to throw off Roman control, Rome was constantly on the alert against invasion or uprising. Hence a charge that Jesus was trying to make himself king (Luke 23:2) was something to take seriously.

PALESTINE'S RELATION TO SYRIA

Only to the north was there direct contact with Roman territory and strength. To be sure, not far to the southwest lay Egypt (XIII, E-3), constantly in communication with Palestine and securely under the control of Rome. But the Nabataeans broke the land link between Egypt and Palestine. The basic political connection of Palestine was with Syria on the north.

It was the task of the Roman governors in the more stable province of Syria to exercise supervisory control of Palestine in critical times. Palestine was definitely under their protection and watchful oversight. A vivid illustration of this occurred in A.D. 36; Pontius Pilate, the Roman procurator ruling Samaria, Judaea, and part of Idumaea, was under suspicion of acting unwisely in crushing a Samaritan disturbance, and Vitellius, the governor of Syria, deposed him and sent him to Rome for trial.

Further facts show the close interlocking of Palestine with Syria. The Roman province of Syria extended down the coast to include Phoenicia and Mount Carmel (XIV, B-C 1-3). Gaza (XIV, A-6), located in southwest Palestine, was detached from its setting and made a part of the province of Syria. An even more striking evidence of the subordinate relation of Palestine to Syria is the fact that the governor of Syria protected and watched over the Decapolis (XIV, C-F 1-5).

THE DECAPOLIS

To those who think of first-century Palestine as a strictly Jewish country, the facts about the Decapolis will bring a startling correction. The word "Decapolis" is Greek; it combines the words *deka*, "ten," and *polis*, "city," and refers to a federation of cities marked by Hellenistic organization and culture. The original league of ten cities probably came into being under Roman protection after Pompey took over the region in 63 B.C.

The earliest mention of the Decapolis is in the Gospels (Mark 5:20; 7:31; Matt. 4:25), Josephus' *Wars of the Jews* (c. A.D. 75), and the *Natural History* of the elder Pliny (c. A.D. 77). Pliny lists the cities as follows (all on Plate XIV): Damascus (E-1), Philadelphia (D-5), Raphana (E-3), Scythopolis (C-4), Gadara (D-3), Hippos (D-3),

FIG. 61. The Jerusalem-Jericho Road. Between these two cities, fifteen miles apart in a direct line, the road descends 3,300 feet through wild country which has always offered hiding places for robbers (cf. Luke 10:30).

Dion (E-3), Pella (D-4), Gerasa (D-4), and Canatha (F-3). Ptolemy, a second-century writer, names eighteen cities; he omits Raphana and includes not only Abila (XIV, D-3) but also eight other cities. This fact, and a late reference to a fourteen-city federation, proves that the number varied from time to time. The map shows the ten cities named by Pliny and in addition Abila, which may have a better claim than Raphana to be one of the original ten.

Scythopolis, which Josephus calls the greatest city of the Decapolis, was the only member west of the Jordan. The other cities were all on the east side, spread out from Damascus on the north to Philadelphia on the south. It is impossible to represent this league clearly on the map. Each city evidently controlled the region immediately surrounding it, but how far such control extended cannot be determined. Plainly, however, the Decapolis was not a compact and definitely bounded political unit. Damascus was in Syria; Dion, Raphana, and Canatha were in the territory ruled by Philip; and Herod Antipas must have had some recognized and lawful way to move troops and messengers freely from Galilee (XIV, C-3) to Peraea (XIV, D 4-5). The Decapolis seems, therefore, to have been a league of independent cities under the protection of the governor of Syria, each controlling a greater or smaller area immediately about it. The region from Hippos to Philadelphia was so largely dominated by these cities that it may be regarded as in a particular sense the region of the Decapolis.

Why did these cities band together in this way? The answer may be in part that since they were on the frontier they needed to protect themselves from Nabataeans, Parthians, or other enemies who might attack them or cut their lines of trade. Probably, however, they banded together mainly to defend their interests and the cause of Hellenistic culture against the Jewish and other Semitic interests which were strong around them. For this was not merely a political frontier; it was also a cultural borderland.

Centuries before the days of Jesus the infiltration of Greek influence into the land of Palestine had begun. By the time of Jesus, this Hellenistic influence was operative in almost all parts of Palestine. Along the coast and in the Jordan Valley many cities were Greek in organization and cultural connection. No doubt Jewish and other Semitic influences were found in them, but the dominant features were Hellenistic. For example, outposts of Greek culture were present in Caesarea (XIV, B-4), Pilate's capital city during his rule in Palestine; Tiberias (XIV, D-3), built by Herod Antipas to be the capital of his tetrarchy; Samaria (XIV, C-4); and Jericho (XIV, C-5), near the Old Testament site but a little south of it.

Of all the expressions of this penetrating Greek influence, however, the Decapolis was the most powerful and impressive. Excavations at Gerasa have made clear the Greek plan of the city. The

Greek theaters, temples, stadium, forum, colonnades, and inscriptions reflect the Greek manner of life (Fig. 41). Although these remains date almost entirely from a time later than the ministry of Jesus, their earliest portions reach back into his day. They show what a city of the Decapolis was like, and how different it was from a truly Jewish city.

Against the background of this cultural clash between Hellenistic and Jewish elements we must understand the situation of Jesus' day. The visible challenge to Jewish faith and customs probably does much to explain why the Pharisees were so strict in the observance of their ceremonial laws. It also added to the fiery spirit of revolt which the Zealots showed against the Romans. Many Jewish patriots felt that Roman power, which supported Hellenistic influences, was directed against both their liberty and their entire way of life. Palestine had become a battleground of two cultural worlds. Jesus could not have been ignorant of Hellenistic forces. If he shunned them, he must have done so deliberately.

THE POLITICAL DIVISIONS OF PALESTINE

With the exception of the areas under the rule or protection of Syria, Palestine in Jesus' day fell into three main political divisions. This partition was based on the will of Herod the Great. When he died in 4 B.C., he bequeathed to his son Archelaus his title of king, and gave him control of Samaria, Judaea, and the northern part of Idumaea (cf. Matt. 2:22). To his son Herod Antipas he left Galilee and Peraea. To another son, Philip, he left the region east of the upper Jordan, from Mount Hermon (XIV, D-2; see Fig. 55) to the River Yarmuk (I, D-3). The Roman emperor Augustus, whose right it was to approve or reject this division of Herod's kingdom, approved it except that he granted Archelaus merely the rank of ethnarch. Ten years later, however, in A.D. 6, complaints against the rule of Archelaus became so serious that Augustus deposed him, and in his place appointed a Roman procurator, directly responsible to the emperor but dependent upon the Roman governor of Syria for military help and emergency supervision. This arrangement lasted until A.D. 41.

PONTIUS PILATE, "GOVERNOR OF JUDAEA"

The fifth in the line of succession of these procurators was Pontius Pilate (Luke 3:1). He was appointed by the Emperor Tiberius in A.D. 26, and remained in office until Vitellius, Roman governor of Syria, sent him to Rome in A.D. 36 to stand trial on the charge of unfair sternness toward turbulent Samaritans. While his control extended over Samaria, Judaea, and part of Idumaea, the city of Gaza, as noted, was detached from this district and joined to Syria. Other small areas also were under special control—always, of course, by the decision and under the final control of the emperor. Ascalon (XIV, B-5) continued to be an independent city of Hellenistic culture, as it had been for over a century. Nominally free, it actually depended upon the Roman Empire for its liberties and protection. Jamnia and Azotus (XIV, B-5), Phasaelis (XIV, C-4) and Archelais (XIV, C-5) were left by Herod the Great to his sister Salome. Upon her death, some time between A.D. 9 and 12, she left this possession by will to Livia, the wife of Augustus. Upon Livia's death these places passed into the hands of the Emperor Tiberius (A.D. 14-37), who controlled them by a specially appointed officer. Probably such areas depended upon the Roman procurator for military defense. The purpose in granting them to an individual was not so much to give political power as to provide a source of income and prestige for some favored person.

To the modern Christian, as to the first-century Jew, the outstanding city under Pilate's rule was Jerusalem (XIV, C-5). This was not the Roman view. Other cities, such as Samaria and Jericho, were more important as centers of Graeco-Roman life. Other religious centers, such as Mount Gerizim, where the Samaritans gathered, and Samaria, where a magnificent temple of Augustus crowned the western brow of the hill, probably seemed more important to a Roman than they do to a modern Jew or Christian. Moreover, for political purposes Caesarea took first place. It was the residence of the governor. Built by Herod the king, provided with a man-made harbor, and equipped with a royal palace, it was an attractive location for the Roman procurator, and he lived regularly in the palace which Herod had built. However, at Passover time, when nationalistic feelings might cause the Jews to think of revolt, the procurator took up temporary residence in Jerusalem. It was this custom which explains Pilate's presence there when Jesus came up to keep the Passover (Mark 15:1).

HEROD ANTIPAS GOVERNS GALILEE AND PERAEA

From 4 B.C. to A.D. 39 Herod Antipas was tetrarch of Galilee and Peraea (cf. Luke 3:1). These districts appear separated on the map by territory under the influence of the Decapolis cities Gadara, Scythopolis, and Pella. It may be taken for granted, however, that Herod Antipas had free passageway from Galilee to Peraea.

The region of Peraea was less thickly populated than Galilee and figures little in the Gospel story. It began a little below Pella and ended just south of the border fortress Machaerus (XIV, D-5), where, according to Josephus, John the Baptist was imprisoned and executed.

The main attention of Herod Antipas must have been devoted to Galilee. His capital and residence were there. At first he governed from Sepphoris (XIV, C-3). This city had participated in the revolt against Rome in A.D. 6, and as a result the Romans ruthlessly destroyed it. Shortly thereafter it was rebuilt. All this occurred during the boyhood of Jesus, and he must have known the entire tragic story, since he lived not far to the south in Nazareth (XIV, C-3). At a later time, perhaps about A.D. 20, Herod Antipas built the city of Tiberias, on the western shore of the Sea of Galilee, and moved his capital and residence thither. Built on the site of a cemetery, and peopled by foreigners and lax Jews, it was at first shunned by most loyal Jewish people.

Galilee was bounded on the east by the Jordan River and the Sea of Galilee. In practice, however, the northern part of the sea's eastern shore was reckoned to Galilee. Gaulanitis (XIV, D-3) was a high plateau region over two thousand feet above the level of the Sea of Galilee. The steep, forbidding slope on the east side of the sea discouraged contacts between the lake region and the upland. It was easier for inhabitants on the eastern shore to communicate with residents on the other sides of the lake than to deal with people in Gaulanitis.

On the north, Galilee extended to Thella (XIV, D-2) and Gischala (XIV, C-2). The western border ran just west of Baca (XIV, C-3), Cha-

bulon (XIV, C-3), and Gaba (XIV, C-3). On the south, Josephus places the border at Xaloth (XIV, C-3); but, since he speaks of Ginaea (XIV, C-4) as the northern limit of Samaria, it is probable that the border ran through the plain between these two towns.

THE TETRARCHY OF PHILIP

From 4 B.C. until his death in A.D. 34 Philip was tetrarch of the region northeast of the Sea of Galilee (XIV, D-F 2-3). It is not possible to fix accurately the eastern borders of his territory. Moreover, his control of the area marked on the map cannot have been complete and rigid. Three cities of the Decapolis were in his tetrarchy; each had its local sphere of influence and its free lines of communication with other Decapolis cities.

Philip seems to have been a good ruler, conscientious, fair, and respected. In honor of the emperor he built a city at Paneas; to distinguish it from other cities of the same name he called it Caesarea Philippi, i.e., Philip's Caesarea (XIV, D-2; cf. Mark 8:27). Pagan shrines marked its non-Jewish character; indeed, the region ruled by Philip was prevailingly Gentile. For his capital Philip rebuilt Bethsaida, on the lake, and named it after Julia, the daughter of the Emperor Augustus. It is sometimes called Julias or Bethsaida Julias; in the Gospels the older name Bethsaida is still used (XIV, D-3; cf. Mark 6:45).

THE BASIC UNITY OF PALESTINE

The existence of so many separate units of political administration may give the impression that Palestine was a group of entirely distinct areas. In fact, however, Rome's control of the entire region gave it essential unity. All rulers held their power by grant from Rome and only so long as they furthered her interests. All were under the eye of the Roman governor in Syria.

Hence travel was free and constant between all sections of Palestine. Jesus could go freely, not only throughout Galilee, but also into Philip's territory (Mark 8:27), into the Decapolis (Mark 7:31), and into the region ruled by Pilate. He could even go without challenge into regions which were part of the province of Syria (Mark 7:24).

One caution, however, is in place. We often read of the excellent Roman roads. But these Roman roads of Palestine are later than the time of Jesus. What are shown on the map as roads are not the solidly constructed highways of Roman engineering genius but, rather, regularly used ancient lines of travel. Some of these were not capable of year-round use. The road down the west side of the Jordan Valley, for example, was probably not passable in the wet season of the year, at least in the district south of Scythopolis.

THE SCENES OF JESUS' MINISTRY

The modern tourist has no difficulty in finding the sites where Jesus lived and taught. Indeed, he is sometimes embarrassed to find two or more sites for the same event! There is in human nature a deeply rooted desire to know exactly where significant Biblical events occurred, and traditions confidently provide explicit answers to such desires.

As a matter of sober historical fact, however, the student of the Gospels must confess that he cannot locate some of the sites mentioned in the narrative. This becomes painfully clear when we begin to study the work of John the Baptist. He is said to have baptized at Aenon near to Salim (John 3:23). Aenon cannot be found. It is not even certain where this Salim was located. An ancient tradition favors a site six miles south of Scythopolis (XIV, C-4); strong arguments are also made for the Salim east of Mount Gerizim (XIV, C-4). Both are shown on Plate XIV; no decision is possible. Similarly, Bethany beyond Jordan (John 1:28) is a puzzle. It is even disputed whether this is the correct name of the place; Origen, a third-century Christian scholar residing in Palestine, insisted that the name was Bethabara. Early Gospel manuscripts do not appear to support him, however, and we may conclude that a place named Bethany was meant. In the very nature of the case, a place used for baptism would be hard to

FIG. 62. Gethsemane. In the center of the picture, just east of the Brook Kidron, is one traditional site of the Garden of Gethsemane (Mark 14:32; John 18:1). To the right is a church built to commemorate Jesus' struggle in the Garden. To the left, in a semicircular area, is the Grotto of the Agony, where another tradition places the event. Quite probably the original Garden into which Jesus entered was in the area pictured. The Mount of Olives rises to the east. Running across the Kidron and up the slope to the right is the road to Bethany and Jericho.

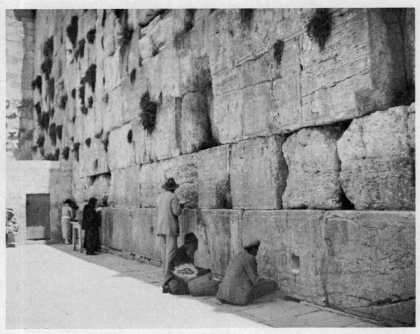

FIG. 63. The Wailing Wall in Jerusalem. This is the outside western wall of the ancient Temple area. Note the size of the hewn stones. Jews here lament the loss of their Temple and national home.

locate in later times, and all we can do is to show on a map the place which from ancient times was regarded as the place where John baptized (XIV, D-5).

In like manner places referred to in the story of Jesus' ministry are often impossible to locate. He is said to have delivered a sermon on a "mount" (Matt. 5:1); none of the rival sites west and north of the Sea of Galilee appear to be more than early guesses.

Some have sought the scene of the transfiguration on Mount Hermon. Others have upheld the claims of Mount Tabor (XIV, C-3), where two churches have been built to commemorate the event. Both sites are mere conjecture.

Nor can a definite decision be made about Gergesa (XIV, D-3). The name itself is uncertain; in all three Gospels the manuscripts vary greatly, offering three alternatives, Gergesa, Gerasa, and Gadara (Matt. 8:28; Mark 5:1; Luke 8:26, 37). Even if, as seems probable, Gergesa is original, the location is doubtful. The modern *Kursi*, where Gergesa is placed on the map, shows the approximate location, but this Arabic name is not the exact equivalent of the Greek word "Gergesa." Even more baffling is Dalmanutha (Mark 8:10); no town of this name is known, and ancient manuscripts of Mark vary greatly in their spelling of the name; so the mystery seems incapable of solution.

Once such limitations of knowledge are honestly confessed, it is gratifying to find that we can identify the main sites of Jesus' life and ministry. The birthplace, Bethlehem (XIV, C-5), and the childhood residence, Nazareth (XIV, C-3), are certainly known. Concerning the Sea of Galilee, Cana (XIV, C-3), Nain (XIV, C-3), Capernaum (XIV, D-3), and Chorazin (XIV, D-3) there can be no reasonable doubt. There was long a dispute about the location of Capernaum, but it seems clear now that this center of Jesus' Galilean ministry was at *Tell Hûm*. It must be added, however, that the synagogue whose ruins are seen today at *Tell Hûm* is not that mentioned in the Gospels, but was built later, possibly in the third century (Fig. 37). Bethsaida (XIV, D-3) may be two miles north of the Sea of Galilee, at *et-Tell*, but is most probably at *el 'Araj*, on the shore of the sea.

On most of his trips to Jerusalem, Jesus probably followed the usual Galilean custom, journeying down the Jordan Valley on the east side of the river, crossing the river near Jericho (XIV, C-5; cf. Matt. 19:1; Mark 10:1; Luke 19:1), and going up the road from Jericho to Jerusalem (see Fig. 61). The Gospel of John tells of one journey through Samaria, and mentions a stop near Sychar (John 4:5). The usual location given for this town is at the modern village *'Askar* (Fig. 6). It is at least clear that Sychar must have been close to Jacob's Well (XIV, C-4), the location of which is certain.

The sites in Jerusalem appear on Plate XVII:B. It is important, however, to note the location of Bethany (XIV, C-5), southeast of Jerusalem; there Jesus found a welcome and refreshment in the home of friends (Mark 11:11; John 12:1). Bethphage was not far from Bethany, probably just northwest (XIV, C-5), but no certainty is attainable. The beautiful resurrection story in the Gospel of Luke (ch. 24:13 ff.) seems to refer not to the Emmaus close to Jerusalem (XII:D, C-5), but to *'Amwâs*, where Emmaus appears on this map (XIV, B-5).

GENERAL CONCLUSIONS

One gains from the study of the geography of the Gospels three strong impressions. First of all, we know the general framework of the life of Jesus. The political background is plain. The places of his birth, childhood, and death are known; the center of the Galilean ministry was at Capernaum; the major portion of his ministry was exercised north and west of the Sea of Galilee (see Fig. 60).

A second observation, however, is not so often made. In spite of the definite framework of the ministry, few places are definitely named as scenes of the activity of Jesus. Most of the sayings and actions which the Gospels report are not located in a particular place, and it is usually wrong to assign such incidents to the place mentioned in a neighboring paragraph of the Gospel story. Only fourteen or fifteen places in all Galilee are named as places where Jesus lived or worked. That he visited numerous other cities and towns may be regarded as certain; what those places were we do not know.

The third observation is that Jesus worked consistently in centers of Jewish life, and had very little to do with the many Hellenistic centers which dotted the landscape of Palestine. He avoided Sepphoris and Tiberias, outstanding Hellenistic cities of Galilee. There is no mention that he went to the coastal cities of Judaea, almost all of which were strongly Hellenistic in organization and culture. He never more than touched or passed through the region of the Decapolis, and no passage reports that he entered a Decapolis city (cf. Mark 5:1, 20; 7:31). He had nothing to do with the notably Hellenistic city of Samaria.

Apparent exceptions do not prove valid or significant when examined. It has been asserted that Jesus went to Tyre (XIV, C-2) and Sidon (XIV, C-1). The fact is that this journey into "the parts of Tyre and Sidon" (Matt. 15:21; Mark 7:24) was a retirement into rural seclusion; he went, not into those cities, but into the "parts" or regions connected with them. That is, he withdrew northwest from Galilee into a lonely region, and spent some time there with his disciples. Similarly, the romantic pictures which writers sometimes draw of Jesus at Caesarea Philippi, a city noted for Greek temples and other signs of Hellenistic culture, are without foundation. What the Gospels say is that he went into the "parts" (Matt. 16:13) or outlying "villages" (Mark 8:27) of Caesarea Philippi. There also he was alone with his disciples in a time of withdrawal from public ministry. He is said in Mark 8:22 to have touched at Bethsaida (XIV, D-3). This city, however, was not only Philip's capital; it included a Jewish settlement, composed partly of fishermen, which antedated Philip's time. Undoubtedly Jesus was interested in the Jewish section of the city. Jesus passed through the Hellenistic city of Jericho, it is true; but he had to do this to go to Jerusalem, and he lodged there in the home of a Jewish taxgatherer, Zacchaeus (Luke 19:5). The Gospels report but few contacts of Jesus with Gentiles, and such occasions are clearly represented as exceptional (e.g., Mark 7:27; cf. Matt. 15:24). When Jesus heals a Gentile, he does so without entering a Gentile home (Matt. 8:5-13; Mark 7:24-30).

Had the writers of the Gospels, who were providing writings intended in part at least to appeal to Gentiles, been able to tell that Jesus ministered freely to Gentiles in Galilee and elsewhere, they would certainly have done so. The conclusion is clear. The ministry of Jesus was deliberately limited to the Jews, and was confined almost entirely to centers free from strong Gentile influence. There is no trace of a planned effort to reach the Gentiles who were all about him. The mission to Gentiles had roots in the teaching and attitudes of Jesus, but its actual inauguration waited until the Apostolic Age.

THE JOURNEYS OF PAUL

Plate XV

THE Apostle Paul was providentially prepared to lead the early missionary expansion of Christianity. He was a Jew, thoroughly grounded in his ancestral faith. But he was a Jew of the Dispersion; hence he knew something of the larger world of his day. He not only knew the Hebrew in which the Old Testament was written and the Aramaic in which most residents of Palestine conversed, but he was most at home in the common Greek tongue which was then used almost everywhere in the Roman world. He was a Roman citizen (Acts 22:25, 28) as well as a citizen of Tarsus (Plate xv, F-3; cf. Acts 21:39). It was therefore no unprepared development when Saul—to use his Jewish name—became the leading missionary of the Apostolic Age.

EARLY PREPARATION

Although the famous Christian scholar Jerome wrote in the fourth century that Saul was born in Galilee at Gischala (VIII, F-4), it is said in The Acts that he was born in Tarsus of Cilicia (ch. 22: 3). This city was noted for its vigorous intellectual and commercial life, and many have thought that Saul was greatly influenced by its Gentile thought. The apostle, however, states quite definitely in Phil. 3:5 that he was brought up in the strict Jewish tradition and became a Pharisee. He went to Jerusalem (xv, G-5) and with Gamaliel as teacher (Acts 22:3) took up the systematic study of the ancestral tradition (Gal. 1:13, 14). This faith he jealously championed against the newly arisen Christian movement. Not content with active efforts to suppress the new sect in Jerusalem (Acts 8:1, 3), he set out for Damascus (xv, G-4), where "the Way" was making inroads into the synagogues (Acts 9:1, 2). On the road, near Damascus, he had the vision of the living Christ which transformed his life and affected the course of history. Soon, while lodging in the street called Straight (Acts 9:11; Fig. 65), he made contact with Christian disciples and was baptized.

For a period of unknown length, Saul then withdrew into Arabia (Gal. 1:17). Writers of romantic temperament often picture him going far south to Mount Sinai (cf. Gal. 4:25). Arabia, however, was a vast desert area which reached almost to Damascus itself (xv, F-G 4-5). It is doubtful that Saul went on a long journey, since he next appeared in the same city of Damascus (Gal. 1:17). When Jewish hostility threatened his life there, he escaped with the help of friends, who during the night let him down to the ground through a window in the wall (Acts 9:25; II Cor. 11:33).

Thus three years after conversion (Gal. 1:18) Saul came to Jerusalem, met Peter and James, and according to Acts 9:29 preached to the Greek-speaking Jews (cf. Fig. 64). In fifteen days he aroused such hostility that the leaders of the Jerusalem Church urged him to leave. Christians conducted him to Caesarea (xv, G-5), where he took ship for Tarsus.

During the next few years Saul's vigorous personality impelled him to active Christian work. He himself writes in Gal. 1:22, 23 that his evangelistic work was reported even in Jerusalem. The Churches in Cilicia (xv, F-G 3; cf. Acts 15:23, 41) almost certainly owed their existence to his work.

When, therefore, Barnabas, in need of an able helper at Antioch in Syria (xv, G-4), journeyed to Tarsus to induce Saul to join him (Acts 11:25), he was seeking a man of proved energy and ability. Saul went to Antioch, the capital of Syria and third city of the Roman Empire, and for a year assisted Barnabas. When a famine brought the Christians of Judaea into severe straits, and the energetic Antioch Church sent relief, Barnabas and Saul were entrusted with the funds. They fulfilled the trust and brought back with them John Mark, son of a devout and well-to-do Christian lady of Jerusalem (Acts 12:12, 25). Saul then continued his work as a prophet and teacher in the Church at Antioch.

THE FIRST MISSIONARY JOURNEY

Through an unnamed leader, recognized as the spokesman of the Holy Spirit, the Church at Antioch was called upon to surrender Barnabas and Saul for wider activity (Acts 13:2). Barnabas was the Antioch Church's most trusted leader, Saul his most promising assistant. These men, with John Mark as helper, set out to spread the Christian faith.

From Antioch, located inland upon the Orontes River, the party went some sixteen miles west to Seleucia (xv, G-4). It was five miles north of the mouth of the Orontes, where the roadstead would not be silted up by deposits from the river. Thence the missionaries took ship for Cyprus (xv, F-4), important for copper mines and timber and governed by the Roman senate through a proconsul. They landed at Salamis (xv, F-4), chief business center of the island (Acts 13:5). Their method was to preach in synagogues as opportunity opened; nothing is yet said of a direct mission to Gentiles.

By what route the apostles crossed the island is not reported, nor are we told how much they preached as they went. In general, it appears to have been Paul's policy throughout his journeys to establish himself in cities of importance and let the Gospel spread from such central places. In any event, the next definite word of his work is connected with Paphos (xv, F-4), the capital of the province (Acts 13:6). There the apostles were called to preach before the proconsul, Sergius Paulus, and in connection with this occasion The Acts begins to call the apostle Paul. The change to this name suggests that Paul had become the real leader of the party.

From Paphos, Paul and his companions crossed to the small Roman province of Pamphylia (xv, F-3). They may have landed at Attalia (xv, F-3). Perga (xv, F-3), the first city they are said to have visited (Acts 13:13), was several miles inland. Without John Mark, who returned to Jerusalem for some reason which Paul thought distinctly inadequate (Acts 15:38), the party struck north into the higher country of central Asia Minor. Was it due to illness that they made this journey? So Ramsay thinks, supposing that Paul suffered from malaria along the coast land. Or did they stop in central Asia Minor on account of an illness which first seized Paul there? We cannot say (cf. Gal. 4:13).

The cities to which Paul came contained many Jews, and Paul found synagogues in which to begin his work. The cities in which missionary preaching now occurred were Antioch, Iconium, Lystra,

FIG. 64. Theodotus synagogue inscription. Theodotus built a synagogue and guest rooms for the convenience of Jewish pilgrims to Jerusalem. The inscription which told of his generous act was found in 1914 during excavations on the hill Ophel. It is in Greek, and reflects the presence of Greek-speaking Jews in Jerusalem. In such a synagogue Saul of Tarsus may have disputed with Christians (cf. Acts 6:9).

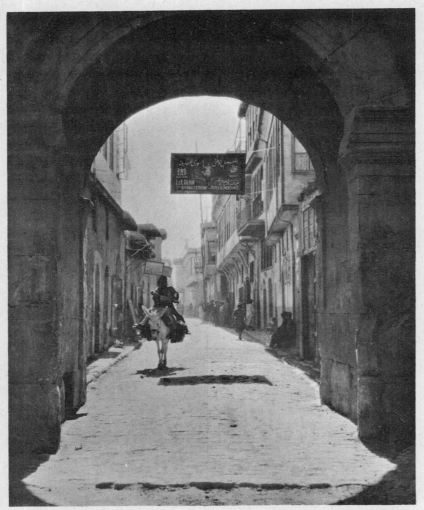

FIG. 65. "Straight Street," Damascus. A modern view of one of the most ancient streets in the world. Cf. Acts 9:11.

and Derbe (xv, F-3). All four were in the Roman Province of Galatia (xv, F-G 2-3), and probably it was to these Churches that Paul later wrote his letter to the Galatians. Further north, in the valley of the Halys River, lay the section settled by Gauls who came from Europe in the early third century B.C. Their chief cities were Ancyra (xv, F-2), the modern Ankara, capital of Turkey; Pessinus (xv, F-3); and Tavium (xv, F-2). It was long held that Galatians was written to these cities, but more likely it went to the Churches that Paul had founded on his First Journey and later revisited (Acts 13:14 to 14:23; 16:6; 18:23).

At Antioch—often called Pisidian Antioch (Acts 13:14) to distinguish it from Antioch in Syria—the great majority of the Jews refused to hear Paul. He turned directly to the Gentiles and invited them to accept the Christian Gospel without observing the distinctive rites of Judaism. In Iconium, the modern Konya, he again won both Jews and Gentiles to the faith. In Lystra there may have been fewer Jews; the lack of mention of any Jewish synagogue and the fact that Timothy had not been circumcised (Acts 16:3) suggest that the Jews were not so numerous or strict here. Yet they could hardly have been entirely lacking, since Jewish leaders from Antioch and Iconium were able to stir up a mob against Paul in Lystra (Acts 14:19). After preaching with success at Derbe, on the southeastern border of the Province of Galatia, the apostles retraced their route, came down to Attalia, and sailed to Seleucia (Acts 14:20-26). At Antioch they were able to report the conversion of a modest number of Jews and large numbers of Gentiles.

THE COUNCIL AT JERUSALEM

Strict Jewish Christians soon challenged Paul's practice of accepting Gentiles into the Church without requiring them to observe the Jewish law (Acts 15:1). Since the Church at Antioch was itself a mixed group, in which both Jews and Gentiles joined in worship and fellowship, its existence, as well as the results of Paul's wider mission, was thus threatened. The issue was taken to Jerusalem. Paul, Barnabas, and others apparently journeyed by land, since they "passed through both Phoenicia and Samaria" (Acts 15:3); but it is possible that they went on a ship stopping at the Phoenician ports and disem-

barked at Ptolemais (xv, G-4) or Caesarea (xv, G-5). When Paul's mission to the Gentiles had been essentially approved by the conference in Jerusalem, the Antioch representatives returned home and reported the result (Acts 15:30).

THE SECOND MISSIONARY JOURNEY

On the Second Journey, in which Paul had Silas to help him, the route led north by land through Cilicia to the Cilician Gates (xv, G-3; Fig. 48), a pass leading through the Taurus Mountains into the high country of inland Asia Minor (Acts 15:40, 41). The travelers visited the Churches of South Galatia, and from Lystra took with them Timothy, who probably had been converted on the First Journey (Acts 16:1-6). Then followed a period of uncertainty. Paul was seeking a new field, but felt led to avoid for the time both the Province of Asia (xv, E-F 2-3) and Bithynia (xv, E-F 2). Finally, after moving north through Phrygia (xv, F-3) and west through Mysia (xv, E-3), he came to Troas (xv, E-3), an important port on the Aegean Sea, not far south of the Hellespont (Acts 16:6-8). Here Paul saw in a dream a man in Macedonian garb, who urged him to preach in Macedonia (xv, C-D 2). This he took to be the divine guidance he needed. Since The Acts begins at this point to use "we" and "us" (Acts 16:10), it seems that at Troas Paul enlisted the help of Luke, the writer of The Acts.

The party sailed for Macedonia. One day's journey took them to the island of Samothrace (xv, E-2); the next day they reached Neapolis (xv, D-2) in Macedonia. They went immediately ten miles northwest to Philippi (xv, D-2), a leading city in that part of Macedonia, and a Roman colony with special privileges. No synagogue is mentioned at Philippi, and at the Jewish place of prayer, located outside the city at a place convenient for the washings which Jewish ceremonies prescribed, Paul found only a group of women. Among those won to the faith by Paul's preaching was Lydia, a Gentile of Thyatira (xv, E-3) in Asia Minor. She was a seller of purple cloth (Acts 16:14). Paul restored to sanity a slave girl whose mysterious psychic powers were being exploited by her masters, and they made frantic complaint. The Philippian authorities stripped Paul and Silas, and ordered them beaten and imprisoned. The apostles were soon released, however, and the magistrates forced to apologize for having dealt illegally with Roman citizens (Acts 16:16-40).

Following the Egnatian Way westward, the evangelists passed through Amphipolis and Apollonia (xv, D-2) and came to Thessalonica (Acts 17:1). This city (xv, D-2), on the main road, with a good harbor and sustained by a rich valley behind it, was inevitably a commercial center, and has remained so into modern times. The unusual title "*politarchai,*" which The Acts uses to designate the rulers there (ch. 17:6), has been proved correct by inscriptions. Jews were numerous there as well as at the next stop, Beroea (xv, D-2), which was some forty miles southwest of Thessalonica, and not on the Egnatian Way. When Jewish opposition forced Paul to leave Beroea, friends conducted him to Athens (Acts 17:14 f.). Whether they took him by the land road or by ship is disputed, but a man who had been shipwrecked three times before writing II Cor. 11:25 must have used the sea route whenever possible.

In its golden age Athens (xv, D-3) had been the center of the classical culture of ancient times. On its Acropolis stood famous masterpieces of art and architecture. In Paul's day Athens was less brilliant, but it was still a city to thrill any lover of culture. Objects of art abounded; interest in poetry, mythology, and philosophy continued; tradition was rich. All this made little impression on Paul, who knew but one God and one Lord (I Cor. 8:6). According to The Acts, he tried to catch and mold the mood of this polytheistic and philosophical city, but with little success (Acts 17:16-34; Fig. 66). No letter to Athens survives; he mentions no Church there; his work had little fruit. He moved on to Corinth (xv, D-3).

Corinth was the political and commercial center of the Province of Achaia. It was located around a rocky citadel at the southern end of the isthmus which connected the Peloponnesus with the Grecian mainland. Much traffic crossed the isthmus to avoid rounding the storm-haunted capes at the southern tip of Achaia (see p. 80). There were ports on the west and east sides of the isthmus; on the west was Lechaeum, on the east Cenchreae (xv, D-3). Paul passed through the latter port (Acts 18:18), and the existence in it of a Christian group is attested by Paul's reference to Phoebe as active in the Church there (Rom. 16:1). Corinth itself, after a century of eclipse due to its destruction in 146 B.C., was rebuilt by Caesar in 46 B.C. and soon became a populous and thriving center of trade. The contents of I Corinthians make it clear that there were Jews in the Church Paul founded there, and their presence in Corinth is also indicated by a Greek inscription, which, though fragmentary, seems to read, "Synagogue of the Hebrews."

In Corinth Paul was brought before the Roman proconsul, Gallio, and excavations have uncovered the rostrum on which Gallio may have appeared before the mob. Gallio is mentioned as proconsul of Achaia in an inscription found at Delphi (XIII, D-2). This inscription gives one of the few dependable clues to the chronology of the life of Paul. It indicates that Gallio came to Corinth for his year as proconsul in either A.D. 51 or 52. Paul then, according to Acts 18:11, 12, must have arrived there about A.D. 50.

When Paul left Corinth, he sailed from Cenchreae to Ephesus (xv, E-3) and visited the synagogue there (Acts 18:19), but apparently only to determine the desirability of a future visit; for he refused an invitation to stay longer and sailed to Caesarea. The Church which he then "went up and saluted" was probably that in Jerusalem. Very soon, however, he went north to Syrian Antioch; this rather than Jerusalem was his home base.

THE THIRD MISSIONARY JOURNEY

After a stay in Antioch, Paul again went north by land through the Cilician Gates and visited the Churches in Southern Galatia (Acts 18:23). From Pisidian Antioch he went westward to Ephesus (Acts 19:1), his chief center of work on this Third Journey. Beginning in the synagogue, as was his custom, he moved after three months into a lecture hall which he rented. Thus he opened a successful two-year mission to Gentiles. He also sent out workers into other cities of the Province of Asia; in this way Churches were established in Colossae, Hierapolis, and Laodicea (xv, E-3; Col. 1:2; 4:13).

As at Philippi, so at Ephesus commercial greed ended Paul's work. Demetrius, a silversmith who made shrines of the goddess Artemis for sale to pilgrims to the great temple in Ephesus, saw that his business was suffering by reason of Paul's work. He aroused the silversmiths, by a blended appeal to religious fanaticism and business profits, and drew a great mob into the large theater (Acts 19:29; Fig. 67). Some of the Asiarchs, officials who had responsibility in the religious festivals of the city, urged Paul not to brave the mob, and

the town clerk quieted and dismissed the crowd without bloodshed (Acts 19:31-41).

The situation, however, made impossible effective preaching in the immediate future. Paul, therefore, soon left for Macedonia (Acts 20:1), either by land to Troas and thence by sea to Neapolis, or by ship from Ephesus to Neapolis. He then followed the Egnatian Way west to Thessalonica, and proceeded south to Greece. He may have followed the route of his Second Journey, encouraging the Christians in Beroea, and thence going south to Athens and Corinth. Since, however, he later says that he had preached as far as Illyricum (xv, C 1-2; Rom. 15:19), and since we find embedded in the Pastoral Epistles a reference (which may date from this time) to his purpose to winter at Nicopolis (xv, D-3; Titus 3:12), the possibility remains that from Thessalonica he went west by the Egnatian Way to Dyrrhachium or Apollonia (xv, C-2), south to Nicopolis for the winter, and later to Athens or Corinth. We do not know the exact route of Paul's journeys; in most cases the map can show only a possible or probable route. The certain thing is that Paul spent three months in Greece (Acts 20:3), most of it perhaps at Corinth, and made his plans for his last visit to Jerusalem. His purpose was to take thither a collection for the poor Christians of Palestine.

His plan had been to go by ship to Syria and thence—from Ptolemais, perhaps, or Caesarea—to Jerusalem. A plot against his life by some Jews led him to change his plan and double back through Macedonia. He then crossed from Neapolis to Troas (Acts 20:3-5). Here he joined representatives of the Churches who were to go with him to take the collection to Jerusalem. When the ship left Troas, going south, Paul for some reason went by land as far as Assos (xv, E-3), where he boarded the ship (Acts 20:13, 14). Then began Paul's last voyage to Jerusalem. The first day the ship came to Mitylene (xv, E-3), chief city of the island of Lesbos (Acts 20:14). The next day they reached a point by Chios (xv, E-3); the third day they touched at Samos (xv, E-3); on the following day they came to Miletus. Here the ship stopped long enough for Paul to send to Ephesus, thirty miles away, and summon the elders of that Church to Miletus for final instructions (Acts 20:17). From Miletus the voyage led straight to the island or city of Cos (xv, E-3), then to Rhodes (xv, E-4), and next to Patara (xv, E-4), a port in Lycia (Acts 21:1). There they boarded another ship, sailed southeast, passing within sight of the west end of Cyprus, and came down to Phoenicia at Tyre (xv, G-4), where Paul visited Christian disciples before the ship went on to Ptolemais (Acts 21:3-7). From Ptolemais the party went on to Caesarea, the capital city of Palestine, either by sea or on the land route rounding Mount Carmel and following the coastal road south. After a few days in Caesarea they went up to Jerusalem (Acts 21:8-10, 15), to present the collection and to observe Pentecost.

FIG. 66. Areopagus, Athens. The smaller hill in the center of the picture is the Areopagus, "Mars' Hill," where Paul may have spoken to the Athenians (cf. Acts 17:22). Behind it is the Acropolis, on which stand the remains of the Parthenon.

FIG. 67. Ruins of the theater at Ephesus. Scene of the riot described in Acts 19:29–41. In the lower left center is the orchestra, around which the spectators' seats rise in semicircular tiers. The theater is said to have had a capacity of nearly 25,000. Note the street running toward the sea.

PAUL THE PRISONER

After the Roman guard seized Paul during the riot scene in the Temple court, they took him to the "castle" or Tower of Antonia at the northwest corner of the Temple area (Acts 22:24). When a plot against his life became known, the centurion sent him by way of Antipatris (xv, G-5) to the governor, Felix, in Caesarea (Acts 23:31-33). He was kept a prisoner in the palace which Herod the Great had built. After two years Festus replaced Felix (c. 60 B.C.). Festus desired to take Paul to Jerusalem for examination; but Paul, a Roman citizen, appealed to Caesar (Acts 25:11). He then had to be taken to Rome for a hearing before the emperor or his representative.

THE VOYAGE TO ROME

Luke's account of Paul's voyage to Rome is a marvel of graphic description. The centurion Julius and his soldiers embarked with Paul and other prisoners on a boat that touched at Caesarea. The vessel was going to Asia Minor and, as it seems (Acts 27:2), intended to go up the western coast to its home port, Adramyttium (xv, E-3). Since the winds were not favorable for travel to the west, the ship went north to Sidon (xv, G-4), where Paul was permitted to visit Christian friends. Thence the ship continued north, keeping east of Cyprus, and sailed west along the southern shore of Asia Minor to Myra in Lycia (xv, F-4). There the centurion transferred his charges to an Alexandrian ship headed for Italy (Acts 27:5 f.).

By slow sailing the ship worked westward until it was just south of the island of Cnidus (xv, E-4). It then struck south to come under the lee of Crete, passing by the promontory of Salmone (xv, E-4; cf. Acts 27:7). Under the protection of Crete the ship worked west to Fair Havens (xv, E-4), an anchorage near Lasaea. Winter, when sea travel was too dangerous for sailing vessels, was at hand, and the problem was to find the best place to stay during the stormy winter months. Fair Havens was too open to storms, and the sailors, with full knowledge of the risk, tried to sail west to Phoenix (xv, D-4), a safe harbor (Acts 27:12, 13). But a violent wind caught the ship and drove it away from the land. It came under the shelter of the small island of Cauda (xv, D-4), and the crew sought to strengthen the ship for the strain of the storm (Acts 27:16, 17). Then, for fear that they might be driven into Syrtis Major (xv, C-5), the treacherous shallows off the northern coast of Africa, they permitted the ship to be driven west in the sea called Adria, a name which then applied not only to the Adriatic Sea between Italy and Illyricum but also to the open sea west of Crete (xv, C-D 3-4).

After fourteen days of wild buffeting the ship drew near to land during the night (Acts 27:27). Anchors warded off disaster until dawn. Then a bay with a beach appeared (Acts 27:39), and the one chance of safety seemed to be to beach the ship. When this was attempted, however, clashing currents "where two seas met" drove the ship aground, and it broke up under the beating of the waves. The soldiers wanted to kill the prisoners lest they escape; but the centurion, friendly to Paul, vetoed this plan and permitted all to try to reach land. Some could swim; the others clung to wreckage and were washed ashore by the waves (Acts 27:43, 44).

They found (Acts 28:1) that the island was Melita or Melitene (xv, B-4), the modern Malta. There they were forced to winter. Fortunately for them, another ship of Alexandria was wintering there. When spring permitted, this ship, carrying the centurion and his party, sailed for Italy (Acts 28:11). The first stop was at Syracuse in Sicily (xv, B-3), an excellent harbor where they stayed three days. Then they made a circuit to Rhegium (xv, C-3), on the Italian side of the Straits of Messina (where were located the mythical Scylla and Charybdis). The final stage of the voyage was from Rhegium to Puteoli (Acts 28:13), a favored harbor for large ships coming from Egypt. From Puteoli (xv, B-2) the apostle was taken by road to Rome (xv, B-2). At Appii Forum and Tres Tabernae he was met by Christian friends. During the latter part of the land journey to Rome, Paul traveled the famous Appian Way (Fig. 56). Upon arrival, he was permitted to live in his own lodging under guard (Acts 28:15, 16, 30, 31).

Thus ends the book of The Acts. Paul had wanted to go to Spain (Rom. 15:24, 28). There is an ancient tradition that after two years he was released from prison, traveled in East and West, was again imprisoned, and finally was executed in Rome. Indeed, if the Pastoral Epistles in their present length come from Paul, they seem to require us to accept this tradition. But the authorship of the Pastoral Epistles is disputed. Perhaps only in a shorter form did they come from Paul. Yet, even if Paul took such journeys, we can say nothing definite about his itinerary.

Certain facts, however, are clear. Paul found the Christian movement a small fellowship, little known outside of Palestine and Syria, and left it a growing movement planted in almost all of the important provinces of the empire. He found it a movement just beginning to take root among Gentiles and left it a greatly enlarged Church open to Jew and Gentile alike. The Apostle Paul did more than any other man to plant the Church in the centers where it was destined to shape the future of Europe and America.

FIG. 68. Pompeii and Vesuvius. In A. D. 79 a violent eruption of volcanic Vesuvius covered with cinders and ashes the famous Italian resort city of Pompeii. Excavations during the last two centuries have thrown much light on the architecture, art, amusements, and daily life of the ancient Romans. This view looks across the forum.

THE EXPANSION OF CHRISTIANITY

PLATE XVI

I T IS often futile to ask why history happened as it did, but the student of Christian missions will understand the expansion of Christianity better if he inquires why the new faith so promptly spread west to find its center and greatest future in Europe. Certainly such a result could not have been clearly foreseen. Although the Apostle Paul is reported to have said that "this thing was not done in a corner" (Acts 26:26), a sophisticated Roman citizen residing in the capital of the empire might have asserted the very opposite, for Christianity arose on the far eastern border where the empire met and clashed with Oriental powers and influences. It originated in an obscure and apparently backward region of the empire, in a very small subdivision under the rule of a minor official. It emerged among a people who were constantly drawing criticism but from whom no empire-molding was expected.

Moreover, these Jews among whom Jesus appeared were by no means confined to the Roman Empire. They were also found in regions to the east, which were under Parthian control (Plate XIII, E-H 2-3). This fact is forcefully emphasized by the Pentecost story in Acts, ch. 2. When one carefully examines the list of places from which the Jews present at Pentecost had come, it is found that almost half of the regions mentioned are located outside of the eastern borders of the Roman Empire, and, with the exception of the city of Rome, those parts of the empire that are included in the enumeration are in the eastern half.

Palestine seemed poised between West and East, and there was no outward sign to guarantee that the rising Christian Church would move mainly to the west. Jesus in his ministry had seemed to shun cities of Hellenistic connection. Basically untouched by influences from the west, he had confined himself almost entirely to a ministry among Palestinian Aramaic-speaking Jews. These facts give added interest to the question, Why did the Church almost immediately turn westward?

WHY CHRISTIANITY SPREAD WESTWARD

Five factors go far to explain this somewhat unexpected development. In the first place, the possibility of such a growth was implicit in the purpose and program of Christ. For all his faithful loyalty to his people, he presented a message concerned with basic human needs and traits, and exhibited freedom from external, divisive elements of current religious life. He thus laid the foundation for a Church which made a universal appeal and increasingly transcended racial barriers.

A second factor was the wide westward dispersion of the Jews. In the first century, many more Jews lived outside of Palestine than in their homeland. While they were found in regions farther east, particularly in Babylonia, they were notably numerous in Egypt, Syria, Asia Minor, Africa, and Italy. Indeed, in almost every important center of the empire were Jews to whom Jewish Christians could take their Gospel appeal.

Still a third factor was the presence in Palestine, even among many of the Jews, of a strong strain of Hellenistic culture or influence. Here is probably the greatest significance of the Hellenistic expansion into Asia which Alexander the Great so greatly furthered and promoted. That eastward expansion of Hellenistic life established in the Semitic world a bridgehead which, although not permanent, furnished a transition point from which a religious movement arising among Aramaic-speaking Jews could find its way into the entire Roman Empire.

Basic to this transfer was a fourth factor, the widespread use of the Greek language, not only by most Gentile residents of the Roman Empire, but also by great numbers of its Jews. Most of these members of the Dispersion spoke Greek. Indeed, so did many Jews who lived in Palestine, and from this group came some of the members of the very early Church. This tie of common language, present in

FIG. 69. Coliseum and Arch of Constantine, Rome. The Coliseum, begun in A. D. 75 by Vespasian and completed in A. D. 80 by Titus, seated 80,000 spectators around an arena 282 x 148 feet. In this arena gladiatorial combats took place and during times of persecution Christians were forced to fight with wild beasts. The Arch of Constantine was erected by the Senate and People of Rome in A. D. 315 to commemorate Constantine's victory over Maxentius three years earlier. Constantine was the first Christian emperor; his victory over Maxentius, in which he is said to have seen a vision of the cross, gave him mastery of the western part of the Roman Empire.

Palestine, led out into all parts of the empire and even beyond, and enabled missionaries to go everywhere without the necessity of acquiring a new tongue before presenting the Gospel message.

The fifth important factor which promoted the westward trend of Christianity was the Roman Empire itself. Even though the new faith appeared on the very frontier, it was still within the sphere of Roman control and contacts and could move into other parts of the empire without international complications.

Plate XVI shows four stages in the expansion which Christianity made in the first three centuries. It must be confessed that the information one needs to make such maps is often far from adequate. The student of the ancient Church frequently has the feeling that there must have been Christian groups in a certain place at a given time, yet he lacks the evidence to support the surmise. He is often attracted by general references which early Christian writers make to the spread of the faith, but such statements are too vague to give real help. At other times there are full and confident traditions; but they are late and open to grave suspicion, which prevents their use in serious study. Yet, with all the drawbacks which the character and incompleteness of our sources create, evidence suffices to enable us to trace the general lines of the development in a dependable way.

THE CHURCH BEFORE PAUL'S JOURNEYS

Because the Apostle Paul brought about so great an enlargement in the territory touched by Christianity, it is well to begin by seeing what the Church had done before he entered upon his systematic mission. In this earliest period, the center of the Christian movement was in Jerusalem. Galilee, which had been so prominent in the ministry of Jesus, is mentioned but once in this connection in The Acts (ch. 9:31) and played no controlling role in the Apostolic Church. From Jerusalem the Christian Church spread out into Judaea, Samaria, and the coastal plain, where Lydda, Joppa, and especially Caesarea (XVI:A, E-3) became centers remembered in Christian tradition (Acts, ch. 8). Churches arose in Phoenicia, evidently at first among Jews (Acts 11:19; 15:3). Tyre and Sidon (XVI:A, E-3) were apparently early Christian centers there (Acts 21:4; 27:3). Greek-speaking Jews driven from Jerusalem after the martyrdom of Stephen founded a most important Church in Syria at Antioch (XVI:A, E-3), where there were large numbers of Jews. Here a Church containing both Jews and Gentiles marked a new stage in the growth of the Church (Acts 11:20). At some very early date a group of believers was formed in Damascus (XVI:A, E-3). When Saul, i.e., Paul, went to his home city Tarsus (XVI:A, E-3) after his conversion, he preached and founded Churches there and elsewhere in Cilicia (Gal. 1:21, 23; Acts 15:41).

Although men of Cyprus (XVI:A, E-3) and Cyrene (XVI:A, D-3) are mentioned in this period of the Church (Acts 11:20), there is no reason to suppose that Churches already existed in these two areas. Neither does the mention of the conversion of the Ethiopian eunuch (Acts 8:38) warrant the conclusion that there was already a Christian movement in his country by A.D. 45. Moreover, there is no trustworthy witness that Christianity had reached Egypt (XVI:A, E-4) in this early period.

It may be assumed with considerable probability, however, that a Christian group existed in Rome by A.D. 45. To be sure, the tradition, so widely circulated in later times, that the Apostle Peter founded the Roman Church must certainly be rejected. Yet other evidence more substantial must be heard. About A.D. 49 the Emperor Claudius expelled the Jews from Rome for rioting over "one Chrestus," and this is quite likely a reference to disputes in the synagogues over Christian claims that Jesus was the Christ. In the middle fifties, when Paul wrote a letter to the Church at Rome, he implied that it had been founded a considerable number of years before. These facts, combined with the fact that messages from all parts of the empire naturally traveled to Rome, make it probable that by A.D. 45 there were Christians in the capital. Whether the Christian Gospel was brought there by Jews who had been present at Pentecost (Acts 2:10), or by immigrants who had been converted in the eastern parts of the empire, or by travelers or traders temporarily in the capital, cannot be determined.

The overwhelming proportion of the Christians in this earliest period were Jews, although a large proportion of the Jewish Christians were Greek-speaking. Groups of believers were found in Palestine, Phoenicia, Syria, Cilicia, and probably in Rome. As yet, however, they constituted an apparently negligible fraction of the empire's population.

AT THE CLOSE OF PAUL'S MINISTRY

The wide extension of the Church in the next fifteen years was due largely to the energetic and statesmanlike work of the Apostle Paul. He developed a strategy of following main trade routes and stopping in important cities, from which the Gospel could spread out into adjacent territory. His journeys may be traced on Plate XV. Here we need only survey the extent of his achievements.

Paul and Barnabas brought Cyprus into the Christian circle. In this island, as in other regions which Paul touched, there was no thorough approach to the entire population. What the apostles did was to establish centers in Salamis and Paphos (XVI:B, E-3), and probably in other points (Acts 13:5 f.). In Asia Minor Paul's work took place in southern and western regions. He probably founded Churches in the province of Pamphylia (XV, F-3; Acts 13:13 f.; 14:25). The Churches of Galatia (Gal. 1:2) were probably those in Antioch, Iconium, Lystra, and Derbe (XVI:B, E 2–3; see Acts, chs. 13;14); the alternative theory that they were farther north in Ancyra, Pessinus, and Tavium (XV, F 2-3) is less likely. But the greatest work of Paul in Asia Minor was in the Roman province of Asia. The chief center was Ephesus (XVI:B, D-3), from which the Gospel was carried out to other cities of the province, such as Colossae (XVI:B, D-2), Laodicea, and Hierapolis (XV, E-3; Col. 4:13). The existence of a Christian group at Troas (XVI:B, D-2) is also clearly attested, and one at Assos is implied (XV, E-3; Acts 20:6-13).

In Macedonia and Achaia Paul founded Churches in Philippi (XVI:B, D-2), Thessalonica (XVI:B, D-2), Beroea (XVI:B, D-2), Corinth (XVI:B, D-2), and likewise at Athens (XVI:B, D-2), although the extent of his success there was limited (cf. Acts 17:32-34). In minor places also, such as Amphipolis and Apollonia in Macedonia (XV, D-2), and Cenchreae in Achaia (XV, D-3), it is likely that groups of believers were formed. Paul's reference to saints in "all Achaia" (II Cor. 1:1) suggests a rather vigorous outreach of influence from his center at Corinth; indeed, such outreach may be assumed to have occurred from every center where the apostle made a stay of any length.

Since Paul says that he preached the Gospel "round about unto

Illyricum" (XVI:B, C 1-2; Rom. 15:19), it is clear that there were then Christians on the western border of Macedonia. Whether Paul himself went there or whether he sent assistants to preach in that region is not easy to decide, but the existence of Churches on the west coast of Macedonia and probably also of Achaia must be accepted. If, as seems probable, the personal references in the Pastoral Epistles are historical, Paul evidently extended his work to the island of Crete (XVI:B, D-3; Titus 1:5) and took thought for a further ministry there.

The fact that The Acts centers its attention so largely upon Paul may give us a somewhat misleading picture. That Paul's work was the outstanding and permanently significant missionary achievement of the period is indisputable, but he certainly was not the only Christian actively engaged in such pioneer mission preaching. Yet the names and accomplishments of these contemporaries of Paul are unknown, and we cannot be sure how far their labors extended. No clear evidence survives of early work east of Syria. Egypt still receives no mention; the reference to Apollos as an Alexandrian does not prove the presence of a Church in Alexandria (XVI:B, D-4), since it does not appear that he had a clear understanding of Christianity when he came to Ephesus (Acts 18:25).

In two regions, however, we find an extension of the Church beyond the area covered by Paul. One is in northern Asia Minor. Indeed, if The First Epistle of Peter dated from the lifetime of Paul it would be sufficient to prove that practically all of Asia Minor was sprinkled with Churches at that time; for it mentions Pontus (XVI:B, E-2), Galatia (XVI:B, E-2), Cappadocia (XVI:B, E-2), Asia (XVI:A, D-2), and Bithynia (XVI:B, D-E 2; cf. I Peter 1:1). But even if this epistle is to be dated somewhat later, as is assumed to be the case for the purposes of this map, it still suggests the possibility that there were Christian Churches in northern Asia Minor as early as Paul's time. Hints from other sources support this view. Early in the second century A.D., Pliny wrote to the Emperor Trajan (A.D. 98-117) about conditions in Bithynia, and his letter reflects a long-established and numerically dominant Church whose origin may well extend back into Paul's day. More important is the fact that Paul felt definitely led to avoid Mysia (XV, E-3) and Bithynia (Acts 16:7 f.). In view of his policy of not working where others had laid the foundation of the Church (Rom. 15:20), the most likely explanation of his action is that there were already Churches in these regions.

The other region where further expansion of Christianity can be documented in this time was in and near Puteoli in Italy (XVI:B, C-2). When Paul landed there as a prisoner he found "brethren" (Acts 28:14). It is probable that by this time there were Christians also in the neighboring city of Pompeii (XVI:B, C-2; cf. Fig. 68).

In this second period of the expansion of Christianity the almost exclusively Jewish character of the Church gave way to a mixed membership, a development which was largely effected and successfully defended by Paul. The Church spread through most of Asia Minor, established itself in Macedonia, Achaia, and Crete, and further extended its bounds in Italy. Outstanding centers were Jerusalem, Antioch in Syria, Ephesus, Corinth, and Rome. Numerically the Church still constituted a very small proportion of the inhabitants of the Roman Empire.

THE TIME OF IRENAEUS

For the period which follows Paul's journeys we lack the data to trace even in broad outline the continuous development of the Church. The next three decades are almost a complete blank. From about A.D. 95 on we get glimpses and episodes. A little help comes from First Clement, a letter of the Roman Church to Corinth about A.D. 96. Some time about A.D. 115 Ignatius journeyed from Antioch in Syria (XVI:C, E-3) through Asia Minor, where he met with Christian leaders and wrote letters, still extant, to Churches in the area. He was being taken in chains to Rome, where he anticipated martyrdom. Between one and two generations later Marcion came from Pontus, where he had already become a Christian, to Rome. Other Roman leaders are known; rivalry between Ephesus and Rome is attested; the Montanist movement arose in Phrygia (XVI:A, D-E 2); Polycarp was martyred in Smyrna (XVI:C, D-2); and clues to the life of the Church throughout the empire begin to appear. But a connected, comprehensive story cannot be written.

The situation changes, however, about A.D. 185, when we may date the chief writing of the influential Christian leader Irenaeus. He gives much information about the situation in the Church, and thereafter the evidence of a succession of writers and sources makes it possible to present a more detailed picture of the successive stages in the life of the Church.

When in the time of Irenaeus the information becomes more abundant, it is clear that the Church has made tremendous strides. Extension to the east has begun. There are Churches in Edessa (XVI:C, E-3), the first place where Christianity became the official religion, and in Melitene (XVI:C, E-2), where the faith found adherents among soldiers. Egypt now appears as an important center of Christian life and scholarship. The discovery in recent years of

FIG. 70. Air view of Dura-Europos, on the Euphrates River (XVI:D, F-3). This city, a Roman military outpost on the eastern frontier, was destroyed in or shortly after A. D. 258. Recent excavations have uncovered not only pagan temples, but also a Jewish synagogue, adorned with striking wall paintings of Biblical scenes; a Christian church, built by remodeling a private home and containing not only a room for worship but also a baptistry marked by distinctive wall paintings; and a parchment sheet of Tatian's *Diatessaron* in Greek, clear proof of the presence of Greek-speaking Christians in Dura in the first half of the third century.

FIG. 71. Church of the Holy Sepulcher, Jerusalem. Built on the traditional site of the crucifixion and burial of Jesus. Constantine erected the first Christian church here in the early fourth century. After repeated destructions and rebuildings, essentially the present form appeared after the destructive fire of 1808. The present church is architecturally unsatisfying and structurally weak. Its parts are partitioned among various Christian groups, chiefly the Armenian, Greek Orthodox, and Roman Catholic groups.

Christian papyri dating from the early second century A.D. proves that Egyptian Christianity was not then confined to Alexandria (XVI:C, D-4) and the section near the sea, but extended up the Nile into the dry regions where papyri have been preserved in the sand through the centuries. In Cyrenaica, also, there were Christians in the region about Cyrene (XVI:B, D-3), although the sources mention other cities without including Cyrene itself. Farther west in Africa, the area about Carthage (XVI:C, B-2) was proving to be a fruitful field for Christian evangelism. Asia Minor was dotted with Christian centers. Macedonia and Achaia were likewise largely included in the sphere of Christian influence. A few cities of Thrace are known to have had Churches. North of Macedonia, in Dalmatia on the Adriatic Sea, the faith was beginning to take root. Beginnings at Syracuse (XVI:C, C-3), and further extension throughout Italy, are to be noted.

It is difficult to show on the map the evidence of Early Church writers concerning Christian advances in some portions of the empire. They mention the existence of Churches in a province, but fail to tell in what cities Christian missionaries have successfully preached. This is in part true of their references to the region of Gaul (modern France: XVI:C, A-B 1). It is definitely known that there were Christian Churches in Lyons and Vienne (XVI:C, B-1); for the story of persecutions there, about A.D. 177, makes the fact clear, and suggests that farther south in Gaul there were probably Churches. The mention of Churches in the Rhine River valley, however, is not explicit as to location; the most likely centers in that region may well be Cologne and Mainz (XVI:C, C-5). Christians are mentioned in Spain only a few years after the time of Irenaeus, and it may be taken as certain that Christian centers were found there by A.D. 185. The exact location of such centers is uncertain, but the cities of Astorga (XVI: C, A-1), Leon (XVI:C, A-1), Merida (XVI:C, A-2), and Saragossa (XVI:C, A-1) appear to be the most likely choices.

The early history of Christianity in Britain is obscure. It is entirely possible that there were Churches in the southeast portion of Britain in the latter part of the second century, but it is not possible to be certain of this.

Thus by the close of the third period which our survey covers the Church was established in many centers over the Roman Empire and had also crossed the eastern border. The predominantly Gentile character of the Church had long been a fact, and the center of leadership had moved westward. Jerusalem, rebuilt by the Romans as a Gentile city and renamed Aelia Capitolina, had dropped from its commanding role shortly after Paul's ministry. Antioch in Syria was not so dominant as in Paul's day. Alexandria, Ephesus, and Rome were outstanding centers. The remarkable geographical extension of the Church, however, must not obscure the fact that as yet the Christian group constituted but a small portion of the total population. It was a vigorous minority movement.

THE AGE OF CONSTANTINE

The fourth period witnessed both intensive and extensive advance of Christianity. For this period the evidence is gratifyingly full and explicit. Such documents as the lists of bishops who attended the Council of Arles (XVI:D, B-1) in A.D. 314 and the Council of Nicaea (XVI:D, D-2) in A.D. 325 provide clear proof that the Christian movement was not confined to key cities of provinces, but had taken root in most of the important centers of population in every portion of the empire. The cities shown on Plate XVI:D are only part of those in which it is known that Christian bishops then had their residence, but they are sufficient to give an impression of the intensive spread of Christianity in the Roman Empire. Practically every province is seen to be well covered with Churches. In Mauretania (XIII, A-B 2), in the provinces along the River Danube (XVI:D, C-D 1-2), in western Gaul and in England (see XVI:D, Inset) there is now clear evidence of a firmly established Christian life.

In addition to the intensive growth of the Church in regions previously reached by Christian missionaries, there was also in this period a considerable geographical expansion into new areas, particularly in the east. Evidence appears of Christians in Arabia, for example at Aila (XVI:D, E-4). There were Churches in Mesopotamia, Babylonia, and even farther east, beyond the Tigris (XVI:D, F-3), on the borders of Persia. Indeed, suggestions of Christian centers as far east as Bactria and India are not lacking, although it is extremely difficult to know what to make of the traditions concerning these regions. Part at least of the eastward outreach was connected with the Greek-speaking Church, as has been shown by the discovery at Dura-Europos (XVI:D, F-3; Fig. 70), on the Euphrates River, of a Christian chapel and a sheet of Tatian's *Diatessaron* in Greek. Farther north, Armenia (XVI:D, F-2) had become the first country of any size to become officially Christian. On the north side of Armenia, between the southern part of the Black and Caspian Seas, the region of Georgia may have been the scene of missionary work by the time of Constantine. In the region north and west of the Black Sea the Goths had had contact with Christianity, but the exact location and number of Christian groups in that area is unknown.

By the time of Constantine (A.D. 306-337), therefore, the Christian Church had established itself throughout most of the Roman Empire and was reaching out far beyond its eastern borders. The greater number of Christians undoubtedly lived within the empire, where Greek and to a lesser degree Latin were the languages used by Christians. In the eastern extension of the Church the use of Syriac and other tongues was involved, although, as stated, Greek was used even in regions where other tongues were widely employed. The Church was of course by this time strongly Gentile in composition. It was particularly strong in Italy, North Africa, Asia Minor, and Egypt.

It is worthy of note that up to this time the Church had been largely an urban movement. In spite of the fact that the ministry of Jesus was centered in villages and open country, the Church from its early days at Jerusalem took to the cities and preserved its urban emphasis throughout the period of our study.

It should also be held in mind that Christianity was still a minority movement at the close of our survey. Though Churches had been established throughout a wide area, a numerical majority had been attained in few places. With the conversion of Constantine, however, there arose a new situation, in which the former governmental attitude of tolerance or persecution gave way to active support. Thus encouraged, the Church was able in the next two centuries to bring a majority of the residents of the empire into the Christian fellowship.

THE HISTORY OF JERUSALEM

PLATE XVII

JERUSALEM is by far the most important city in the Bible. In it was the Temple, the focal point of Israelite and Jewish religious life and aspiration. Here David and Solomon, Isaiah and Jeremiah, Ezra and Nehemiah, lived and labored. Here too a portion of the ministry of Jesus took place; here he was crucified and raised up, and here the Christian Church was founded. During the seventh century A.D. Jerusalem was conquered by the Mohammedans and became, next to Mecca and Medina in Arabia, the most important holy place of the Moslem world. To Jews, Christians, and Mohammedans, therefore, it is in a special way the "holy city" (cf. Rev. 21:2, 24).

THE TOPOGRAPHY OF JERUSALEM

The site of Jerusalem has never been forgotten. In different periods its limits have varied, but one spot has remained constant. Unbroken tradition fixes the sacred area of the First or Solomonic Temple, the Second Temple, and the Herodian Temple of Jesus' day on the site now called the *Haram esh-Sherif* (Plate XVII:D, D-E 4-5). In Old Testament times the city proper lay chiefly south of this area. In the New Testament period it lay largely west and north.

Jerusalem is located on the central ridge of the hill country, 33 miles east of the Mediterranean and 14 miles west of the northern tip of the Dead Sea. Its highest part is 2,550 feet above sea level. To the east is the Mount of Olives, separated from the city by the Kidron Valley (or "The Brook," II Chron. 32:4). The Valley of Hinnom (this is the original meaning of the New Testament word Gehenna) lies south and west; during the period of the Judges this valley formed the boundary between the tribes of Judah and Benjamin (Josh. 15:8; 18:16; see Plate VI). Between these two main valleys stood a plateau connected with the central ridge on the north. A smaller north-south valley, which Josephus calls the Tyropoeon (i.e., valley of "cheese-makers") divides the plateau into two parts. Of these the Western Hill is larger than the Eastern, and also higher. Hence it was later called the Upper City (XVII: B-C, C 5-6).

Two springs were the main sources of the early city's water supply. The chief one, in the Kidron Valley, was called the Gihon (XVII:A, E-5). Another, just below the juncture of the Kidron and Hinnom Valleys, was called En-rogel (XVII:A, E-7). It may also be the Dragon's (or Jackal's, R.V.) Well of Neh. 2:13.

The location of the water supply determined that the earliest settlements should be located on the Eastern Hill, south of the Temple area and above the Gihon spring. In ancient times this hill was called, in its northern part at least, Ophel (XVII:A, D-E 5; Micah 4:8, R.V. marg.; II Chron. 27:3; 33:14; Neh. 3:26 f.; 11:21). This was also the site of the City of David, or Zion, and of the Jebusite city before it. This part of the Eastern Hill is not formidable in appearance, and since the fourth century A.D. tradition has associated Zion with the southern part of the Western Hill, where guides still show tourists the traditional Tomb of David (XVII:D, C-6). Archaeological investigation, however, has proved that Zion was south of the Temple area, as indeed it had to be in order to be near its water supply. In Old Testament times it was higher than at present; the Hasmonaeans in the second century B.C. removed the top of the Eastern Hill in order that it might not rival the Temple in height. By the time of Jesus the city had spread north and west; because of the use of aqueducts and cisterns, the Gihon spring was no longer the chief source of water (see Fig. 54). It is known that Pontius Pilate, Roman governor of Judaea from A.D. 26 to 36, built or repaired an aqueduct into the city and paid for the work with funds from the Temple treasury. This aqueduct may have run along the general line of the later Lower Aqueduct shown on Plate XVII: D, B-D 4-7.

JERUSALEM DURING THE OLD TESTAMENT PERIOD

Little is known of the history of Jerusalem before the fourteenth century B.C. The earliest archaeological remains on Ophel date from c. 3000 B.C. The name "Jerusalem" first occurs in Egyptian texts dating about 1900 B.C. In the fourteenth and thirteenth centuries B.C., before and during the conquest, the city was one of the main Canaanite city-states (see pp. 34, 44) of southern Palestine, with a mixed population (cf. Ezek. 16:3).

Shortly after 1000 B.C., the city was captured by David, who made it his capital (II Sam. 5:6 ff.; I Chron. 11:4, 5). As his personal property, it was now named the City of David. Plate XVII:A shows its approximate size. It was a small but powerfully fortified "stronghold" (II Sam. 5:7, 9). At its northern end was the Millo, apparently a raised platform on which the palace-citadel of David was erected. This palace, like that of Solomon, was built for David by Phoenician artisans of Hiram of Tyre (II Sam. 5:11).

No certain trace of Davidic building has been recovered. A portion of the Jebusite city wall and one of the gates have been excavated. The wall was exceedingly strong, being twenty-seven feet in width, and so well built that it was repaired and used as the main fortification of the City of David. A tower and revetment added to this wall above the Gihon spring have been excavated; they were probably built by David or Solomon.

Solomon found the City of David too small. He enlarged the city to the north and erected the Temple, his palace, and administrative buildings in the area of the present *Haram*. Near the center of this area today the beautiful "Dome of the Rock" (Fig. 73) covers an old sacred rock on which the altar of burnt offering once stood. The Temple itself was directly west of this point, and the court surrounding it (the Inner Court of I Kings 6:36 and the Upper Court of Jer. 36:10) probably had the approximate extent of the large platform on which the "Dome of the Rock" now stands. Directly south of the Temple, probably on a lower terraced level, were the palace of the king and that of his queen, Pharaoh's daughter. South of the palace were other administrative structures. Solomon thus built a separate governmental quarter in a special walled-in court (the Outer or Great Court; cf. I Kings 7:12).

While the Canaanites still controlled Jerusalem, they dug a rock

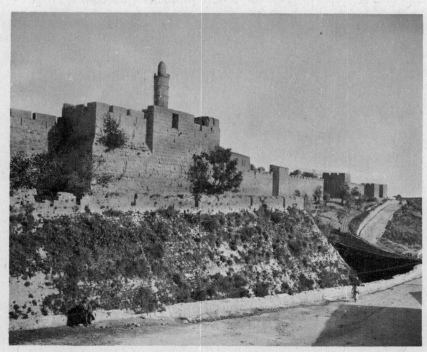

FIG. 72. Citadel and city wall, Jerusalem. On the left, the western exterior of the Citadel. On the right is seen the city wall running to the southwest corner of Jerusalem. The Citadel is on the site of Herod's Palace.

tunnel from near the top of the hill down to the Gihon, to give protection to those who drew water. Perhaps David's men gained access to the city by going up this watercourse, though it is doubtful that the Hebrew of II Sam. 5:8 contains any mention of it. In any event, at some later date, an aqueduct (cf. Isa. 7:3) was constructed along the edge of the hill from the Gihon to the Old or Lower Pool (XVII:A, D-E 5-6). Hezekiah abandoned these older waterworks and built the Siloam Tunnel, to carry the water of the Gihon to the new Upper Pool or Pool of Siloam or Shiloah (Neh. 3:15 has Shelah; XVII:A, D-6). He probably then built an outer wall at the south, enclosing the new pool so that water would be available in case of siege (XVII:A, D-6; II Chron. 32:4, 5, 30; Isa. 22:9 ff.; II Kings 20:20).

Various Old Testament passages seem to distinguish between the city of Jerusalem as a whole and the City of David. Even in Solomon's day, the city was probably spreading to the Western Hill. In fact, the First North Wall mentioned by Josephus (first century A.D.; see below) was perhaps built in part by Solomon. In the time of Manasseh and Josiah (seventh century B.C.), we first hear of the *Mishneh* or Second Quarter, in which were located the Fish Gate and the house of Huldah the prophetess (Zeph. 1:10; II Kings 22:14, R.V.); it was probably west or northwest of the Temple area. We are unable, however, to sketch the westward limits of Jerusalem at that time.

After North Israel fell, in 721 B.C., Jerusalem became increasingly important as the religious center and the symbol of the people's unity. Its capture and devastation by Nebuchadnezzar in 587 B.C. was a severe blow. Under Zerubbabel's leadership a new but smaller Temple was completed in 516 B.C., and under Nehemiah's direction the city fortifications were rebuilt (Ezra, chs. 5; 6; Neh., chs. 2 ff.).

For the next century Jerusalem was small and politically unimportant, although involved in trouble with the Persians which led to stern reprisals or possibly to actual capture and destruction. Two important developments, however, were in process. One was the increase in the proportion of Jewish population located outside of Palestine. Yet Judaism still centered in Jerusalem, and to this focal point its life flowed back in pilgrimages and gifts.

The other development was the increase of Greek influence in Palestine. Contacts and trade between Palestine and lands of Greek culture existed over a century before Alexander the Great appeared in 332 B.C. Under his successors, however, the program of achieving political unity by promoting cultural unity on a Hellenistic basis was purposefully developed. By the first half of the second century B.C. Greek dress, games, and customs were finding favor in Jerusalem. Most Jews, then as always, rejected such practices, yet athletic exercises were carried on in the Tyropoeon Valley, and some priests adopted Hellenistic ways.

When, therefore, in 168 B.C., Antiochus Epiphanes, determined to stamp out the Jewish religion, profaned the Temple and stopped the sacrifices, he must have counted on considerable support among the Jews. Nor did the Maccabean revolt at first appear a serious threat to his plans. He held not only the Temple area, but also the Acra or Citadel, a fortress probably located just south of the Temple precincts (XVII:C, D-5). After three years the Maccabeans regained control of the Temple and rededicated it, an occasion still recalled by Jews in December at the Feast of Dedication (see John 10:22 f.). The Maccabeans also built a fortress called Baris on a strategic rock elevation at the northwest corner of the Temple area. Not until some time after 142 B.C., however, did they expel the Syrians from the Acra. They then destroyed that citadel and cut down the top of the hill so that it no longer threatened the Temple.

The existence of a separate, distinct Judaism was thus assured, and the importance of Jerusalem preserved. But the later Maccabees, also called Hasmonaeans, became as devoted to Hellenistic ways as had been the Syrians. One building of this period which was still in use in Jesus' day was the Palace of the Hasmonaeans, located on the northeast brow of the Western Hill (XVII:B, D-5). The coming of Roman rule in 63 B.C., therefore, marked no decisive cultural break,

although in the decades just before and after this date the city was subjected to several damaging sieges which resulted from the unsettled political conditions. When Rome made Herod the Great king in A.D. 40, he followed the Roman pattern of promoting Hellenistic influence.

JERUSALEM IN HEROD'S DAY

Herod carried out extensive building projects in numerous places, but particularly in Jerusalem. He must have repaired the city walls, which Pompey had breached a few years before. The characteristic masonry of this period can still be seen in many places, as, for example, at the Wailing Wall (XVII:D, D 4-5; see Fig. 63).

At the northwest corner of the Western Hill, Herod built a fortified palace, with gardens, pools, and porticoes (XVII:B, B-C 5). On the north, where gates gave entrance and attacks were most to be feared, Herod built three great towers: Hippicus, Phasael, and Mariamme, named in honor of a friend, a brother, and Herod's favorite wife. Recent excavations show that the tower Phasael was located where the Tower of David now stands (XVII:D, C-5). Hippicus must have stood slightly southwest, Mariamme a little east of Phasael. All three were built into the old city wall.

Herod rebuilt the Baris and renamed it Antonia (XVII:B, D 3-4). At each of its corners was a tower. Two stairways or bridges connected it with the Temple porticoes, to enable its garrison to watch and control the Temple courts. There must have been some space between the porticoes and Antonia, for in the Jewish revolt the Jews isolated the Temple by cutting away the stairs, and Josephus describes fighting between the Temple and Antonia.

Herod erected many other buildings in Jerusalem—a theater, amphitheater, hippodrome, et cetera—but his most ambitious project was the rebuilding of the Temple. He used specially trained priests in the building work and so executed the plan that the worship of the Temple was not interrupted. The rebuilding of the sanctuary proper, begun in 20-19 B.C., was completed in eighteen months, but the complete reconstruction of the entire plan Herod did not live to achieve. Indeed, it was not completed until A.D. 64. For this larger plan Herod prepared a larger Temple area. By the use of massive retaining walls on the slopes of the Temple Hill he extended the area of the outer court, although probably not so far northward as it now reaches.

The main parts of the Temple area are indicated on Plate XVII:B. It had at least eight gates: four on the west, two on the south, and one each on east and north. Around the outer court ran porticoes. The Royal Porch, on the south, was wider than the others. On the east was Solomon's Porch. Inside these porticoes was the Court of the Gentiles, the only court which Gentiles could enter. Signs in Greek at the gates leading to the inner courts warned Gentiles not to go farther. Two such notices have been discovered; they read:

No foreigner is allowed within the balustrade and embankment about the sanctuary. Whoever is caught [violating this rule] will be personally responsible for his ensuing death.

On the east side of the inner structure steps led up to the main gate of entrance; probably this was the Beautiful Gate (cf. Acts 3:2, 10). Within was the Court of the Women, the last court which Jewish women could enter. Here were collection boxes into which gifts were put (Mark 12:41). The men of Israel could go up the steps into the Court of Israel, where they could watch the sacrifices being offered on the altar of burnt offering in the center of the Court of the Priests. West of the altar, steps led up into an ornamental porch, through which ministering priests entered the Holy Place, a room 30 x 60 feet. West of this room, behind a veil, was the Most Holy Place, 30 x 30 feet, into which the high priest entered on the Day of Atonement. Around the sides of the sanctuary were storerooms and treasuries. Special chambers for the priests were located at appropriate places in the Temple area, especially in the northern part. Meetings of religious leaders were held on occasion in the Council Chamber just west of the Temple area (XVII:B, D-4), and a viaduct across the Tyropoeon Valley gave easy access to the Upper City (XVII:B, D-5).

JESUS IN JERUSALEM

Jerusalem was the scene of comparatively little of Jesus' ministry, but his dramatic and momentous experiences there merit careful attention. His visit to Jerusalem when twelve years of age (Luke 2:42) recalls the fact that great throngs went there for the three great festivals of the Jewish year. It also reminds us that pilgrimages and religious devotion gave Jerusalem much of its economic support.

Of places mentioned in the Gospels, the Pool of Siloam is certainly known (XVII:B, D-6). The Pool of Bethesda is probably not the Pool of Israel (XVII:D, D-E 3) or the Virgin's Spring (Gihon) or the Pool of Siloam, but the pool, now many feet below the surface, near the present Church of St. Anne (XVII:B, D-3). Solomon's Porch, where Jesus walked in December for protection from wintry winds (John 10:23), was the east portico.

In the triumphal entry Jesus used a gate located approximately where the walled-up Golden Gate now stands (XVII:D, E-4). When he cleansed the Temple he drove traders and money-changers from the Court of the Gentiles; only this part of the Temple area was a "house of prayer for all the nations" (Mark 11:17). The place of the Last Supper is not certainly known; strong ancient tradition fixes the site at the modern Coenaculum (XVII:D, C-6). The modern Grotto of the Agony and the Gethsemane Church (XVII:D, E 3-4) show approximately where Jesus withdrew for prayer on his last night (Mark 14: 26, 32). Dubious tradition locates the house of Caiaphas just north of the Coenaculum (XVII:D, C-6).

The Praetorium where Jesus stood before Pilate was probably in the Palace of Herod rather than in the barracks at Antonia. If this is so, the traditional Via Dolorosa (XVII:D, C-D 3-4) cannot have been the path from Pilate's residence to the crucifixion. To take Jesus to Herod Antipas (Luke 23:7), then, the guard would have taken Jesus from the Palace of Herod to the Palace of the Hasmonaeans.

The traditional site of the crucifixion, continuously identified as such since the time of Constantine (C.A.D. 325), is where the Church of the Holy Sepulcher now stands (XVII:D, C-4). A recent rival claim for a hillock called Gordon's Calvary (XVII:D, C-3) has little strength, and the "Garden Tomb" near by, in which some hold that Jesus was buried, probably dates several centuries later than the first.

THE FIRST-CENTURY WALLS

Discussion of the site of the crucifixion requires a study of the walls of first-century Jerusalem. On the south, the wall ran approximately as seen on Plate XVII:C. Later, however, the south wall, as excavations show, ran northeast to the Temple area along the line JKLMN, leaving the southern Tyropoeon and the ancient City of David outside the wall. Another later course followed much the line of the modern wall.

On the north were at least four ancient walls. The earliest ran eastward from the Palace of Herod to the Temple area. The second north wall is discussed below. Herod Agrippa I began a third wall about A.D. 42; it enclosed the hill Bezetha and other sections north of the second wall. This third wall was long thought identical in course with the present north wall. A century ago, however, traces of it were found much farther north, and in the last twenty years nearly 800 yards of it have been discovered. The rest of its course can be plotted with little error by noting the elevation of the land. The tower of Psephinus, at its northwest corner, was probably on the edge of high ground northwest of the city.

Ancient remains along the course of the present north wall are proved by recent soundings to be from a wall built by Hadrian about A.D. 135. Before that date there was no wall along this line.

The second north wall began at the Gate Gennath, which was probably between the towers Hippicus and Phasael, encircled a section north of the first wall, and ended at Antonia. Four courses for it have been suggested. The circular course indicated by the letters ABCDP is unlikely; some evidence indicates this wall ran west, not north, from Antonia. The course AEFH encloses too small an area, and places the Gate Gennath too far east. Prevailing tradition favors the course AEFGP. Some debated remains of walls and a line of ancient cisterns appear to support this view. This, however, is a queer course for a city wall. Walls were built for defense; yet this line runs on low ground as compared with the ground outside it. Moreover, the traditional view assumes that the wall left a hill, Golgotha, just outside. Military judgment would have dictated the inclusion of such a hillock within the wall. On the whole, and with considerable hesitation, one may conjecture that the wall which ran west from Antonia and north from Phasael followed more nearly the line marked AEGP. If so, the traditional site of Golgotha cannot be authentic, and we do not know where Jesus was crucified and buried.

EARLY CHRISTIAN JERUSALEM

Apostolic Christianity was closely linked with Jerusalem and the Temple. The disciples met in Solomon's Porch; Peter and John went up to the Temple at the hour of prayer; they healed the lame man at the Beautiful Gate; even Paul the Apostle to the Gentiles was fulfilling a vow in the Temple when his enemies started a riot, dragged him out of the inner court, and caused the Roman guards to rush down from the Tower of Antonia and arrest him. From the stairs leading to the tower he addressed the crowd. Later he was confined in Antonia until sent to Caesarea. It was not until the Jewish revolt began in A.D. 66 that the Christian group, prompted by an oracle, left the city and moved to Pella, east of the Jordan. In A.D. 70 Jerusalem with its Temple was destroyed by the Romans. It was later rebuilt as a pagan city by the Romans, who renamed it Aelia Capitolina.

The Christian emperor Constantine gave the city new prestige as a Christian center and began the building of great churches to commemorate events in the life of Christ. From the seventh century to the First World War, with a few interludes, such as the Crusades, when Palestine was held by Christian armies, Jerusalem was under Mohammedan rulers and the Temple area was a possession, as it still is, of Moslem worshipers. For the last twenty-five years the British, with a mandate over Palestine, have controlled the rest of the city.

FIG. 73. Dome of the Rock, Jerusalem. The sacred rock under the dome is probably the site of the ancient Jewish altar of burnt offering. The beautiful octagonal structure, built late in the seventh century, stands on a raised platform some ten feet above the surrounding area. Just to the right of the Dome of the Rock is the Dome of the Chain. Mount Scopus is seen north and northeast of Jerusalem.

FIG. 74. Panorama of Jerusalem and vicinity, made in 1938, looking northeast. The present walls were built in 1542 by Sultan Suleiman the Magnificent. Within the walls the most striking feature is the *Haram esh-Sherif*, now under strict control of the Moslems, but occupying the site of the ancient Temple area. On an elevated platform in the center stands the Dome of the Rock (Fig. 73), sometimes wrongly called the Mosque of Omar. It was built at the end of the seventh century over the sacred rock where probably was located the Jewish altar of burnt offering. Jerusalem's four quarters reflect the religious faiths of the residents. The Moslems occupy the northeast quarter, the Jews are in the south center, the Armenians in the southwest section, and other Christian groups in the northwest quarter. In the latter section is the Church of the Holy Sepulcher (Fig. 71), on the spot where according to prevailing Christian tradition Jesus was crucified and buried. The tower at the northwest corner of the *Haram* marks the approximate site of Herod's Tower of Antonia. Thence the traditional *Via Dolorosa*, or road which

Christ trod on his way to the cross, runs west toward the Church of the Holy Sepulcher. It is very uncertain, however, that this traditional route was the true one; it is also uncertain that the Church of the Holy Sepulcher marks the spot of Jesus' death and burial (see p. 99).

In recent decades the city has spread north and west. Important business and government buildings cluster near the northwest corner of the city wall. The railroad station is at the bottom, left of center. The Y.M.C.A. and King David Hotel, west of the old city, are recent structures. The American School of Oriental Research, in the top center, is the hub of American archaeological study in Palestine. The splendid new Museum is near the northeast corner of the city wall.

To bring in as many features as possible, the artist has distorted perspective at the extreme upper and lower right. Nevertheless, the panorama is valuable because it shows so many sites and is such a graphic visual aid.

PLATE XVII

A

JERUSALEM IN ISRAELITE TIMES

Copyright, The Westminster Press
International Copyright Secured. All Rights Reserved

SCALE

0 — 150 — 300
METERS

0 — 500 — 1000
FEET

THE CANAANITE CITY
AND THE CITY OF DAVID ———
SOLOMONIC CONSTRUCTION ———
THE WALL OF HEZEKIAH ———

MISHNEH OR
SECOND QUARTER?

(The N and NW extent of
the city after the time
of Solomon is unknown)

Temple □Altar

Solomon's Palace
and Governmental
Buildings

CITY OF DAVID / OPHEL

Millo?
Valley or
Dung Gate

Gihon
←Hezekiah's Aqueduct

Old Aqueduct
(before 700 B.C.)

Upper Pool or
Pool of Shiloah
(Shelah)

The King's Garden?

Lower or Old Pool

KIDRON VALLEY

VALLEY OF HINNOM

En-rogel

B

JERUSALEM IN THE
TIME OF CHRIST

Copyright, The Westminster Press
International Copyright Secured. All Rights Reserved

SCALE

0 — 150 — 300
METERS

0 — 500 — 1000
FEET

WALLS OF JESUS' DAY ———

BEZETHA

Pool of Bethesda?

SECOND NORTH WALL?

Tower of Antonia
Stairway
Stairway
West Portico
Altar of
Burnt Offering
North Portico
Court of Women
Temple
Beautiful Gate?
Solomon's Porch
Council Chamber
Court of Israel
Xystus?
Court of Gentiles

SUBURB

Phasaelus
Mariamme
Hippicus

FIRST NORTH WALL

Palace
of Herod
Palace of
Hasmoneans?
Royal Porch
Viaduct
Huldah Gates

GETHSEMANE

UPPER
CITY

TYROPOEON VALLEY

LOWER CITY

OPHLAS

Gihon

GEHENNA OR VALLEY OF HINNOM

Pool of Siloam

Lower
or Old Pool

KIDRON VALLEY

ACELDAMA?

En-rogel

C

THE WALLS OF JERUSALEM
IN CHRISTIAN TIMES

Copyright, The Westminster Press
International Copyright Secured. All Rights Reserved

SCALE

0 — 150 — 300
METERS

0 — 500 — 1000
FEET

WALLS OF JESUS' DAY ———
LATER WALLS ———

Tomb of Queen Helena

THIRD NORTH WALL

Psephinus?

HADRIAN'S WALL

B

BEZETHA

Pool of Bethesda?

E
A
Tower of
Antonia

C
SECOND NORTH WALL?

D

SUBURB

G

P Mariamme
Hippicus Phasael
Palace
of Herod

FIRST NORTH WALL

H

To Mount
of Olives

UPPER
CITY

N

TYROPOEON VALLEY

ACRA VALLEY

Gihon

L
M

J
K

Pool of Siloam

Lower
or Old Pool

KIDRON

GEHENNA OR VALLEY OF HINNOM

En-rogel

D

JERUSALEM TODAY

Copyright, The Westminster Press
International Copyright Secured. All Rights Reserved

SCALE

0 — 150 — 300
METERS

0 — 500 — 1000
FEET

PRESENT CITY WALL ———

AMERICAN COLONY

Tomb of the Kings

St. George's
Cathedral

American School of
Oriental Research

Abyssinian
Church

Ecole
Biblique

Italian Hospital

Museum

Hadassah Hospital

Gordon's
Calvary

Herod's
Gate

Russian
Cathedral

Damascus
Gate

Church of
St. Anne

Pool of
Bethesda

St. Stephen's
Gate

Grotto
of the Agony

Post Office

Via
Dolorosa

Barracks

Pool of
Israel

Mamilla
Pool

CHRISTIAN
QUARTER

New
Gate

Church of the
Holy Sepulcher

Via
Dolorosa

HARAM

Gethsemane
Church

ESH-SHERIF

Dome
of the Rock

(Golden)
Gate

Old
Post Office

Hezekiah's
Pool

Dome
of the Chain

Gate of the Chain

Tomb
of Absalom

Jaffa Gate
Citadel
David's
Tower

Walling Wall

Mosque
el-Aksa

Solomon's
Stables

Y.M.C.A.

ARMENIAN
QUARTER

King David Hotel

Zion
Gate

JEWISH
QUARTER

(Double)
Gate

(Triple)
Gate

Dung Gate

House of
Caiaphas

Virgin's Spring

Sultan's
Pool

Coenaculum
(David's Tomb)

Siloam

Lower Pool

MOUNT OF
OFFENCE

KIDRON VALLEY

SILWAN

Railroad
Station

VALLEY OF HINNOM

Lower Aqueduct

Job's Well

ACELDAMA?

HILL OF
EVIL COUNSEL

PLATE XVIII

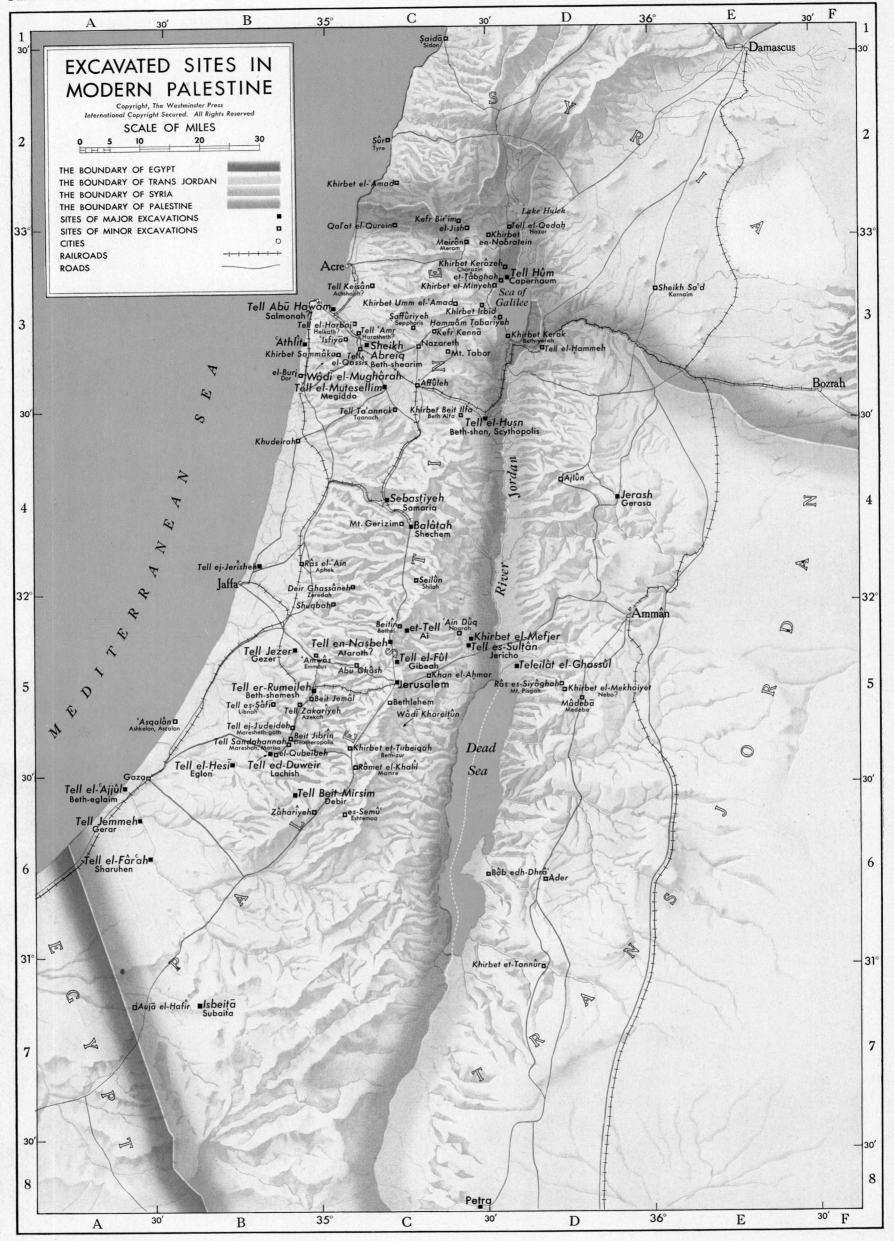

EXCAVATED SITES IN
MODERN PALESTINE

Copyright, The Westminster Press
International Copyright Secured. All Rights Reserved

SCALE OF MILES

0   5   10   20   30

THE BOUNDARY OF EGYPT
THE BOUNDARY OF TRANS JORDAN
THE BOUNDARY OF SYRIA
THE BOUNDARY OF PALESTINE
SITES OF MAJOR EXCAVATIONS
SITES OF MINOR EXCAVATIONS
CITIES
RAILROADS
ROADS

FIG. 75. *Tell el-Ḥuṣn*, the mound containing the ruins of ancient Beth-shan. In the Roman-Byzantine period the town, then called Scythopolis, was situated on level ground mainly to the south (right) of the *tell*, but the cathedral was constructed on top of the mound over the ruins of a long series of earlier pagan temples.

EXCAVATIONS IN MODERN PALESTINE

PLATE XVIII

A LARGE part of what has been written in the pages of this *Atlas* could not have been written, nor could the maps themselves have been prepared, had it not been for the many years of intensive exploration in the Holy Land by scores of devoted students of the Bible. On Plate XVIII may be found the places where excavations have been conducted to determine the nature and history of the ancient towns, though the mere listing of the sites does not tell the complete story, nor does it give any inkling of the problems that have been solved or of the reasons for solving them. Chief among these problems are: how to locate and identify the ancient sites, how to dig the ruins properly, and how to date what is found. These matters have been discussed by Professor Albright on pp. 9-14. Here we need only mention that the journeys of Edward Robinson in 1838 and 1852 and the Survey of Western Palestine by the Palestine Exploration Fund between 1872 and 1878 were the first great achievements in Palestinian archaeology, achievements which formed the basis of all later topographical work.

Between 1920 and 1940 a number of well-trained scholars have studied and traveled extensively through the country and have arrived at a point far beyond that reached by their predecessors. Modern explorers like Albright and Glueck have been able to advance beyond their forerunners, in large part because they have developed new and refined methods for checking conclusions and for 'dating the ruins explored. For example, Num. 33:49 tells us that the Israelites after the conquest of Transjordan "encamped by the Jordan, from Beth-jeshimoth even unto Abel-shittim in the plains of Moab." Study of the places where these towns had been located by former explorers now reveals that the ruins could not be those of the Israelite period because they date from Roman times. The earlier sites have been discovered a little farther back in the hills along the same valleys (IX, H 5-6; the names Besimoth and Abila of the New Testament period are given to the later ruins). When peace prevailed under a stable government, the people moved their towns out into the plain near their crops; but before that they had to live in the hills near good springs at sites which possessed natural features to aid in fortification and defense even though they were some distance from the fields.

EARLY EXCAVATIONS

The ability to date the ancient ruins is the result of years of excavation. It is comparatively easy to recognize the typical site where an ancient city once stood in western Asia. It is in the shape of a truncated cone, possessing a flat top and steep, sloping sides (Fig. 75). This shape is preserved because the stumps of old city walls remain in the slopes and prevent erosion. The name which the Arabs use for such a mound is *tell*, a word which is very old, occurring not only in the Old Testament but in Babylonian literature as well. The Authorized Version of Josh. 11:13 reads as follows: "But as for the cities that stood still in their strength, Israel burned none of them, save Hazor only." The word here translated "strength" is really *tell*, and the words should be translated, "the cities that stood on their *tells*" (cf. R.V.).

When one digs into an ancient *tell*, he usually finds the ruins arranged in layers or strata, one above another. The reason for this is that the typical city was repeatedly destroyed and rebuilt through the centuries of its history. *Tell el-Ḥuṣn* ("Mound of the Fortress"), on which ancient Beth-shan was located, contains eighteen different strata of debris and ruined houses, accumulated during the four thousand years of its intermittent occupation (XVIII, C-4). The depth of the debris from the topmost layer to virgin soil was about seventy-nine feet. The smaller Judaean mound of *Tell Beit Mirsim* (XVIII, B-6), occupied for some two thousand years, has about twenty feet of debris and ten strata.

It is not surprising that the translators of the Authorized Version did not understand the significance of a *tell*. Neither Edward Robinson nor the Survey of Western Palestine understood its full significance. The first demonstration of its true nature came in 1872-1874 with the excavations conducted by Schliemann at Troy (II, D-2). Even so, many years passed before the archaeological world as a whole was convinced. Lacking, therefore, a knowledge of the nature of a mound, and, more important, lacking an ability to date the ruins uncovered, early excavations were little more than treasure hunts. The "Tomb of the Kings" in Jerusalem, for instance, was so com-

FIG. 76. The American School of Oriental Research in Jerusalem. For its location in the city, see XVII: D, C-2.

pletely misinterpreted that, while actually dating from the first century A.D., it was thought to be the mausoleum of the kings of Judah (XVII:D, C-1)! Excavations around the walls of Jerusalem by Warren (1867-1870) were carried out with great vigor, but the information gained was scarcely commensurate with the effort required.

The year 1890 was a turning point in archaeological work, for in that year W. M. Flinders Petrie made a small excavation at *Tell el-Hesi* (XVIII, B-5). Here he showed that the pottery varied greatly in the different levels and that it was possible to set up a chronological scheme by means of it. This was the key needed to determine the date of excavated ruins. In a poor country like Palestine where monumental inscriptions are few, and the moist climate destroys papyrus documents, some other means of dating must be found. In the fifty years since Petrie's work the study of Palestinian pottery has been greatly advanced; and today, given a representative collection of broken fragments, it is usually possible for the expert to date them within a century, though the pottery styles of some periods are better known than others.

Between 1890 and 1914 there were a number of important excavations. In 1891-1893 an American named Frederick Jones Bliss continued Petrie's work at *Tell el-Hesi* for the Palestine Exploration Fund, clearing one third of the mound to bedrock. So little money was available for the publication of the discoveries, however, that neither they nor their stratification were adequately described. Between 1894 and 1897, Bliss conducted excavations in the southern part of Jerusalem to determine the line of the ancient walls and the extent of the city. Ruined fortifications along the southern edge of both the western and the eastern hills were unearthed (XVII:C, B-D 6), but their date was not precisely determined. Those which he found on the western hill probably do not go back to the time of Christ, as many have thought. They date chiefly from the Byzantine and Crusader periods, though they may follow the lines of earlier walls.

In 1898, Bliss was joined by R. A. S. Macalister, a young English archaeologist, and together they examined four tells in the Judaean Shephelah: *Tell es-Ṣâfī*, *Tell Zakarîyeh*, *Tell ej-Judeideh*, and *Tell Sandaḥannah* (XVIII, B-5). Judaean ruins were found in the first three; the most important was a strongly walled citadel at *Tell Zakarîyeh* (Azekah) which may have been built by Rehoboam (II Chron. 11:9), though the exact date was not determined. At *Tell Sandaḥannah* the best preserved Hellenistic town yet found in Palestine was unearthed. None of the discoveries were adequately published, however, and little can be said about them.

Macalister then undertook the first major excavation of a mound at *Tell Jezer* (XVIII, B-5). Most of the site was cleared in five campaigns between 1902 and 1909. This was a great achievement, the more so because Macalister directed the work alone, with no assistance except that of an able Arab foreman. He divided the mound into north-south strips, each forty feet wide, and dug the strips one at a time. At first he was able to keep check on the strata and the objects found in each. As time went on, however, he found it in-

creasingly difficult to correlate the strata of one strip with those of other strips near by and to observe and record accurately the precise level from which the objects came. Hence, the value of his energetic work is largely dissipated. In general terms we can now recount the history of the site and its fortifications, but we cannot be precise. The most interesting discovery was that of a Canaanite sacred area in which there were a number of large, upright stones (Hebrew *maṣṣēbôth*). Similar installations have been found elsewhere, particularly in Transjordan, but their religious function, whether as symbols of deities or memorials erected for ancestors, is not yet clear.

The accomplishments of German archaeologists between 1901 and 1905 at Taanach and Megiddo (XVIII, C-3) were far less even than that of Macalister. They destroyed far more evidence than they recovered. At Taanach the most important discovery was a Canaanite structure which contained a few cuneiform tablets dating about a century earlier than the Amarna period. The meaning of the seemingly chaotic results of the Megiddo expedition has been clarified only in part by recent excavations (see below). Interesting objects were discovered, among which was the official seal of "Shema, servant of Jeroboam." This individual is not mentioned in the Old Testament, but the Jeroboam of the seal was undoubtedly the king who reigned in Israel during the early part of the eighth century. The expression "servant" on this and other similar seals means "royal official."

German work at Jericho (1907-1909) was a great improvement over previous excavations, because for the first time the importance of an adequate trained staff was realized. This was the second major excavation before the First World War, and considerable information was gained about the houses and fortifications of Jericho, though some of the strata were misdated by several centuries (see further below).

The third major excavation of this period, and by far the most important, was the work of Harvard University at Samaria (XVIII, C-4), directed by the Americans George A. Reisner and Clarence S. Fisher between 1908 and 1910. Important discoveries were made, including a magnificent temple built by Herod the Great, under which were the ruins of the palace of the Israelite kings (see further below). Equally important was the development by these excavators of the method of excavation now in use throughout the Near East (see p. 10).

EXCAVATIONS BETWEEN 1920 AND 1940

In the story of Palestinian excavations the period before 1920 must be considered largely as one of preparation for what was to come. There were significant discoveries, but none were so important as the knowledge of how to dig and how to date what was found. Consequently, when excavations began again after the war, far more valuable results were obtained. In addition, a number of organizations now entered the field whose co-operative endeavor and sharing of information made advance more rapid. One of the most significant events occurred in 1920, when the Department of Antiquities in Palestine was established by the British Government. Digging by unauthorized and untrained persons was now forbidden, but the work of trained and well-equipped expeditions was greatly encouraged. Before the war the latter were hampered by a corrupt Turkish Government and oppressive laws.

Another significant organization was the American School of Oriental Research in Jerusalem, which has done much to encourage co-operation between national and religious groups and institutions, serving as a clearing house for information, and providing a place where students can study (Fig. 76). Likewise important was the interest taken by the Rockefeller Foundation, which gave to the Government of Palestine $2,000,000 for the establishment of the Palestine Archaeological Museum. In addition, numerous educational institutions have taken a direct interest in the work on a scale far greater than before 1914.

The largest and most elaborate excavation ever planned in Palestine was that at Megiddo (XVIII, C-3; and Fig. 5) by the Oriental Institute of the University of Chicago. The entire site was purchased so that it could be completely dug as a model excavation for the whole of the Near East. The work began in 1925, and during the following decade the first four strata were entirely removed. These dated from the fourth back to the tenth century B.C. The first stratum contained the scattered ruins of the Babylonian and Persian periods, including the walls of an exceedingly strong building that must have been the palace of the district officer. Stratum II contained the ruins of the palaces used by the Assyrians when they ruled the province of Galilee from this site (Plate VII:C). Strata III and IV were Israelite; the earliest phase of IV dated from the time of Solomon, who made the city the capital of his fifth administrative district in Israel (Plate VII:A). Royal stables for horses (cf. I Kings 9:15 ff.) and the palace built for Baana, the district governor (I Kings 4:12), are among the most interesting discoveries.

After some ten years of work the comprehensiveness of the excavation's plan had to be abandoned. Between 1935 and 1938 sections were dug to bedrock which showed that the city had been founded about 3500 B.C. and throughout its history had been one of the strongest and most important in Palestine. During the time of the Patriarchs, about 1900 B.C., three temples with a large adjoining altar for burnt offerings were erected. The main altar in ancient temple enclosures always stood in an open court (cf. II Chron. 7:7), but this is the first large one yet found intact in Palestine. A later temple and the elaborate palace of the local king during the time of Joshua have also been recovered (Figs. 28 and 29).

Next in importance must be placed the excavation of Beth-shan (XVIII, C-4; Fig. 75) between 1921 and 1933 by the University Museum of Philadelphia. The major discoveries were a Byzantine Church and monastery, a Hellenistic temple of the third century B.C., and a series of Canaanite temples dating between the fourteenth and tenth centuries B.C. The Hellenistic structure is a good illustration of the general type of Phoenician temple plan and is similar in its main features to the Solomonic Temple (Fig. 31). The Canaanite temples and their contents are our most important source of information regarding the material equipment of Canaanite religion. Two of them, the "houses" of Ashtoreth and Dagon, are mentioned in the Old Testament (I Sam. 31:10; I Chron. 10:10), and were probably destroyed by David. In any event, the city was laid waste shortly after 1000 B.C. and remained virtually unoccupied for centuries. Between the fifteenth and early twelfth centuries an Egyptian garrison was stationed there, and at least three Pharaohs left their stelae (monumental inscriptions) in the temple area.

Numerous other excavations vie with each other to be mentioned next. *Tell Beit Mirsim* (XVIII, B-6), dug by the American School of Oriental Research in Jerusalem and the Xenia (now Pittsburgh-Xenia) Theological Seminary, under the direction of W. F. Albright, has become a type site because of the many well-preserved strata and the excellence of the excavation. Few spectacular objects were found, but the detailed history of the site and the significance of its various features as reconstructed by the excavator are a most important addition to our knowledge of ancient Palestine.

Of particular interest to students of the Old Testament have been the English excavations at Jericho (XVIII, C-5) between 1930 and 1936, directed by John Garstang. German excavations before the First World War (see above) had already revealed something of the city's history. Garstang's results have greatly clarified and amplified this information. The center of interest naturally lies in the Canaanite city, the fall of which is described in Josh., ch. 6. About 1500 B.C. the city was provided with a strong double fortification of brick (see p. 36). The evidence of violent destruction was clear. The walls had toppled over down the sides of the mound. The base of the outer wall had shifted, and the debris gave evidence of a terrific conflagration and earthquake. Houses were filled with the burned remains, including charred roofing beams, onions, bread, wheat, barley, oats, and dates. There has been considerable debate over the date of this destruction, but it is now certain that it was some time before 1300 B.C.

The city then remained virtually uninhabited until the tenth-ninth centuries (cf. Josh. 6:26 and I Kings 16:34). Since other evidence points to a thirteenth century date for Joshua, this information concerning the final fall of Canaanite Jericho furnishes the major problem in the historical reconstruction of the Exodus and the Conquest (see pp. 39 f.).

Similarly, the excavation of Ai (XVIII, C-5) in 1933-1934 by Mme. Krause-Marquet furnishes an interesting problem. The name of the site in Hebrew means "The Ruin"; its conquest is described in Josh., chs. 7; 8. The excavator found that it was one of the great cities of Palestine during the third millennium B.C., but that it was destroyed c. 2200 B.C. and never again occupied, except for a small Israelite settlement dating after the twelfth century. An excavation by W. F. Albright in 1934 at Bethel (XVIII, C-5), 1½ miles away showed that it was established to take the place of Ai. The ruins of Bethel bore vivid marks of a violent destruction during the course of the thirteenth century (cf. Judg. 1:22 ff.). The simplest explanation of the situation is that the story of the capture of Bethel was transferred to Ai in The Book of Joshua. When Israelite writers recorded the story, they knew of the great ruin near Bethel, and naturally ascribed its capture to Joshua.

Between 1931 and 1935 excavation was resumed at Samaria (XVIII, C-4) under the direction of the English archaeologist J. W. Crowfoot. The results have necessitated a slight revision in the dating of the strata as proposed by Reisner and Fisher. The first phase, consisting of an elaborate palace and strong fortifications, was undoubtedly begun by Omri as previously thought, though almost certainly not completed until the reign of Ahab. The second phase, consisting of the "ostraca house" and a double (casemate) wall which in the most vulnerable part of the city was nearly 33 feet wide, is now known to have been built, not by Ahab, but by one of the kings of the Jehu dynasty, presumably either Joash or Jeroboam II. These fortifications were so strong that it took the Assyrian army three years to conquer the city in 724-721 B.C. (II Kings 17:5). A number of beautifully carved ivories, probably from Ahab's "ivory house" (I Kings 22:39), and the pool where Ahab's chariot was presumably washed after bearing the king's body from Ramoth-gilead (I Kings 22:38) have been found also.

From 1932 to 1938 exceedingly important work was done at Lachish (XVIII, B-5) by the Wellcome-Marston Archaeological Research Expedition, directed by J. L. Starkey before his tragic murder by Arab brigands early in 1938. Among the discoveries were a Canaanite temple, a strong double fortification with protecting gateway built by Rehoboam (Fig. 33; II Chron. 11:9), a group of letters from the time of Jeremiah, and a Persian palace and temple. The letters were by far the most astonishing find, since they are the first

FIG. 77. A reconstruction of the fortifications of *Tell en-Naṣbeh* (XVIII, C-5). The high wall, some 26 feet wide, was built c. 900 B.C. during the civil war between Israel and Judah. It is a good example of ancient fortifications: see also Figs. 18 and 33.

group of inscriptions of any length yet found in Judah. They were in the ruins of the city gate, and were written by an officer in charge of an outpost between Lachish and Azekah to the commandant at Lachish. They date just before the final siege of Nebuchadnezzar in 589-587, and reflect the same state of tension in the country which is also to be seen in The Book of Jeremiah.

In 1923-1925 and again in 1927-1928 the Palestine Exploration Fund sent new expeditions to explore the City of David. The first, under the direction of R. A. S. Macalister and J. G. Duncan, excavated a portion of the old city wall above the Gihon spring (XVII:A, E-6). A tower and revetment, both probably built by David, were found. The second expedition, directed by J. W. Crowfoot, worked on the western side of the hill and found the massive towers of a Jebusite city gate (XVII:A, E-6). Whether it was the Valley or Dung Gate of ancient Jerusalem is a matter of debate.

Among the minor American undertakings may be mentioned the following: (1) the uncovering of Saul's fortress at Gibeah (XVIII, C-5), the first capital of united Israel, by the American School under the direction of W. F. Albright; (2) the excavation of Beth-shemesh (XVIII, B-5) by Haverford College, directed by Elihu Grant; (3) the excavation of *Tell en-Naṣbeh* (XVIII, C-5) by the Pacific School of Religion, directed by W. F. Badè (see Fig. 77 and p. 49); and (4) the excavation of the Maccabean fortress and earlier remains at Beth-zur (XVIII, C-5; Fig. 53) by the Presbyterian (now McCormick) Theological Seminary in Chicago, directed by O. R. Sellers.

Also of interest is the work of a small Danish expedition at Shiloh (XVIII, C-4) and of Sir Flinders Petrie at *Tell Jemmeh, Tell el-'Ajjûl,* and *Tell el-Fâr'ah* (XVIII, A-6).

Very little has been done in Palestinian towns of the time of Jesus, apart from Jerusalem (see pp. 97-100) and Samaria (where a great temple and numerous houses built during the time of Herod the Great have been found). Numerous important excavations, however, have been made in later Roman and Byzantine ruins. The largest has been at *Jerash* (XVIII, D-4) by the British and American schools and Yale University. Here was laid bare the best-preserved Roman city in Palestine, with its wall and gates, colonnaded streets, temples, theaters, baths, and stadium (see Fig. 41). During the Byzantine Age between the fourth and seventh centuries, the city was filled with a dozen churches, witnessing to a large Christian population. Numerous other churches of the age have also been excavated, among the most interesting of which may be mentioned the Church of the Multiplying of the Loaves at *et-Ṭâbghah* (XVIII, D-3), the Cathedral of Scythopolis (Beth-shan), and the church at *Mâdeba* (XVIII, D-5) which contained a mosaic floor with a large map of Palestine worked in it. The Colt Archaeological Expedition to the Negeb, working on the churches at *'Aujā el-Ḥafîr* in 1935-1936, found a large group of papyri, the most significant documents of the age yet found in Palestine (see pp. 63 f.). Judging from the exceedingly large number of churches, chapels, and monasteries built in the country during Byzantine times, there can be no doubt that the country was predominantly Christian.

Similarly, a wealth of information is now at hand about Jewish synagogues and burial customs. The synagogues of Galilee had attracted the attention of Edward Robinson who described several of them, namely at Capernaum (XVIII, D-3), *Meirôn* (XVIII, C-3), *Kefr Bir'im* (XVIII, C-2), and *Khirbet Irbid* (XVIII, C-3). Two German archaeologists examined these and others by means of soundings in 1905. After the First World War the one at Capernaum, the finest yet discovered in Palestine, was completely cleared and partially restored by the Franciscans (see Fig. 37). Unfortunately, however, it is not the same one which existed there in the time of Jesus, since it dates from about the third century A.D. In fact, there appear to be no synagogues thus far found which belong to the period of the New Testament, probably because most of them were destroyed during the first and second revolts against Rome in A.D. 66-70 and A.D. 131-135. Two of the most interesting and important synagogues

excavated since the First World War are those at *Khirbet Beit Ilfa* (XVIII, C-3) and *'Ain Dûq* (XVIII, C-5). Both contained well-preserved mosaic floors with elaborate designs, pictures, and inscriptions. After the Byzantine period, a reaction against such things set in and they were no longer tolerated in the synagogues. One of the most significant excavations into Jewish antiquity was that at *Sheikh Abreiq* (1936-1940; XVIII, C-3) in burial catacombs filled with pictorial representations and inscriptions. From the latter we learn that between the second and fifth centuries A.D. this was one of the most famous burial grounds of Judaism, and Jews from many parts of the Roman world came there to die and to be buried on sacred soil.

One of the most astonishing results of Palestinian excavations in the period between the two wars has been in the field of prehistoric archaeology, with the result that the country has become a center of the search for Stone Age man. The lowest levels of such sites as Megiddo, Beth-shan, and Gezer show that a number of Palestine's leading cities in the Biblical period had been founded as early as the fourth millennium B.C. The period between 3500 and 2500 B.C. was one of great prosperity for the country. Among the cities then in existence were Ai (XVIII, C-5), Jerusalem, Jericho, Gezer, Beth-shan, Megiddo, and Khirbet Kerak (XVIII, D-3). The last mentioned is a good illustration of the prosperity of the period, for it is a huge site, covering nearly sixty acres. In Roman times a number of Palestinian cities were this large or larger, but during the days of the Old Testament the average city was much smaller, sometimes comprising twelve to twenty-five acres (Megiddo covered thirteen), but usually much less. Excavations at *Teleilât el-Ghassûl* (XVIII, D-5) have uncovered a small agricultural and pastoral village from the fifth and fourth millennia, while the lowest levels at Jericho go back to the Late Stone Age, when villages were first being established, before 5000 B.C.

In the Early and Middle Stone Ages, covering the long dark ages of prehistory, most of the people of Palestine apparently lived in caves. In the *Wâdi el-Mugharah* (XVIII, B-C 3), the *Wâdi Khareitûn* (XVIII, C-5), *Shuqbah* (XVIII, C-5), and Galilee such caves have yielded a great store of information about early man, including the first complete Stone Age skeletons ever found. At *Shuqbah* some forty-five skeletons belonging to the Middle Stone Age probably represent the earliest appearance of the native race which lived in the country during historical times. In the *Wâdi el-Mugharah* seventy feet of deposit, representing mainly the life of Early Stone Age man, were excavated, and from them ten skeletons were recovered. These were the first complete remains of Neanderthal man, the earliest widely scattered European race, though they show evidence of mixture with Homo sapiens.

This by no means completes the story of modern excavations in Palestine; yet enough has been written to indicate that the recovery of the ancient life of the country is still in its initial stages. Many years of intensive effort have had to be spent in solving problems of method. Most of the earlier excavators and many of the more modern, without proper knowledge of how to dig, record, or publish, have unwittingly destroyed or lost much of the evidence needed to discover the meaning of their findings. Today the most pressing of these problems have been solved, and we stand at the threshold of a new era in Biblical study. Neither in Palestine nor in any of the Biblical lands has the point of diminishing returns in exploration and discovery yet been reached or even seen upon the distant horizon. When one considers what is yet to be learned, he can only conclude that the districts of Galilee, Samaria, Philistia, Transjordan, Bashan, Damascus, and Phoenicia have barely been touched. In addition, a vast body of material already discovered needs intensive study and assimilation. After the First World War progress was unprecedentedly rapid, and there is reason to believe that the results will be no less astonishing during the years to come.

For further discussion of these and other excavations refer to the sites listed under Subject Index.

INDEX TO THE MAPS

INCLUDING A TOPOGRAPHICAL CONCORDANCE TO THE BIBLE

THIS index has three purposes: (1) to give the location of the sites and geographical features on the maps; (2) to provide a topographical concordance of all places mentioned in the Bible and indicate their location; and (3) to present accurately (with the aid of Professor W. F. Albright) the modern names of the places where ancient sites are located. (The system of transliteration of Semitic place names is one in use among scholars; the markings on the vowels do not represent the same sounds as in English.)

Where two or more places had the same name, the different sites are indicated by numbers: e. g., Abel 1 and 2. If two or more sites of the same name are mentioned in the Bible, the Biblical references are given for all but one; all other references to that name refer to the site for which no references are given.

Note the use of certain words and phrases:

see—used after the name of a site which does not occur on any map; it introduces another name or spelling for the same site which is found on one or more of the maps.

see also—indicates that the place just named occurs on the maps or in the Bible under the following name or names.

?—The question mark after the identification of a site means that the location is possible or probable but not certain.

uncertain—all proposed locations for the site seem to the Editors quite unconvincing.

unknown—the location of the site cannot be determined.

near—used when only approximate location of site can be given.

Abana, River, *Nahr Baradā:* I, E-1; IV, E-1; VI, E-1; VIII, J-1
Abarim, Mountains of: IX, I-6
Abdon, *Khirbet 'Abdeh:* IV, C-2; VI, C-2; VIII, D-4
Abel
 1—I Sam. 6:18, near Beth-shemesh 1; unknown
 2—*see also* Abel-beth-maachah, *Tell Abīl (ābil):* IV, D-2; VII: A-D, C-3
Abel-beth-maachah, *Tell Abīl (ābil):* VI, D-2; VIII, F-3
Abelcheramim (R.V.), near Rabbath-ammon; uncertain
Abel-maim, *see* Abel-beth-maachah
Abel-meholah, *Tell Abū Sifrī?:* IV, C-4; VI, C-4; IX, G-2
Abel-mizraim, in Transjordan; uncertain
Abel-shittim (in N.T. times Abila), *Tell el-Ḥammâm:* V, G-2; VI, D-5; IX, H-5
Abez, in Issachar; uncertain
Ab-i-Diz, River; III, E-3
Abila
 1—(in O.T. times Abel-shittim), *Khirbet el-Kefrein:* IX, H-5; XII:D, D-5
 2—*Tell Abīl (ābil):* VIII, H-7; XIV, D-3
Abilene, district N.E. of Mt. Hermon: XII: C-D, E-1; XIV, E-1
Abū Ghôsh: XVIII, C-5
Abydos, *'Arabet el-Madfûneh:* II, E-3
Accad, capital of Babylonia, c. 2400 B.C.; unknown
Accaron' (in O.T. times Ekron), *Qatrā?:* IX, C-6; XII: A, B-5
Accho (in N.T. times Ptolemais), *Tell el-Fukhkhâr:* I, C-3; III, B-3; IV, C-3; VI, C-3; VII: A-D, C-4; VIII, C-5
Aceldama, "field of blood," southern side of lower Valley of Hinnom?: XVII: B, D, D-7
Achaia, *cf.* Greece; Roman province: XIII, D-2; XV, D-3
Achmetha, *see also* Ecbatana, *Hamadan:* XII: B, C-2
Achor, Valley of, *Wâdi Daber* and *Wâdi Mukelik:* IX, G-6
Achshaph, *Tell Kisân?:* IV, C-3; VI, C-3; VIII, D-5; XVIII, C-3
Achzib
 1—Josh. 15:44; Mic. 1:14; *Tell el-Beiḍâ,* S.W. of Adullam?
 2—(in N.T. times Ecdippa), *ez-Zib:* IV, C-2; VI, C-2; VIII, D-4
Acra, hill (citadel) S. of temple area in Jerusalem: XVII: C, D-7
Acrabetta, *'Aqrabeh:* IX, F-4; XII: D, C-4
Acre, *see also* Accho and Ptolemais: XVIII, C-3
Actium, *La Punta:* XIII, C-2
Adab, *Bismaya:* III, E-3
Adadah, probably the same as Aroer 3
Adam, *see* Adamah 1
Adamah
 1—*Tell ed-Dâmiyeh:* IV, D-4; VI, D-4; VII: A, C-4; IX, H-4
 2—Josh. 19:36; in Naphtali; uncertain
Adami, *Khirbet Dâmiyeh:* IV, C-3; VI, C-3; VIII, F-6
Adar, *see* Hazar-addar
Adasa, *Khirbet 'Addâseh:* IX, F-6; XII: A, C-5
Addan, Addon, unknown
Ader: XVIII, D-6
Adida, *see also* Hadid, *el-Ḥaditheh:* IX, D-5; XII: D, B-5
Adithaim, near Beth-shemesh 1; uncertain
Admah, near Sodom; unknown

Adora, *see also* Adoraim, Adoreus, *Dûrâ:* IX, E-8; XII: A-B, C-5
Adoraim, *see also* Adora, Adoreus, *Dûrâ:* IX, E-8
Adoreus, *see also* Adora, Adoraim, *Dûrâ:* XII: A, C-5
Adramyttium, harbor, near *Edremit:* XV, E-3
Adria, *see also* Adriatic Sea and Hadriaticum, Mare, XV, C-2
Adriatic Sea, *see also* Adria and Hadriaticum, Mare, XIII, C-2; XV, C-2
Adullam, *Tell esh-Sheikh Madhkûr:* VI, C-5; IX, E-7
Adummim, Ascent of, *Tal'at ed-Damm:* IX, G-6
Aduru, *Dûrâ:* IV, D-3
Aegaeum, Mare, *see also* Aegean Sea: XIII, D-2; XV, D-2
Aegean Sea, *see also* Aegaeum, Mare: XI: D, A-2; XV, D-3
Aegyptus, *see also* Egypt: XIII, E-3; XV, E-5
Aelana, *see also* Aila, c. 1 mi. WNW of *'Aqabah:* XIII, E-3
Aelia Capitolina, *see also* Jebus and Jerusalem, *el-Quds:* XVI: C-D, E-4
Aenon, John 3:23, "near to Salim" (*q.v.*); unknown
Aethiopia, *see also* Ethiopia and Cush: XIII, E-4
Affûleh: XVIII, C-3
Afghanistan: II, H-2
Africa, Roman Province in N. Africa: XIII, B-3; XV, A-4
Afyonkarahisar: III, B-2
Agala, *Rujm el-Jilimeh?:* X, J-2; XII: A, D-6
Agendicum, Agedincum, *Sens:* XIII Inset, D-2
Agrigentum, *Girgenti:* XIII, C-2
Agrippias, *see* Anthedon
Ahava, River or Canal, in Mesopotamia; unknown
Ahlab, Meheleb, *Khirbet el-Maḥâlib:* IV, C-2; VI, C-2; VIII, D-2
Ahnâs el-Medîneh, *see also* Heracleopolis: V, B-4
Ai, original name probably Beth-aven, *et-Tell:* IV, C-5; V, G-2; VI, C-5; IX, F-5; XVIII, C-5
Aiath, *Khirbet Haiyân,* near Ai?
Aija, *see* Aiath
Aijalon or **Ajalon**
 1—*Yâlô:* IV, C-5; V, G-2; VI, C-5; IX, E-6
 2—Judg. 12:12; near Rimmon 2; *Khirbet el-Lôn* or *Tell 'el-Buṭmeh?*
Aijalon or **Ajalon, Valley of,** *Wâdi Selmân:* IX, D-5
Aila, *see also* Aelana, c. 1 mi. WNW of *'Aqabah:* XVI: D, E-4
Ain
 1—Num. 34:11, near Riblah; uncertain
 2—*see* En-rimmon
'Ain Dûq, *see also* Noarah: XVIII, C-5
Ajalon, *see* Aijalon 1
'Ajlûn: XVIII, D-4
Akhetaton, *Tell el-Amarna ('Amârneh):* V, B-6
Akrabbim, Ascent of, *Naqb eṣ-Ṣafâ:* VI, C-7; X, F-4
Alaca Hüyük: III, B-1
Alalakh, *Tell 'Aṭshânah:* II, E-2; III, C-3
Alammelech, near Helkath, unknown
Alashiya, *see also* Elishah, Kittim, Iatnana, and Cyprus: II, E-2; III, B-3
Albis, *see also* Elbe, a river: XIII Inset, F-1
Alemeth, *see* Almon

Aleppo, *see also* Khalab, *Ḥaleb:* II, E-2; III, C-2
Aleria, city in Corsica, near S. side of mouth of R. Rhotanus (modern *Tavignano*): XIII, B-2
Alesia, near *Alise Saint-Reine?:* XIII Inset, E-3
Alexandria
 1—*Iskanderiyeh:* XI: D, A-3; XIII, D-3; XV, F-5; XVI: A-D, D-4
 2—*Gulashkird:* XI: D, E-3
Alexandria Troas, *see also* Troas, *Eskistanbul:* XIII, D-2
Alexandrium, *Qarn Sarṭabeh:* IX, G-4; XII: A-B, C-4
Allon, to be read with Zaanannim as Elon-bezaanannim; near Adami; uncertain
Allon-bachuth, near Bethel 1, unknown
Almon, *Khirbet 'Almît:* IX, F-6
Almon-diblathaim, *Khirbet Deleilât esh-Sherqiyeh?:* IX, I-7
Aloth, I Kings 4:16; text uncertain
Alps, The: II, C-1
Alurus, *see also* Halhul, *Halhûl:* IX, E-7; XII: D, C-5
Alusa, also called Elusa, *Khalaṣa:* X, D-3; XII: A, B-6
Alush, near Dophkah; uncertain
Amad, near Helkath; unknown
Amalekites: III, B-4
Amam, near Beer-sheba; unknown
Amana, Mt., *Jebel Zebedâni:* VII: B-D, D-3
Amasia, *Amasya:* XIII, E-2; XVI: D, E-2
Amastris, *Amasra:* XIII, E-2; XVI: C-D, E-2
Amathus
 1—*Tell 'Ammatâ:* IX, H-3; XII: A-B, D-4
 2—on S. coast of Cyprus; near *Limassol:* XIII, E-2
Amida, *Diyarbekir:* XVI: D, F-2
Amisus, *Samsun:* XIII, E-2
Amki, *el-Biqâ':* III, C-3
Ammah, Hill of, near Gibeon; unknown
'Ammân, near Rabbath-ammon, Philadelphia, XVIII, D-5
Ammathus (in O.T. times Hammath), *Ḥammâm Ṭabariyeh:* VIII, F-6; XII: D, D-3
Ammon, Kingdom of, I, E-5; IV, E-5; V, H-2; VI, E-5; VII: A-D, D-5; IX, J-5
Amorites, Land of the: II, F-2
Amphipolis, *Neochori:* XV, D-2
'Amwâs, *see also* Emmaus 1: XVIII, B-5
Anab, *Khirbet 'Anâb:* IX, D-8; X, E-1
Anaharath, *en-Na'ûrah:* IV, C-3; VIII, E-7
Ananiah, O.T. name for Bethany
Anathoth, *Râs el-Kharrûbeh:* IX, F-6
Anchialus, *Ankhialo:* XVI: C-D, E-2
Ancona: XIII, C-2
Ancyra, *Ankara* (*q.v.*): XI: D, B-2; XIII, E-2; XV, F-3; XVI: C-D, E-2
Anem, *'Olam ('ôlam)?:* VI, D-3; VIII, F-7
Aner, *see* Taanach
Anim, *Khirbet Ghuwein et-Taḥta?:* X, F-1
Ankara, *see also* Ancyra: III, B-1
Ankuwa, *Aliṣar Hüyük?:* II, E-2
Anthedon, also called Agrippias, *el-Blâḥiyeh:* IX, A-7; XII: A-B, D, A-5
Antioch
 1—*see also* Antiochia 1; *Anṭâkiyeh:* XII, D-2; XV, G-4; XVI: A-D, E-3
 2—*see also* Antiochia 2; Acts 13:14; 14:19, 21; II Tim. 3: 11, *Yalvaç:* XV, F-3; XVI: B-C, E-3
Antiochia
 1—*see also* Antioch 1, *Anṭâkiyeh:* XIII, E-2
 2—*see also* Antioch 2, *Yalvac:* XIII, E-2
Antipatris, *see also* Aphek and Pegae, *Râs el-'Ain:* IV, D-4; XII: A-B, D, B-4; XIV, B-4; XV, G-5
Antiphrae, close to the coast in W. Egypt: XIII, D-3
Antium, *Anzio:* XIII, C-2
Apamea
 1—*Qal'at el-Muḍiq:* XVI: D, E-3
 2—*Diner:* XIII, D-2; XVI: D, D-2
Aphairema or **Apherema;** *see also* Ephraim; *same as* Ophrah 1?, *eṭ-Ṭaiyibeh?:* XII: A, C-4
Aphek
 1—*see also* Pegae and Antipatris, *Râs el-'Ain:* IV, D-4; VI, B-4; IX, D-4; XVIII, B-4
 2—Josh. 13:4; *Afqâ* E of Byblos
 3—Josh. 19:30, *Tell Kurdâneh?:* VI, B-4
 4—I Kings 20:26, 30; II Kings 13:17; *Fiq:* VI, D-3; VIII, G-6
Aphekah, near Hebron; uncertain
Aphik, *see* Aphek 3
Aphrah, to be read Beth-leaphrah (R.V.); *eṭ-Ṭaiyibeh* near Hebron?
Apollinopolis, *Edfu:* XIII, E-3

Apollonia
 1—*Arsûf:* IX, C-3; XII: A-B, B-4
 2—*Sizeboli:* XI: B-D, A-1; XIII, D-2
 3—several miles N. of Valona: XIII, C-2; XV, C-2
 4—in Cirenaica, *Marsa Susa:* XIII, D-3
 5—S. of Lake Bolbe; uncertain: XV, D-2
Appii Forum, i.e., Market of Appius, near *Foro Appio:* XV, B-2
Aqabah, Gulf of: V, F-5
Aquileia: XIII, C-1; XVI: D, C-1
Aquincum, *Buda (Budapest):* XIII, C-1
Aquitania, Roman province in southwest Gaul: XIII, A-1; XIII, Inset, C-3
Ar, *el-Miṣna?:* VI, D-6; VII: A-C, C-5; X, J-2
Arab, *er-Râbiyeh?:* IX, E-8; X, F-1
Arabah, *el-Ghôr* (Jordan Valley) N of Dead Sea and *Wâdi el-'Arabah* S of it: I, C-8; III, B-4; V, G-3; IX, H-4; X, G-6
Arabah, Sea of, *see* Salt Sea
Arabia, Arabian Desert: II, F-3; III, C-3; V, H-4; VII: A-D, E-4; XI: B-D, C-3; XIII, F-3; XV, G-5; XVI: A, E-4
Arabian Gulf, *see also* Sinus Arabicus, Red Sea: XIII, F-4; XVI: A-D, E-4
Arabs, *see* Arubu and Arabia
Arabs, Arabians, mentioned in Neh. 4:7, 6:1: VII: D, B-6
Arachosia, district on W. side of R. Indus: XI: C-D, E-3
Arad, *Tell 'Arâd:* IV, C-6; V, G-2; VI, C-6; X, F-2
Aral Sea: II, H-1
Aram, *see also* Syria, Zobah, Ube: II, Inset; VII: B, D-3; VIII, J-2
Aram-maachah, *see* Maachah
Aram-naharaim, *same as* Padan (Paddan)-aram
Aram-rehob, district around Beth-rehob
Aram-zobah, *see* Zobah
Ararat, *see also* Armenia, Urartu: XI: A-B, C-2
Arbah, City of, *see* Kirjath-arba
Arbela
 1—*Khirbet Irbid* (*q.v.*): VIII, F-6; XII: A-B, D-3
 2—in Assyria, *Erbil:* III, D-2; XI: A-D, C-2; XIII, F-2; XVI: D, F-3
Archelais, *Khirbet 'Aujâ et-Taḥtâni:* IX, G-5; XII: C, C-5; XIV, C-5
Archi, not a place, but a clan which owned Ataroth 3
Ardata, *Ardat:* VII, B-4
Arelate, *Arles* (*q.v.*): XIII, B-1
Argentoratum, *Strassburg:* XIII Inset, E-2
Argob: VI, E-3
Aria: XI: C-D, E-2
Ariel, *see* Jerusalem
Arimathaea, *see also* Ramathaim-zophim, *Rentis?:* IX, E-4; XIV, C-4
Ariminum, *Rimini:* XIII, C-2; XVI: D, C-1
Arles, *see also* Arelate: XVI: D, B-1
Armenia, *see also* Ararat, Urartu: III, D-2; XI: C-D, C-2; XIII, F-2; XVI: C-D, F-2
Armenia Minor: XIII, E-2
Arnon, River, *Wâdi el-Môjib:* I, D-6; IV, D-6; V, G-2; VI, D-6; IX, H-8; X, J-1
Aroer
 1—Josh. 13:25; Judg. 11:26, 33; near Rabbath-ammon; uncertain
 2—*'Arâ'ir:* VI, D-6; IX, I-8; X, J-1
 3—I Sam. 20:28; *'Ar'arah:* IV, B-6; VI, B-6; X, F-3
Aron, *Tell 'Arâ ('ârâ):* IV, C-4
Arpad, Arphad, *Tell Erfâd:* III, C-2; XI: A, B-2
Arrapkha, *Kirkûk:* II, F-2; III, D-2; XI: A, C-2
Arretium, *Arezzo:* XIII, C-2
Arsinoe, *see also* Crocodilopolis, *Medinet el-Faiyûm:* XIII, E-3; XVI: D, D-4
Artacoana, at or near *Herat:* XI: D, E-2
Artaxata, *Ardashir:* XIII, F-2
Arubboth, or **Arruboth,** *'Arrâbeh?:* IV, C-4; VI, C-4; IX, F-2
Arubu, *see also* Arabs, Arabia: VII: C, B-5; XI: A, C-3
Arumah, near Shechem; uncertain
Arvad, *Erwâd:* II, E-2; III, C-3; VII: A-D, C-2; XI: A-C, B-2
Arzawa: III, B-2
Ascalon (in O.T. times Ashkelon), *'Asqalân* (*q.v.*): IX, B-7; XII: A-D, B-5; XIV, B-5; XVIII, B-5
Asdudu, Assyrian Province: VII: C, B-5
Ashan, *Khirbet 'Asan:* VI, B-6; X, D-2
Ashdod
 1—Persian Province, VII: D, B-5
 2—(in N.T. times Azotus), *Esdûd:* IX, B-5; V, F-2; VI, B-5; VIII: A-D, B-5; IX, C-6
Ashdoth-pisgah, *see* Pisgah

Asher
 1—Tribal District: VI, C-3
 2—Josh. 17:7; near Shechem; unknown
Ashkelon (in N.T. times Ascalon), *'Asqalân:* II, E-3; IV, B-5; V, F-2; VI, B-5; VII: A-D, B-5; IX, B-7; XVIII, B-5
Ashkenaz: II, Inset
el-Ashmûnein, *see also* Hermopolis: V, B-6
Ashnah
 1—Josh. 15:33; near Zorah; uncertain
 2—Josh. 15:43; *Idhna,* near Mareshah?
Ashtaroth, *Tell 'Ashtarah:* III, C-3; IV, E-3; VI, E-3; VII: A-D, D-4; VIII, I-6
Asia, Roman province in western Asia Minor: XIII, D-2; XV, E-3; XVI: A, D-2
Askelon, *see* Ashkelon
Asochis, *Khirbet el-Lôn:* VIII, D-6; XII: A, C-3
Asophon, or Asaphon; *cf.* Zaphon; at or near *Tell es-Sa'îdiyeh?:* XII: A, D-4
Asor, *see also* Hazor), *Tell el-Qedah* (or *Waqqâṣ):* VIII, F-4; XII: A, D-3
Aspendus, c. 7 mi. from mouth of Eurymedon R.: XVI: D, E-3
Asphaltitis, Lake, *see also* Dead Sea and Salt Sea, *Baḥr Lûṭ:* IX, G-7; X, H-1; XIV, C-5
'Asqalân, *see also* Ashkelon and Ascalon: XVIII, B-5
Asshur
 1—*see also* Assyria: II, Inset
 2—*Qal 'ât Sherqâṭ:* II, F-2; III, D-2; XI: A, C-2
Assos, *Behramköy:* XV, E-3
Assyria, *see also* Asshur 1: II, F-2; III, D-2; XI: C, C-2
Astorga, *see also* Asturica: XVI: C-D, A-1
Asturica, *Astorga* (*q.v.*): XIII, A-1
Atad, in Transjordan; unknown
Atania, *Adana:* III, C-2
Ataroth
 1—Num. 32:3,34, *Khirbet 'Aṭṭârûs:* IX, I-8; XI, H-7
 2—Josh. 16:7, *Tell Sheikh edh-Dhiyâb?:* IX, G-4
 3—of the Archite clan, *Tell en-Nagbeh?:* IV, F-5; XVIII, C-5
 4—I Chron. 2:54, near Bethlehem; unknown
Ataroth-addar (or -adar), *see* Ataroth 3
Atbach, *see* Ether 2
Athenae, *see also* Athens, *Athênai:* XIII, D-2
Athens, *see also* Athenae, *Athênai:* XI: A-D, A-2; XV, D-3; XVI: B-D, D-2
'Athlit: XVIII, B-3
Athone, *see also* Thone, *Khirbet eṭ-Teniyeh?:* X, I-3; XII: A, D-6
Athribis, *Tell Atrib:* V, C-3
Atlantic Ocean, *see also* Oceanus Atlanticus: XIII, A-1; XIII Inset, B-3
Atropatene, a district: XI: D, C-2
Atroth, read Atroth-shophan; near Jogbehah; unknown
Attalia, *Adalia:* XV, F-3
Augsburg, *see also* Augusta Vindelicorum: XVI: D, B-1; XVI: D, C-6
Augusta Rauracorum, *Augst:* XIII, B-1; XIII Inset, F-3
Augusta Treverorum, *Trier* (*q.v.*): XIII Inset, E-2
Augusta Vindelicorum, *Augsburg* (*q.v.*): XIII, C-1; XIII Inset, F-2
Augustodunum, *Autun* (*q.v.*): XIII Inset E-3
'Aujâ el-Ḥafir: XVIII, A-7
Aulona, *Valona:* XIII, C-2; XV, C-2
Auranitis, *see also* Hauran; southeastern *Ḥaurân:* XII: B-D, E-3; XIV, E-3
Autun, *see also* Augustodunum: XVI: D, B-1; XVI: D, B-6
Ava, *see* Ivah
Avaricum, *Bourges:* XIII Inset, D-3
Avaris, *see also* Rameses, Tanis, and Zoan, *Ṣân el-Ḥagar:* II, E-3; III, B-4; V, C-3
Aven
 1—Ezek. 30:17, *see* On
 2—Hos. 10:8, *see* Beth-aven
Aven, Plain of, north of Damascus; uncertain
Aventicum, *Avenches:* XIII, B-1; XIII Inset, F-3
Avim, same as Ai?
Avith, in Edom; uncertain
Ayyanu, *'Ayyûn:* IV, D-3
Azal, unknown
Azekah, *Tell ez-Zakariyeh:* IV, B-5; V, F-2; VI, B-5; IX, D-6; XVIII, B-5
Azem, *Umm el-'Aẓam?:* VI, B-6; X, E-3
Azmaveth, *Ḥizmeh:* IX, F-6
Azmon, *Qeṣeimeh?:* VI, A-7; X, B-6
Aznoth-tabor, *Umm Jebeil* near Mt. Tabor?
Azotus: IX, C-6; XII: A-D, B-5; XIV, B-5; XVI: A, E-4
Azzah, *see* Gaza

INDEX TO THE TEXT